During The War

and other encounters

GW00584713

An autobiography

Buster Merryfield

SUMMERSDALE

Copyright © Buster Merryfield 1996

Reprinted 1997 (three times)
Reprinted 1998

No part of this book may be reproduced by any means, nor transmitted, nor translated into a machine language, without the written permission of the publisher.

Summersdale Publishers
46 West Street
Chichester
West Sussex
PO19 1RP

A CIP catalogue record for this book is available from the British Library.

Printed and bound in Great Britain by Biddles Ltd.

ISBN 1 873475 54 3

Cover Photo courtesy of BBC Picture Library.

Contents

To my Mother and Father,
Iris,
Karen and Rodney,
Stuart and Jonathan.
Also to John Dawson,
who I insist must share
the blame for this infliction.
Finally to Ron and Betty Mumby,
Founder and Secretary of the
Eastcote Fan Club.

Chapter 1

Musjid Road

I'm not claiming to have been a child prodigy or anything, but as a baby I did seem to have an acute awareness of my surroundings that went well beyond normal expectations. My earliest recollection is of my mother, out shopping, pushing me down Battersea High Street in my pram. I couldn't have been more than about four or five months old at the time. Battersea was not a bad place to be born in, even in mid-November, which was when I first saw the light of day - not that there was much light about on that dull, drizzly morning. But now it was early Spring and I still vividly recall the weak afternoon sun casting a dancing shadow on the inside of my pram from the rattle hanging on the canopy fringe.

As I grew up, I was to become increasingly fond of Battersea and the colourful people who lived there in the 1920s, but for the moment my world did not extend beyond my parents, Lily and Harry Merryfield, and my sister Irene who was two years my senior.

Harry Merryfield was one of seven brothers and, were it not for his weak chest, he would undoubtedly have followed the rest into the Army as a professional soldier. He still made his contribution to the Great War by working for two years on munitions in Canada before returning to London to become a packer for a high class catering firm. He had married Lily Stone in 1916 and she proceeded to take charge of his life from the day after the wedding, when they moved into their terraced council house in Musjid Road. In the middle of a war, there was no room for frivolities like honeymoons for working class folk.

Lily came from a background where one had to be tough to survive and it was from her that I inherited the dogged determination which was to see me through the many difficult times in my life that I am about to recount. But let's not leap ahead.

On that spring afternoon in 1921, Lily was enjoying herself as she dawdled from window to window looking at the things she would love to buy. She was in no hurry, as Harry would be late home for his tea that night. Before leaving in the morning he had told her of the job that would keep him busy until gone six thirty that evening. His firm were providing all that was necessary for a grand lunch at the Mansion House. Harry would be busy packing and transporting crockery, cutlery and other accoutrements, as well as the food which was prepared at the company's depot. And then when it was all over, he would have the job of clearing up and bringing it all back again. She was glad that he would be able to spend the evening with her and the children. Many times when there were evening functions to be seen to, it would be daylight again before he was able to return. Neither of them complained about this, as he would then be paid an extra two shillings and the money was very welcome.

She gazed at the fishmonger's marble slab and wondered whether to get a pint of shrimps, which were Harry's favourite, or a pair of kippers which would be cheaper. With a sigh she elected for the kippers and hoped Harry might bring a cream cake or Swiss roll home from the banquet leftovers, as he often did. The depression was at its height and she was thankful for all she could get to feed four hungry mouths - not that I was into kippers and Swiss rolls at that tender age.

I was a bonny baby, weighing in at nearly nine and a half pounds and my mother was justifiably proud of me.

"Isn't he a right one?" she asked, the first time relatives came to see the new baby.

"Yer, he's a right buster," joked Grandfather Merryfield. And from that day on, 'Buster' it was, despite a formal christening to the contrary some months later.

I think it was Thomas Aquinas who said, "Give me the boy and I will show you the man." As a Battersea boy, I had never heard of Thomas Aquinas, I don't think he came from round our way. But looking back, the characteristics that were to shape my life were apparent from a very young age. The egotistical streak that made me want to be the centre of attention; my love of sport and anything competitive; my determination to come out top; my bad temper which occasionally got the better of me; all will become apparent in due course.

I started school, as all children did in those days, a few months before my fourth birthday. Even in the nursery class, I had a few playground skirmishes, often with boys older than me, but this was usually done with a cool head, having assessed the chances of victory before entering the fray. Much to Mum's consternation, I often went home with cuts and bruises but quickly learnt the foolishness of getting into fights I couldn't win. I soon became respected as a 'tough nut'.

The following summer I attended my first school sports. I was really wide-eyed at the occasion of it all. During earlier games periods, each form practised their running and jumping. On the big day, those that were any good were allowed to enter the appropriate events. There was an additional race for all those children who had not been picked to compete in any other event, called the 'Catch the Train' race. For this, each competitor brought a case to school filled with a shirt, trousers, jumper, coat and hat. These were placed at the far end of a thirty yard course down which we raced, opened the case, put on the clothes as fast as possible and raced back to the start.

In those days, I was still living up to my Buster image and was not nimble enough to make any of the real races and was duly informed by the teacher the previous day that I would be a candidate for 'Catch the Train'. I went home that night and explained to Mum the sporting equipment I required for the next day. She had no trouble finding the clothes but the case presented a bit of a problem. She had never been on a real holiday since she married and had no occasion to need a case - until now. After a few moments thought, I was despatched to my Gran's and proudly returned carrying a brown compressed-board attaché case. Happily, I filled it up ready for the next day. We had normal lessons in the morning and rushed excitedly home at lunch time to collect our kit. Those parents who were able were invited to attend, and my mum somehow managed to get the afternoon off from her job as a waitress at Lyon's Corner House.

I had no idea how the sports were organised and it seemed that they would never get around to Catch the Train. I spent much of the afternoon wandering about and taking in the atmosphere. I was particularly fascinated by the miniature cups and other prizes all set out on a dark grey army blanket thrown over a trestle table. Whilst the cups looked interesting, I couldn't see much use for them. They were so small you would have to keep filling them up to get a decent drink of lemonade or whatever, so I decided they were not for me. All the other prizes seemed to have come from

7

the school stock cupboard, consisting mainly of exercise books, rulers, pens and - gosh, just look at that - packs of plasticine. From that moment, I was determined I would win and select plasticine for my prize.

There were about eight or nine children from each class entered for Catch the Train, which was run off in heats by age. Being in the first year, my heat came first. Having carefully placed Gran's case in position, I stood on the start line with the concentration of Lindford Christie and was off the mark the moment Miss Tuck, the games mistress, shouted "Ready, steady," and fractionally before she was able to say "GO!". Today, it would definitely qualify as a false start, but Old Tuckie was just glad to get nine four-year-olds into line and away. Head back, I puffed down the track, but was not really built for speed. By the time I reached the case, the others already had their lids open.

Fortunately, I had had the foresight to carefully lay my clothes in the order in which they had to be put on, so that whilst those around me were throwing things out on to the asphalt, desperately searching for their shirts, I had mine on and was back into the case for the jumper. Well you can guess the rest. I was dressed before you could say Jack Flash. Off I went, back down the track, with the cheers ringing in my ears. This was great and I had a wonderful feeling of elation as I burst through the paper tape.

I wanted my plasticine there and then and bright as I was, could not understand the concept of heats. I had won fair and square hadn't I? It took Mum some time to calm me down and explain that I had to race again against the other heat winners.

To me, this seemed most unfair, particularly as they were all bigger and older than me. However, when it came to the final, the older children were handicapped in a staggered start.

Now I don't know if it was a miscalculation, or whether it resulted from all the fuss I had made after the heat, but the start I was given seemed rather generous and there were one or two mutterings from parents who could see their offspring's chance of glory fast disappearing. Undaunted, I took full advantage and was off like a shot, into my carefully arranged clothes and back down the track before the others had even shut their cases. Now I would get my plasticine.

There was only the tug-of-war between staff and fathers to come before the prize giving started. Quite naturally, the names of winners were called out in the same order as the races and one by one the boys and girls went up to collect their cup and select a prize from the table. After a lifetime, the deputy head, Miss Bradshaw, called out, "And last but not least, we have the winner of the Catch the Train Race, Buster Merryfield!" I proudly stepped forward for my prize. There was no cup to be awarded but having had my hand formally shaken, I was invited to take my pick from the table. I walked round behind her and couldn't believe it. There was no plasticine. It had all gone. This was wrong. That was MY plasticine they had taken.

"Where's my plasticine?" I shouted.

"Oh, I'm sorry, it's all gone," she replied, "Here, why don't you have this nice exercise book?" And with that she picked up a blue covered book with 'Mantua Street School' emblazoned in gold across the front and forced it into my hand. But all I could see was red. I had been cheated out of my plasticine. Back came my arm and in a storm of tears I threw the book at her face - not easy to do when you are only three foot two inches tall. But I managed it and before I could be restrained, I had run out of the school gate and home to my bed where I was still sobbing when Mum came home a few minutes later. Having made her so proud of me by winning the race, I knew I had then let her down by my conduct. My tears were a mixture of remorse and frustration.

My sister, Irene, was completely opposite to me in every respect. I took after our mother, she took after Dad. I was rough, she was gentle. I was robust, she was sickly. I showed off, she was humble. I desired success, she was content with her lot. I scowled, she smiled. Most of all, she exuded love.

My mother's job meant that she was generally not at home when we came out of school. Irene was charged with looking after me until Mum returned. Each afternoon, she would wait for me by the school gate and shepherd me round to Aunt Daisy's house, a couple of streets away. Aunt Daisy had three girls of her own, Doris, Daisy and Kathleen. They were much the same age as Irene and the four girls would play together for an hour or so before it was time to go home. My three cousins considered it irksome to have a four-year-old boy tagging along but Irene was very conscientious over her mothering job and would not hear a word said against me. As in all things, she showed me nothing but kindness and love. Although I didn't realise it at the time, I was very fond of my sister.

One thing she did inherit from Mum was a love of music and dancing. Mum was a natural dancer and always said that had she not got married, she would have gone on the stage. All I know is that when there was music on the radio she would often take hold of the sides of her skirt and twirl around the kitchen. If the beat was right, she would even lift her skirt and do a good old Cockney knees up. Irene was equally light on her feet and was selected to be part a team of dancers in the school Christmas concert. Each Saturday morning she went with her cousins Doris and Daisy for rehearsals in the school hall with nine other girls.

Sometimes, Mum was able to get extra work at the tea shop on a Saturday morning, and on those occasions 'Rene would take me along to the rehearsal. I really loved this and cried on the weeks I couldn't go. I was enthralled by the sight of the girls tripping in line across the stage, all singing to the accompaniment of Miss Jones on a very out-of-tune upright piano.

For these rehearsals, the girls wore their normal everyday dresses but as Christmas approached Miss Jones produced drawings of the costumes the girls were to wear in the concert. They were all to be elves and Mum undertook to make the costumes for Irene and her cousins. There was no money for exotic materials such as silk or chiffon so they were all fashioned from coloured crepe paper which came out of the school stock cupboard. Surprisingly, they stood up very well to the wear and tear of the concert and looked gorgeous. The girls dressed up at our house so that Mum could make last minute adjustments and insert a few strategic safety pins before they set off for the concert. She was so pleased with the end results that she had a professional photographer come round to take their photograph. Needless to say, I managed to get into the picture.

Eventually, 'Rene had to give up dancing as it was taxing her strength too much. She was not strong and often had to have time off school. Usually she recovered sufficiently after a few days in bed and was able to return to school. But once, when she was eight, she did not pick up in the usual way and Mum had to call in the doctor. He examined her carefully, taking her temperature, tapping on her chest and listening to her heart with his stethoscope. Eventually he looked up.

"I'm sorry to tell you this, Mrs Merryfield, but I think Irene might have rheumatic fever and it's affecting her heart. I think it would be better if she went into hospital for a few days so that we can do some tests and keep an eye on her."

Shortly after, 'Rene was wrapped in a blanket and carried out to a waiting ambulance and taken to the 'Anti-vivi', which was the popular name for the local hospital. My parents visited her in the evenings whenever they were not working, having first dropped me off at Aunt Daisy's. 'Rene and I slept head to tail in the same bed and I really missed her when she was away. One evening, I complained vociferously to my parents that I wanted to go with them to the anti-vivi to see my 'Rene, but children were only allowed to visit on Sunday afternoons. I was placated with the promise that I could go the following weekend.

It was then only Tuesday, and it seemed that Sunday would never come. During the week I got the idea that I would like to take her some flowers as I had seen my parents do. I expected opposition to this because of the expense, but Mum thought it was a good idea. With the normal impatience of a six year old, I couldn't wait until weekend to buy the flowers and insisted on having the money straight away. Mum quietly found her purse and took out a shilling piece.

"Now I want you to take great care of this and tomorrow you can go with Daisy down to the market." Since 'Rene had been taken ill, Daisy had been bringing me home from school. So the next day I hurried her down to the market, where I insisted on carefully surveying every flower stall there was before making my choice. Only the best was good enough for my 'Rene.

I was familiar with most of the common garden flowers, but was fascinated to see on one stall some beautiful cascades of orange blossoms I had never seen before. They reminded me of the lanterns 'Rene and her cousins had carried in the school Christmas concert. Daisy explained to the stall holder why a six year old boy was buying flowers and he was extremely sympathetic, giving me far more blooms than my shilling warranted.

Proudly I carried them home, my heart full of happiness; joyful that I would be able to show 'Rene how much I cared for her. When Mum came home from work she was delighted. I insisted that until Sunday the flowers should stay in a vase in the bedroom that 'Rene and I shared with Mum and Dad. She readily agreed but had difficulty explaining to me that Chinese Lanterns were everlasting flowers, and didn't need water in with them.

That Friday night, Mum and Dad made their usual visit to the 'Anti-vivi'. An hour or so later, there was a knock at the door as they returned to collect me. When Aunt Daisy opened it, I could hear that my mother was quite excited. She came through into the kitchen and told me why. 'Rene was coming home.

As soon as breakfast was over the next morning, I ran to the end of our street and stood watching out for the ambulance that was to bring her home. I had a long wait, but about eleven o'clock, it turned the corner and I ran alongside as it slowly made its way to the small crowd which had gathered around our front door. I expected Irene to jump out fit and well and was disappointed when they opened the doors and brought her out on a stretcher. She was still very weak and was put straight to bed. I spent the rest of the day in the bedroom with her and insisted that Mum brought my meals through so that I could eat them off a tray, like 'Rene was doing.

A few nights later, I was awoken by the sound of low voices in the room. Opening my eyes I could see that Mum and Dad were by our bedside with a strange man, who I suppose must have been the doctor. Mum was very upset but I couldn't tell why as 'Rene was propped up on pillows at her end of the bed playing a game, or so I thought.

"Goodbye Mummy", she whispered, and blew her a kiss. "Goodbye Daddy," and another kiss. "Goodbye Buster. Goodbye Gran. Goodbye Aunt Daisy. Goodbye Doris. Goodbye Daisy. Goodbye Kathleen." On and on she went through all her relations and friends, blowing each one a kiss. When she paused, I lay there thinking who she might have left out.

"Goodbye Billy Sharpe," I echoed, but seeing I was awake, Mum turned and lifted me out of the bed. Holding me close to her, she left the room and climbed the stairs to the flat above where she rapped on the door. Without a word, Mrs Foster took me from my mother, carried me through and tucked me into one of her beds.

I never saw my 'Rene again and it was only the comforting presence of her Chinese lanterns in our bedroom that enabled me to get through those next few months without her. Buster was growing up.

Chapter 2

Billy

Although I was extremely upset at 'Rene's death, it was as nothing compared with the anguish felt by my parents who each in their own way blamed themselves. I mentioned earlier that Dad had a weak chest, but in reality it was a heart defect. He was convinced' therefore, that Irene's heart trouble was hereditary, despite reassurances from the doctor that rheumatic fever was caused by a germ.

Mum put the blame squarely on the poverty and poor environment she had been forced to bring the family up in. Mum had a hard upbringing herself, being one of five children. Her father had died when she was a young girl and her mother had then married again, producing a further six children. Being the eldest girl out of eleven children, with the youngest some twelve years her junior, Mum was allowed no free time of her own, being permanently occupied as surrogate mother to her step-sisters and brothers. Then, as soon as she was twelve years old, she was sent out to work for ten hours a day, six days a week, bringing in a few extra shillings to supplement the family income. When she arrived home exhausted at the end of each day, she still had to help feed, bath and bed the young ones. She was permanently tired and had little interest in any outside activities. Consequently, she missed out on the close friendships that are a necessary part of teenage girls' lives. She looked on her marriage as a blessed escape from the drudgery and although her lot improved considerably she knew that her existence was still well down the social scale. But she was happy bringing up her family and running her own life, at least she was until Irene died. Now she felt shattered and from that day changed from the carefree mother I loved to see, twirling round the room to the sound of the radio, into a sad, sombre, unsmiling figure.

She was convinced that the dirt and squalor and lack of proper nourishment had made the main contribution to Irene's death. She made a silent vow that she would do all in her power to change things by getting what remained of her family into a better environment. From her contact with the clientele at the teashop where she worked, she somehow knew that money was the answer. She would buy her way to a better life, but had no idea where the money would come from.

She was a devout, religious woman and prayed to God for help, and in the fullness of time her prayers were answered. The revelation came to her while she was looking at the small advertisements in the newsagent's window. She would take in a lodger. She went in, wrote out a card in her small neat handwriting and handed over tuppence for one week's display. She considered it a good investment and was proved right. Within the week, it paid off with a knock at the door.

In front of her stood a tall good-looking youth about eighteen or nineteen years old. "I've come about the room you have," he said, smiling at her.

"Come in," she replied, opening the door wider, and with that ushered him into the front room where she had installed a single bed, bought for a few shillings from the second-hand shop.

At this stage, I had better explain the layout of the house, or at least our part of it. With very few exceptions, all the houses in our road were occupied by two families, one on each floor. Everything on the ground floor was ours and the upstairs belonged to the Fosters. Their stairs were immediately behind the common front door. Sharing houses like this was so common that everybody knew, when out calling on each other, that it was one knock for downstairs, and two knocks for up. Running parallel to the stairs was a dark passage in which we hung our coats. This led through to our kitchen at the back. To the left of the passage were first the front room, and behind that the bedroom in which all three of us slept. To reach our toilet, we had to go out into the small concrete yard which ran alongside the kitchen. There was an indoor toilet, but that belonged to the Fosters.

And that was how Billy Waller came to move into our front room. At the time I found it quite exciting and didn't query why he should be there. Looking back it seems strange, as his proper home was only a few hundred yards away. He was on good terms with the rest of his family and would visit them regularly, so I can only assume that he had grown too old to share a room with his siblings and had been pushed out of the nest.

Billy worked as a baker's roundsman. For this he had a small cart which he would take down to the bakery several times a day to be refilled with loaves which he then delivered around the neighbouring streets. It was a peculiar cart, being completely enclosed, with a small door at the rear through which Billy would take out his wicker basket full of loaves in order to visit the next row of houses. At the front of the cart were two shafts, but instead of a horse, it was Billy who got between the shafts and pulled the cart behind him.

During the week, many houses were empty, with the parents at work and the children at school. The people would then leave notes or else had regular orders. Billy would open the door and pop the bread inside on the kitchen table. But on Saturdays, when people were home, Billy would open the door and shout "Baker ho!", whereupon the lady of the house came to the door and hopefully paid him for the week's bread.

On Saturdays the round took much longer and he would leave the house before breakfast, coming back an hour or so later for something to eat when his round took him past our front door. I would be up by then and waiting excitedly for his return. This was because for the second part of his morning round he would take me with him. Having already delivered some of the bread, there was space in the enclosed cart and he would pop me through the little door in with the bread.

There was no window, but a little light did filter in through small ventilation ports on either side. It was eerie and exciting to be in there with the Hovis and Coburgs and the smell was heavenly. To this day I cannot pass a bread shop without thinking of Billy and his cart.

As we went round the streets, I used to play a little game. By putting my eye to the ventilation port I could see outside, but nobody could see me. When Billy was off with the basket delivering bread, if somebody walked past on the pavement I would suddenly whistle or call out. I found it most amusing to see them start and then look up and down the street with a puzzled look on their faces. I gave no thought to the heart attacks I might be inducing in the old ladies I frightened in this way.

On the shelves inside the cart were odd scraps of crust which had become detached from the loaves. I would avidly search for these and eat them, even though I had only just had my breakfast. When there were none, I would pick at a loaf until a bit fell off for me to eat, but as I got bolder, the tattered corners became apparent to Billy and his customers and I got told off. After that, I left the loaves alone for a while but eventually temptation got the better of me again. I hit upon the idea that nobody could detect what I had been up to if I loosened the top of a cottage loaf, ate some of the soft bread inside and then pressed the top down again. My theory was correct and nothing was noticed when the loaf was sold to an unsuspecting customer. However, when she cut it open, all was revealed and Billy had to refund her money. My mother had to compensate Billy and it was the last time I was allowed a Saturday morning ride in the bread cart.

In his spare time, Billy played the ukulele in a small band that provided the music for local dances. Some evenings, he used to let me join him in the front room when he was practising. He was quite gifted musically and, with my mother's permission, would sit and play popular tunes on our harmonium which sat in the front room under the window. In the summer, the sash window would be open and adults and children alike would gather round to hear him play, often joining in with a sing-song.

I suppose he must have been with us about three years in all and I've no idea why he eventually left. It's possible he was getting married and setting up his own home. Many years later I tried to trace him by making enquiries from folk who were still living in the area. I was told that he was married and was working as a fireman in Walton-on-Thames. The next time I had reason to go that way I went to look him up but he had long since moved on so I've no idea where he is or even if he is still alive. If he is, he is now at least 87 years old.

One final memory of Billy before I move on is of him pulling hairs out of my head one at a time. Although most people in the area tried their hardest to keep themselves and their houses clean, life was not very hygienic and all the infections and infestations imaginable were rife. At school we would have regular head inspections carried out by 'Nitty Nora', the visiting school nurse. We would have to line up one behind the other and on reaching the front of the queue, kneel down in front of her. She would then pull your head forward and carefully comb through your hair so that any head lice present would fall on to a large sheet of paper spread across her knee. At the same time she looked for the eggs clinging to the hairs.

When she had completed the inspection of each child she would call out "One" or "Two" and a teacher would record this in an exercise book. I used to think this was the numbered of nits she had found, but discovered later it was code for 'clear' or 'infected'. I usually got a 'One' but on one occasion, instead of the usual call, she turned and engaged the teacher in low conversation. That afternoon, I was given a note to take home to my mother who read it and immediately took me over to the doctor. I had contracted ringworm.

Very few people come across ringworm today, so I had better explain its symptoms and treatment. It is caused by a parasitic fungus which attacks the skin, commonly on the scalp. It starts as a small pimple which develops into a boggy swelling. This gradually travels out across the scalp in a ring, destroying the hair as it does so. I suspect that by now there is an effective antibiotic that cures it in no time, but the standard procedure then was to create a 'firebreak' as it were, by pulling out a circle of hair outside the infected area. This is where Billy came in. Each evening he would patiently sit and pull my hairs out one at a time and then apply a horrible smelling ointment to the infected area, made from sulphur and carbolic acid.

Despite Billy's attentions, the ringworm continued to spread until as a result of it and Billy's enthusiastic defoliation, I was completely bald. To cover my embarrassment, my mother gave me a flat cap to wear which I was allowed to keep on in class when I went to school. Naturally, this was a great curiosity to the other children. Those in my class were sympathetic but older boys took great delight in running up behind me in the playground and snatching my cap. They would then stand around jeering and throwing it from one to the other as I tried in vain to retrieve it.

On one occasion, I became so incensed I clenched my fist and took a swing at one of the boys, although he was nearly a foot taller than me and about two years older. I missed, but to my surprise he turned and ran away. I ran after him until he suddenly stopped and threw an open penknife at me. I don't think he had any particular knife-throwing skills but the blade went straight into my thigh and there was blood everywhere.

The wound had to be treated by the teachers and he was severely punished. The incident gained me respect and status amongst the other children and I developed a bit of a swagger. Unfortunately, I became overconfident. By way of his friends, I sent a threat to this boy saying that I would 'get him' outside the school gates at four o'clock that afternoon after school. Having issued the challenge, I began to have serious doubts, particularly when the message came back saying he was looking forward to it and detailing all the things he was going to do to me when he got there.

It was with some trepidation that I left school that afternoon. I deliberately hung back helping the teacher to close the windows and tidy up, in the hope that he would have given up and gone home by the time I emerged. Finally, I could delay no longer, and trying to appear nonchalant, sauntered across the playground and out into the street. I was amazed to see that there were twenty or thirty boys gathered around the school gates. Word of the impending slaughter had obviously spread throughout the school. Enthusiastically, they had already borrowed skipping ropes from the girls and tied them between lamppost and school railings to form a crude boxing ring. One of my classmates rushed up and offered to be my second and they had already appointed a referee. I was flattered but knew that there would be little adherence to Marquis of Queensbury rules if my opponent carried out his threats. There was no escape. I took of my jacket and rolled up my shirt sleeves in preparation, but as yet my adversary had not arrived. I was pushed under the rope and my second stood outside the ring trying to tell me how to get the better of my opponent.

Ten minutes went by and he had still not arrived. Perhaps he wasn't coming. I began to grow in confidence. Another five minutes and he was still not there. I moved out of my corner and began to shadow box as I skipped around the ring and the crowd began to cheer. After a few minutes of clowning like this I decided I had given them a good enough showing of my prowess and it was now time to leave. Clasping my hands together above my head I acknowledged their applause as though I had just won the world championship. Then picking up my coat, I left with dignity. After that incident, there was no more bullying over my bald head and a few weeks later the ringworm had all cleared up. I suppose that having expanded its circle until it completely covered my head, there was nowhere else for it to go. The curious thing was that when my hair regrew, it was completely different in character. Before, it had been coarse, straight and dark brown in colour. Now it was curly, auburn and fell in a soft cowlick across my forehead.

After Billy left, I persuaded Mum to let me sleep in the front room in his bed. She readily agreed as I was now nine years old and becoming too curious and aware to continue sharing a bedroom with them. Having my own room gave me a real sense of importance and of being grown up, but eventually I did have to share it as I will shortly explain. But first, the harmonium. I had envied the way Billy had been the centre of attention when he gave his impromptu Summer evening concerts. When I took over his room I decided to teach myself how to play the harmonium so that I could continue in his place. At first I found it much more difficult than I thought it would be, but slowly I unravelled the sequence of notes necessary to pick out recognisable tunes such as 'Three Blind Mice' and 'God Save The King'. Being impatient, and the show-off I was, I would play in front of the open window, and whenever anybody walked past on the pavement, I would stop the laborious one-finger sequence I was engaged in, and pull out the Forte stop. I would then play with all fingers, on as many keys as possible, hoping the passer by might recognise a tune in what I was doing and think I was a gifted musician.

On reflection, I must have had some musical talent, probably inherited from my mother, as I eventually mastered the keyboard. Today, if I know a tune, I can sit down and play it by ear, but I can read not one note of music.

I also envied Billy's skill on the ukulele and longed to imitate that as well. At the end of every Battersea backstreet, the last house in the terrace was a shop. In Musjid Road where we lived, it was a pawnbrokers, probably the most frequented shop in the area. As children, we were fascinated by the jumbled assortment of unredeemed goods in the window which were now up for sale. One could understand the occasional gramophone or radio finding their way there, having been bought in a moment of optimism and then pawned when money was short. But it was difficult to see how things such as false teeth and spectacles, of which there were rows and rows, could have been abandoned by their owners.

The window was also home to a number of musical instruments. There were trumpets, clarinets and saxophones stood on their stands, and along the top of the window a succession of banjos and ukuleles. We would stand in front of the window and play a game of 'bagsies'. Taking it in turns, each child would say, "I bagsy that gramophone," or whatever took his fancy. This continued until either between us we had bagsied everything in sight or we became fed up. Whenever we played this game, I always started by bagsying a beautiful chromium plated ukulele which had pride of place at the top of the window. Oh how I wanted that ukulele. It was coming up to my ninth birthday and I pestered my parents day and night trying to extract a promise that I could have the uke. I was most disappointed when I didn't get it and showed my displeasure in my usual display of bad temper. I did not give up and continued to badger Mum and Dad through into December with my sights set on getting it as a Christmas present.

Around mid-December, Dad started to drop the odd hint with remarks like, "You'll just have to wait and see, won't you." Heartened by this I eased the pressure, confident that at last I had won through. When Christmas morning came, I could see there was something unusually bulky poking against the inside of the pillow case I had hung up in anticipation. Eagerly I shot to the end of the bed and plunged my hand in and was overjoyed when my fingers came into contact with the strings. Excitedly I pulled it out but my joy turned to misery and anger. It was a ukulele all right, but it was home-made from a cigar box. With tears in my eyes I stamped through into Mum and Dad's bedroom.

"I think you're both horrible," I shouted. "This is rubbish. I don't want this." And with that I dashed it to the floor. I could see that my poor old dad was extremely upset by this but I didn't care. I found out later that he had been to the pawnshop to try and buy the ukulele I wanted so much, but the price was way beyond anything he could afford. I might just as well have asked for a Rolls Royce. In the end, so as not to disappoint me, he had bought the home-made instrument from somebody he worked with, paying money he could ill-afford.

It wasn't until I was much older that I found all this out and realised how much I had hurt him. Many years later, after I had brought all that I could afford for my own family at Christmas, my daughter pestered me in a similar way for a Cliff Richard's album. The memories of that ukulele came flooding back to me. Knowing the deep disappointment I had felt, I went out on Christmas Eve and bought the album for her. Although I couldn't afford it, I have never regretted that decision.

Chapter 3

Pastimes

Talking of Christmas takes me back to one incident when I must have been about six years old. As a treat I was taken up to Clapham Junction where there was a fairground. I found the noise and the music and the lights and the people so very exciting. For a long time I was satisfied just to wander round in awe, holding my Mum's hand. Eventually, it came to me that people were having rides on these wonderful machines and I begged to join them. Mum agreed and took me across to a large roundabout full of wonderful dappled white horses on twisted golden poles which pranced up and down as the roundabout rotated. This was great, but hang on, there were lots of horses and any child could go on one of them. I had spotted that amongst the horses there were one or two gigantic chickens. I would go on one of them. Dad lifted me up and I proudly sat astride the chicken clasping the cold metal pole in front of me. After what seemed an age, the hurdy-gurdy music started and the roundabout slowly started to move. As it did so I felt the chicken gently lowering then lifting me again as we circled slowly round. My parents waved as I came past and I smiled back at them. This was fun. The speed picked up and the wind began to blow my hair. I was really enjoying this, when without warning my chicken gave out an ear-shattering "COCK - A DOODLE - DOOOOH". I was frightened out of my wits and immediately started to cry and scream.

"I want to get off. I don't like it Mum. GET ME OFF!" But by now the roundabout was going at full speed and there was no escape. "COCK - A DOODLE - DOOOOH," it went again. I clung to the pole screaming in terror, closing my eyes to blot out the whirling lights around me. I was sure I was going to be sick. In the end, I wasn't, but I had to endure absolute hell for another three minutes before it eventually slowed and stopped. I must have been an awful disappointment to my parents.

I promised to explain about sharing my room. It started when a near neighbour brought home an old motorbike and sidecar. I can't for the life of me remember his name, so let's call him Mr Jones. He worked in a garage, and a customer who had bought a new bike abandoned his old one at the garage. The garage owner had agreed that Mr Jones could have it. This was the first motorised form of transport ever to be owned by anybody in Musjid Road. Prior to that, we hardly ever saw even a car in our road. There was a Mr Fisher opposite who worked as a delivery man for Achille Serre, the Dyers and Cleaners, who would occasionally bring his van home, but apart from that, the only visitor was the ice lorry which used to make regular deliveries to some of the shops in the area. When it came, we kids used to run after it and jump on the back as it slowed to round the corners. The objective was to get any piece of ice that might have broken off the corner of one of the blocks. It tasted diabolical but it was a real feather in the cap to get a piece and suck it in front of others who hadn't been successful.

But I'm digressing. This motorbike and sidecar were the envy of all the fathers in the street. Seeing the interest, and having an eye for business, Mr Jones let it be known that he might be able to get hold of more, that is if anybody was interested! Other fathers, not wishing to lose face in front of their sons, succumbed, although their money would have been better spent on other things. Gradually, BSA, Triumph, Matchless and Harley-Davison bikes appeared along the street. Even my Dad managed to persuade Mum that they should have one, on the grounds that they would be able to use it for holidays.

And so he put his order in and shortly after took delivery of a very ancient Royal Enfield, complete with sidecar, but not in working order. At first, in keeping with the other fathers, he used to work on it every Sunday morning outside the house. But winter approached and after he had come in a couple of times wet and shivering, Mum feared for his health. Although she didn't fully approve, she had no option but to let him bring it into the house.

I've already explained that our part of the house was not exactly spacious. Having looked at all the options, newspaper was spread over the floor in the front room and he worked there on both bike and sidecar. To give him his due, he stripped it all down meticulously to the last nut and bolt, cleaning and polishing it all before putting it back together again. I had to live with this each night and found the smell appalling. It was a mixture of petrol and the paraffin which he used to clean the old grease off everything.

By the time Spring came, the bike was back together again. Taking it outside, Dad kicked it over and it started first time, issuing clouds of blue smoke from the back. A few adjustments soon reduced this to a tolerable level and after a short trial run, Dad pronounced it ready for outings. It was decided that the three of us would go off the following Sunday for a day at Brighton. I could hardly wait.

When Sunday came, the weather couldn't have been better. There wasn't a cloud in the sky and for the time of year it was quite warm. Soon after nine o'clock, the picnic lunch was all prepared and we were ready for the off. Naturally, Dad was to drive and Mum would sit in the sidecar. I was put in a Tansad child's seat behind my father and strapped in. Off we went and all went well for the first mile or two, but as we passed sedately by Wandsworth Common, the front forks snapped.

The front of the bike immediately dropped and dug into the

road, catapulting me out of my seat, over a row of iron railings and into the field beyond. The accident had been witnessed and it wasn't long before an ambulance arrived and we were all taken to the 'Anti-vivi'. Having been protected by the sidecar, Mum was not badly hurt and was able to go home a few hours later. Dad and I were kept in for several days and I thoroughly enjoyed being the centre of attention, with lots of relatives and friends coming to visit us. There were no permanent injuries, but that was the last we ever saw of the bike.

I suppose it could have been our way of imitating our fathers with their motor bikes, but all the boys around started building their own scooter soon after this. Being a bit of a handyman, Billy Sharpe's father made the first one and we just copied the design. They were not difficult to make once you had been shown how. It needed two planks of wood each about thirty inches long. One formed the upright at the front and the other the horizontal runner to stand on. A slot was cut out of one end of each and a ball-race was hammered on to a wooden shaft and nailed across the slots as a wheel. Just above the front wheel, two large metal eyelets were screwed one above the other into the upright. A further pair were screwed into a block of wood which was fixed firmly on to the front of the runner, and a long metal bolt passed through the four eyelets to join the two parts together and provide the steering mechanism. The final touch was a piece of lino nailed to the runner so that it lay above the back wheel. This enabled you to lift your scooting foot and press the lino down on to the wheel when you wanted to apply the brakes. I'm sure that modern children would get the same sense of achievement as we did by making scooters in this way, and all the more enjoyment from them being home-made.

When we became proficient at scooting, we started to see who could scoot the fastest and gradually the races became more organised and sophisticated. One boy, called Lenny Ogden, managed to get hold of an old speedway programme from Stamford Bridge. We all tied numbers on to the front of our scooters and adopted the names of our heroes. Those I remember were Vic Huxley (1), Frank Arthur (8), Gus Kuhn (9), Arthur Warwick (10) and best of all, Lionel Van Prague (15). One of the neighbours who was a speedway fan came out and helped to organise the races, chalking a circular track for us on the road and acting as starter and adjudicator for the races.

In those days, dads used to take a great interest in their children's games. I suppose it was because there were not so many organised activities as there are now, and even if there had been, we couldn't have afforded them. I remember Billy Collins' father used to organise a skating race every Christmas and give sixpence to the winner. Roller skates were a very popular possession and I used to look forward to a new pair every Christmas, costing ten and sixpence from Beards, which was a camping and outdoor activities shop.

The seasons for various street games would come and go with annual regularity. One time we would play nothing else but tops and whips, seeing who could chalk the prettiest coloured pattern on the spinning surface, then a week later not a top would be seen and we were all bowling hoops. Some games didn't require any equipment at all. Our favourite amongst these was called 'Release'. It was actually a variation on 'Hide and Seek'. One side would go out and hide and after a suitable interval, the others would come looking, but leave one person behind as den keeper. If your hiding place was discovered, you were tapped on the head three times and were then duty-bound to return and become a prisoner in the den. However, if one of the hiding side could creep up to the den unobserved, he could release a prisoner by tagging him before he could be stopped by the den keeper. You can imagine that with these rules a game could go on for ever, and some games actually did last several evenings. Occasionally, when we finished for the night somebody would be inadvertently left in his hiding place long after we had all gone home.

Saturday mornings were now devoted to the cinema. More specifically, the Savoy, where on Saturday mornings they ran a children's club. The main feature would be something like an 'Our Gang' film or a Tom Mix, which was followed by a serial which went on for ever, ending each week with the hero in a situation that was impossible to get out of. It was called "The Indians are Coming." The next week when they re-ran the previous ending as a link into the new episode, his predicament had been subtly changed and he escaped once more, getting into dire straights again by the end of the episode. We readily accepted this and still cheered and whistled him, whilst booing the villains with equal enthusiasm.

It was at one of these Saturday morning sessions that I got my first experience of being on a real theatre stage. I had previously been in plays at school, one in particular being worth a mention. There was a lanky youth called Joey Clark who lived in our street and although born in the backstreets there was a different air about him. He kept himself to himself and didn't join in the usual street games with us. He wore steel rimmed spectacles, talked a bit posh and we called him 'The Professor'. He was actually quite intelligent and used to write plays which he took to school and showed to the teachers. One Christmas, they decided to include one of his short plays in the Christmas concert. It was called, "The Hooded Spy". It only lasted about ten minutes and I played the part of a pirate.

So I suppose that was really my first stage appearance, but being on stage at the Savoy on that Saturday morning was something entirely different. Firstly, I hadn't appreciated how high up the stage was off the ground and the fact that with the spotlights on and house lights down, it's impossible to see much of what's happening out in front. I was most interested to see the footlights and all the mechanisms above me that lowered and raised curtains and scenery.

The reason I was on stage was that during the interval, there was usually a children's talent competition of some sort. This particular week it was prowess with the yo-yo. Now I'm not one for boasting, but I fancied myself as a bit of a specialist on the yo-yo, probably amongst the country's leading nine-year-old experts I shouldn't wonder. Most boys had a cheap affair made out of pressed tin-plate. They were manufactured in two halves which snapped together. The trouble was, they didn't carry much weight in them and quickly lost their momentum. The more expensive devices were much more effective. They were made of wood and carved all in one piece on a lathe. The heavier the wood, the more it would maintain its speed which gave you more time to do fancy tricks. I had the Rolls Royce of yo-yos, made out of mahogany, although I can't for the life of me recall how I came by it. It must have been relatively expensive and way beyond my means, but recalling my desire to always get the best, I probably swapped it for a pile of comics or cigarette cards.

So, whilst I usually sat and watched others performing, on this particular Saturday I fancied my chances and up I went. The trouble was, so did half the kids in south London and the stage was jam packed. The judges were pretty adept and quickly eliminated those who had only just about mastered the basics of making their yo-yo go up and down. Gradually the crowd thinned and those left on stage had more room to show their skills. You should be aware by now, from the 'Catch the Train' race I had won some years before, that I was a good tactician. I quickly saw that there was no point in delivering your best material in the early stages. So I waited until we were down to the last eight or ten before coming up with my specialities. At this point in the competition, we were placed in line across the stage and each competitor had to give a solo performance. The audience clapped and cheered each boy in turn and the one gaining the most applause was the winner. I was next to last in the line and whilst keeping my yo-yo going with fairly commonplace stuff, I carefully watched my rivals out of the corner of my eye. As each did their thing my confidence grew and when my turn came I stepped forward with my black mahogany whirlwind and put it through its paces. I started with the tricks I had seen the others doing, flicking it out in front, round my back and through my legs. Then as a finale I gave them a sequence of the Cat's Cradle and Rocking the Baby, two of my specialities. These require the spinning yo-yo to be balanced on the taught string and then dropped through until it was suspended in the cradle underneath. Then by tensioning the string, it could be made to climb back up again where it could be rocked back and forth as the baby. Even without the whistles and shrieks of my close friends, the applause was deafening and I knew I was the clear winner so far. Only one more to go, a boy I knew called Freddy Fry, who was no mean performer. The mistake he made was trying to copy my performance. If he had tried the Cat's Cradle and Rock the Baby as separate routines with his yo-yo being speeded up again in between, he might have got away with it. As it was, with one immediately following the other, his cheap yo-yo didn't have the impetus to keep it going. As he tensioned his string to make it climb again, it went slower and slower until it fell back down accompanied by jeers from the unsympathetic audience. My prize was a camera but the cheers and acclaim that went with it meant far more to me than any prize.

I mentioned cigarette cards, which we referred to as fag cards, 'fag' having then a completely different meaning from its modern usage. In my youth, all packets of cigarettes carried a card inside, and most boys were avid collectors. We had no fear of talking to strangers and would go down the market or into strange streets begging them from smokers. In those days that meant everybody.

Sometimes we would receive a rare gem that we were seeking towards a complete set, but more often than not it would be a 'swapsie' and there was a thriving market in cards. Those that couldn't be bartered were used to play a variety of games. These all involved considerable skill at flicking the wrist so that the card would be propelled from between the fingers. The game might be 'furthies', where the winner was the one who could flick the furthest, or 'knock down dolly', where cards were lined up against the wall and one had to knock them down with the flicked card. Other variations were 'nearest the wall' and 'tops' where you endeavoured to land your card on top of another that had already been flicked.

I also feel we learned a lot from cigarette cards, particularly from sets such as 'Industries', 'Military Uniforms' or 'Flags of the World'. Each card had a picture on the front and a descriptive paragraph on the back which were a valuable source of information. It's possible that the demise of cigarette cards heralded the start of the decline in children's general education.

My favourite sets were 'Film Stars' and 'Footballers'. I don't know if I collected the Film Stars because of my latent interest in the theatre or because they were larger, glossier cards. I managed to get the full set of fifty but have no idea what eventually became of them. Everybody collected Footballers. This was because you could send off a full set in exchange for a football. I never knew of anybody who got one. We all seemed to be missing Number 43, Manchester United. We were quite naïve and didn't realise that the manufacturer must have deliberately issued very few Number 43s. We were sure that up north somewhere there was a glut of 43s but a shortage of 17s, which was Chelsea. We had hundreds of them.

Chapter 4

Boys Will Be Boys

Through my collection of cigarette cards I developed a keen interest in football and by the time I was ten could name most of the players in the First Division. Like most men, Dad would have a weekly sixpence on the football sweep at work and I enjoyed taking the football scores down for him from the radio every Saturday evening. One night, when yet again he hadn't won anything, he remarked,

"The only people that make any money out of this is the organisers." I got to thinking about that and decided to become an organiser. I persuaded people living in the neighbouring streets to enter my football sweep. Each Thursday evening I would write out the names of all the football teams on slips of paper. Including the Scottish divisions, I think their must have been about 130 teams in all. Then I went from door to door letting the neighbours pick a team at a penny a time. The winner was based on the highest score the following Saturday. There was just one prize of ten shillings, leaving me with a profit of ten pence a week. Naturally, if any other teams equalled the top score, the prize would be split.

On the first Saturday night, I eagerly awaited the scores, every ticket having been sold. I hoped there would be a clear winner, as giving out a prize of ten shillings would be good publicity. After the response my scheme had received the first week I had visions of doubling up my profit in following weeks by selling every team twice. At the appointed time nobody was allowed to move or speak whist I took down the all-important results. I was in luck. Torquay had surpassed all others by putting eight into the net.

I consulted my notebook to ascertain the lucky winner so that I could rush round and present the prize. I needn't have bothered - it was my dad. I did not look forward to going round collecting the following Thursday and this initial setback did no good at all to my circulation figures . However, most people were understanding and thought it a bit of a laugh. I ran it throughout the season, ending up with about two pounds profit. This was more than the average man in Musjid Road earned in a week.

Whilst we're on the subject of Saturday nights, I must tell you about a most unusual series of incidents. What I'm about to relate happened soon after my tenth birthday. It started on a cold November Saturday afternoon; the kind of day when you are glad you are not out there in the mist and drizzle. Although it was only just teatime, the daylight had gone and the pavements reflected the weak yellow light of the gas lamps. Inside I felt warm and cosy as I waited for high tea, only we didn't call it that in the 'thirties, it was just tea. But we always had something cooked, and hopefully to follow, a cream sponge, Swiss roll or what ever my dad had been given as leftovers from work.

We had just sat down to faggots and peas, and my dear old mum was pouring the tea, when there was an urgent pounding at the front door. Dad put down his knife and fork and disappeared down the passage to the front door, returning a few moments later with my cousin Kathleen, who was in a very agitated state.

"Mum says you must come round straight away Aunty Lil, something awful has happened," she gasped out. We managed to get from her that something had crashed into their house. 'Mum' was my mother's sister, Daisy, who lived with her husband, Arthur and my three cousins just a couple of streets away in Falcon Grove.

We were a close family who shared all our troubles, and so without hesitation we all left our tea, donned our macs and hurried round to Aunt Daisy's. I was too young to be of any help, but my parents were loathe to leave a ten-year-old boy at home alone - especially with a whole cream sponge on the table.

When we arrived we solemnly trooped through to the back of the house and into the glass lean-to which Uncle Arthur had added some time back. Very proud of it he was, growing tomatoes in pots in the summer and chrysanthemums in the winter. It also housed Aunt Daisy's large wooden mangle so that she could work under cover on wash days. Everything was now in a very sorry state with broken glass and fragmented flower pots everywhere, and lying in the middle of the scattered soil and crushed chrysanths was a large boulder about the size of a bucket. It must have weighed the best part of a hundredweight and had smashed straight through the lean-to roof.

Immediately, Mum sized up the situation. "Daisy," she said, "you must send Arthur for the police straight away. And you children, this is no place for you. Take yourselves off to the front room and stay there. We don't want you running around destroying evidence, do we Dais?" And with that I was despatched with my three cousins into Aunt Daisy's front room where the table was all set for tea. Having just had my faggots snatched from under my nose so to speak, I was getting ravenous and really fancied the cakestand full of fancies. I suppose that's how they got their name because people fancied them, but despite some very strong hints my cousins seemed impervious to my impending starvation.

Meanwhile, Uncle Arthur had been up to Lavender Hill police station and had returned with a large constable complete with dripping cape, notebook and pencil. He surveyed the scene, looked at the boulder from every angle, took copious notes and then asked for a tape measure with which he carefully measured the size of the boulder and its position in the lean-to. When this was all over, he pointed up to the roof and solemnly announced to Uncle Arthur,

"Don't worry sir, we'll soon apprehend whoever was responsible. Got to have been a big chap to get this here rock up there. Can't be many around like that". And with that he disappeared out of the door.

How he thought anybody could have got a rock that size ten foot into the air without a crane beats me but he was deadly serious. The house stood in the middle of a terrace which had fifty-foot-long gardens backing on to similar gardens of houses in the next street. There was no rear access without climbing over several neighbouring fences.

Once PC Plod had gone we stayed discussing where the boulder could possibly have come from. I was sure, from what little I had learned from my cigarette cards, that it was a meteorite. But although they could come up with no better explanation, nobody else was convinced. One thing I do clearly remember about that night is that I got to sample the delights of my first ever cream horn.

Uncle Arthur heard no more from the police and during the week had his roof repaired. We would have thought no more about it, except that the following Saturday, comes five o'clock, the same thing happens again. There's cousin Kath pounding on the door and off we go again to Falcon Grove. Once more PC Plod was summoned to repeat his preliminary investigation. This time he came up with an idea to solve the mystery.

" 'ooligans," he pronounced, "on their way home from Craven Cottage." We were somewhat sceptical as this was long before football hooligans had been thought of and it would have taken at least half a dozen of them to even pick up a rock that size let alone launch it the length of the garden. "Next Saturday," he continued, "we'll be waiting for 'em. Catch 'em red handed, you see if we don't."

And so it was that the next Saturday saw my dad, Uncle Arthur and the constable crouching in the garden at the appointed time. Naturally, the rest of the family didn't want to miss out on the excitement and Aunt Daisy's house quickly filled up with all her close relatives. By that I mean those relatives living close to her rather than those close by birth, although there wasn't much difference in those days. I wonder if that was how they got to be called close relatives.

Anyway, there we all were, tucked away out of danger in the front room and I'm slowly sucking the cream out of my second cream horn when there's this almighty crash. Running through to the back, there was the regular delivery sat squarely on the floor of the lean-to. As we stood round gazing at it in awe, in came the ambush party from the garden looking very shaken and pale.

"Did you see that?" they asked each other. "It came right over our blinking heads". They were convinced that they had seen a one hundredweight boulder fly at least fifty feet at a height of twenty feet or so before crashing through the lean-to roof, but they saw or heard nothing that could have projected it.

The story aroused great local interest and Uncle Arthur and my dad were interviewed by a reporter from the South Western Star. However, the mystery of the flying boulders was never solved and there were no more occurrences - unless of course the happenings next door some months later have a bearing.

Next door to Uncle Arthur and Aunt Daisy, lived an old lady of eighty-odd who had been recently widowed. One Saturday in the September following the boulder incidents, she went up to Battersea High Street shopping, carefully locking up the house before she left. Even in those days it wasn't wise to leave property insecure in south London. Soon after her return, she went to her front room intending to water the aspidistra. But to her surprise, she couldn't get the door open. It wasn't stuck, but something seemed to be jammed behind it, preventing it from opening more than an inch or so. No matter how hard she pushed it would not budge.

Without ado she shuffled round to next door and elicited the help of my Uncle Arthur, but try as he might the door remained firmly shut. The next ploy was to try the windows, but old Mrs Wyatt had made a good job of locking up and the sash was well and truly secured. He tried peering through but the curtains had been drawn to keep the afternoon sun off the furniture and although there was a small gap it was too gloomy inside for anything to be seen.

Eventually, he did manage to force the window catch with a screwdriver to gain access and was amazed to find that furniture from inside the room was piled up behind the door. The table, sideboard, chairs, even pictures off the wall were all part of the heap.

Mrs Wyatt was a bit eccentric and swore it was her dead husband Albert's way of getting in touch with her, although why he should want to do that was beyond me as they had spent a long quarrelsome life together. The local press got to hear of the incident and she also had a visit from one of the psychic papers. They were convinced the incident was connected with the flying boulders next door, which had arrived soon after Albert's death. All I can say is that if Albert was responsible for the boulders, he was a rotten shot.

The following Summer, I was glad I had saved the profits from my football sweep, when dad proudly announced we were going on holiday. When the time came to start the holiday we had to get up quite early in the morning and catch the first tram of the day, that would take us from the end of our road down to London Bridge. It was a Number 34, driven by Billy Sharpe's father. From London Bridge we had to carry our luggage as far as Tower Bridge Pier which was the terminus for ferryboats which ran along the Thames estuary. The largest of these was The Royal Eagle, which went as far as Southend, but that morning, we boarded a smaller vessel, The Laguna Belle, which took us to Clacton. I found the boat trip most exhilarating and would have happily spent the entire week just cruising backwards and forwards on it. As it was we were booked into digs a few hundred yards behind the pier at Clacton.

I used some of my savings to purchase fishing tackle. It was nothing fancy, just a handline wound on a square wooden frame, with a large hook and lead weight on the end. Most days my parents were glad to give me the penny needed to get on to the pier so that they could spend the day by themselves. The landlady wrapped me up some sandwiches in greaseproof paper and I would happily fish until half past four when Mum and Dad would meet me near the pier entrance. In this way they didn't have to pay out unnecessarily to come on to the pier to get me.

I soon established my own fishing spot halfway down some steps at the side of the pier that went down to a small landing stage used for speedboat trips. I remember hooking the odd herring or mackerel but mostly my line would come up with a crab on the end busily pinching my bait. I think my hook must have been the wrong size and too near the bottom but I was content just to be there with grown-up fishermen.

I didn't own a watch, so when I thought it was getting near time to go, I asked somebody the time. I then threw all my line into the water and wound it neatly back on to the wooden frame, ready to go and meet my parents. Towards the end of the holiday I was busy winding in from my final cast when the line went tight. I had got a fish and it felt like a big one. With nothing but the line to hang on to, I was quickly in trouble and had to shout for help. Seeing my predicament, a couple of men put down their rods and ran down the steps to help. Taking the line from me they quickly pulled on to the steps the strangest creature I had ever seen.

"It's a swordfish," I cried, for I could plainly see a six inch blade protruding from it's snout. The fish leapt about on the steps and the men found it difficult to get hold of, being wary of the flashing blade. In an attempt to hold it down, one of them put his foot on it and promptly broke the blade in half. After sparring with it for a few more minutes he managed to stamp on its head and broke its neck. It turned out to be a garfish, about eighteen inches long in all - that is, before it had its blade broken. The men looped my handkerchief through its gills so that I could carry it back to show my parents. I walked down the pier in a delirious state, heady with the attention as everybody turned to see this genius who had made such a rare catch. Excitedly, I greeted my parents outside the pier.

"Look Dad, look what I've caught".

"Hmm, that's a funny old thing," he replied, and then after a few moments thought, "I'll bet the shop that sold you the line never thought you would catch anything like that."

That was it. I would take it back to their shop and they would probably have it stuffed and put on display for all their customers to admire. Although we were due back at the digs for tea, I insisted we all went immediately round to the fishing tackle shop. I felt quite dejected when we arrive just before closing time and they showed not the slightest interest.

One other event sticks in my memory from that holiday. On the beach there was the usual Punch and Judy show. The puppeteer also ran a children's talent competition every week which used to attract quite big crowds of children and parents. There was no charge for entry but quite worthwhile prizes. He made his money by passing the hat around the large audience. The competition was divided into two parts. The main section was for those who had talent, and was followed by a funny-face contest for those who hadn't. Not having my yo-yo with me, the only way I felt I could compete was in the funny-face contest. I already had a head start with a mouth that was too big and slightly protruding ears. I entered and managed to win first prize which was a large box of chocolates. When I opened it up, I was surprised to see there was a gramophone record inside the lid. We didn't own a gramophone at the time, but after my usual pestering, my father managed to get one from our local second-hand shop. That record was my introduction to classical music. It contained excerpts from Gilbert and Sullivan musicals. I loved every note and played it over and over again. Even now I can still sing most of the songs that were on it, word perfect.

I haven't said very much about school, probably because I wasn't very good at it. I had to see an immediate reason for learning something or else I didn't bother. One example of this was spelling. We had what must have been a very forward-looking English teacher, who organised spelling in quite a novel way. Each day she would line us up around the walls of the classroom. Then she broke the circle at an arbitrary point to establish an initial order of merit as it were. The child at the front was then given a word to spell and if correct, maintained position. A new word would then be put to the next in line. If a word was spelt incorrectly, it was offered down the line until somebody got it right. He or she then moved ahead of all those who had been unable to spell that word. I took great delight in this game and got a lot of satisfaction out of moving up the line. The beauty of the game was that on the face of it you were never sent down the line, only up, so there were no failures, only successes. I put a lot of effort into learning words in order to succeed at it and remain good at spelling to this day. I commend the method to any modern teacher who cares to use it.

My favourite lesson, if you can call it a lesson, was swimming. Every Friday afternoon at three o'clock we were marched in a crocodile down to the Latchmere Road Baths, our costumes rolled up inside our off-white towels. For some reason that escapes me, we were always anxious to be the first one into the water, and as we neared the building we would bend down and undo our bootlaces and all the buttons on our shirts in readiness. If we could get away with it without the teacher spotting us we would also remove our jackets. Why this went on I don't know, but it did. After the session was over we would dress with equal haste as we were allowed to find our own way home as soon as we were ready.

For many kids, these sessions were the only complete immersion in water they ever got, as nobody had bathrooms at home. In my younger days, Mum used to give me a weekly scrub in a galvanised bath on the kitchen table, but when I reached the age of eight or nine I suddenly became too embarrassed to appear naked in front of her. She then let me go with my friends down to Latchmere Road where they had hot baths as well as the swimming pool. These were operated by a giant of a man who must have weighed all of twenty stones. He always seemed to be in a sweat. I used to wonder if it was him that heaved the boulders through Uncle Arthur's lean-to; he was big enough. When a bath became empty he would call the next in line forward and fill the bath from taps which were operated from outside the cubicle. Whilst the bath was filling he peeled a clean towel for you from the top of the pile. There is no other word to describe his action as the towels were all heavily starched and stuck together. They contained so much starch that you could fold one down the middle and then stand it on end like a miniature tent. Having got your towel, you then tested the temperature of the bath water before he shut the door with a grunt and moved on with a "Next please!" If we got adjacent cubicles, and sometimes even if we didn't, we would throw idle boyish chatter to each other over the partition walls. "What colour's your cubicle door? mine's green." "How are you getting on, are you out yet?" "Fancy the pictures on Saturday?" Occasionally we would shout to the attendant, "A drop more hot for Number Five please," a request which might or might not be met depending on how often one had called before and how busy he was. When we emerged, he would enter with a large cloth and a bucket containing Lysol, which he proceeded to slosh all round the bath before crying out yet again, "Next please."

One other school subject that I enjoyed was Nature Study and was for ever taking in odd things that I had found such as crickets or cockroaches. The most notable was a lizard that my father bought from a colleague at work. It came in a wooden box about three inches deep with a glass cover which slid along grooves cut into the sides of the box. To be honest the lizard was a bit of a disappointment as it just lay immobile in the bottom of the box, no matter how much I prodded it.

Anyway, anxious to show it off, I asked Dad if I could take it to school and he agreed, warning me to be careful it didn't escape as the wood at one side of the box was split across. This didn't matter too much if you were careful, as the glass top held the loose piece in place.

Come Monday morning, off I went with Dad's lizard and quickly gathered a crowd around me on the way to school. I showed it to the teacher, who was interested, but after I had milked maximum attention out of the situation, I was told firmly to put it out of sight on the lower shelf of my desk. I say, "my desk", but I actually shared it with my best friend of the time, Jim Kempster, a ginger haired, freckle faced lad. The desks were flat-topped with two slots at the front in which we could stand slates or exercise books, with everything else being slid under on to the lower shelf.

Halfway through the lesson, Jim gave me a nudge and pointed

to his slate slot. Peering out of the top was Dad's lizard. The warmth of the radiator next to our desk had brought him out of hibernation and he had escaped from the broken box. You can imagine the fun we had trying to recapture him. He certainly wasn't the same docile creature Dad had brought home. He was like quicksilver darting between the desks to avoid capture. After avoiding our lunges for about five minutes, he made a bid for freedom under the classroom door. Wrenching the door open, we continued the chase across the corridor and into the washroom opposite. Before we could do anything about it, he disappeared down a drain hole and was never seen again. That night I had the job of explaining to my father what had happened to his recent purchase.

And so, although I enjoyed my junior school days, when it came to the Junior County examinations, I failed. This was no great disgrace as most of the boys in the school were expected to fail. In my year only one boy, William Bachelor, gained a scholarship to the Sir Walter St John's School. This was a grammar school situated at the other end of Battersea High Street, not far from where we lived. It had was held in high esteem, had a very good academic record and a smart school uniform. It was the only school around which insisted on 'all whites' for cricket. It was also possible to attend the school as a fee paying pupil but the only children who had ever gone there from our neighbourhood were scholarship winners.

Ever since my sister Irene had died, my mother had harboured secret dreams of sending me to 'Sinjuns', as it was commonly called. This was the next part of the plan for the better life that she had initiated when Billy Waller came to lodge with us five years before. She was all the more disappointed that I hadn't passed the scholarship, in that two of my cousins had previously done so and she hoped that intelligence ran in the family. She sought the advice of my old headmaster, Mr Weatherly. Would it be worth spending money to give me a good education? Mr Weatherly was frank. He described me as an intelligent, enthusiastic time-waster who liked fun and games. He considered it would only be worthwhile if I was prepared to put my mind to my studies. At Mum's insistence, he agreed to give me a good talking to, to see if he could instil in me the importance of a good secondary education.

This he duly did and a couple of weeks later, I went to Sinjuns to sit intelligence tests. I was adjudged fit to go straight into Form 1B, being too old for the Prep Form. Immediately Mum knew I had been accepted, she went to the Post Office and drew out some of Billy Waller's rent money that she had secretly salted away over the years and used it to pay for my school uniform and fees. Buster was going to Sinjuns.

Chapter 5

Sinjuns

The clothes that were required for Sinjuns must have cost my mum an arm and a leg. It wasn't just a case of going down to the market in Battersea High Street and picking out something cheap. We were given a list by the school of what was required and the name of the approved stockist of the blazer, who then expected to sell you the rest of the gear at the same time. This included the sort of things one would wear at any school, such as shirts, shoes and trousers, but in addition, a full set of sports clothing.

Even in the First Form, all boys were expected to have cricket whites, including boots, as well as football kit, gym shoes and shorts. The white cricket flannels were full length, whereas my normal school trousers were knee-length grey flannel shorts. In keeping with school regulations, we all wore short trousers until we were old enough to enter the Fourth Form at the age of about fifteen. By then, many of the boys were almost six foot tall and shaving every day. It was quite a funny sight to see them in short trousers, but rules had to be obeyed. The final items Mum bought to complete my school kit were a leather satchel and a Platignum fountain pen, complete with gold nib, costing one shilling and threepence.

A few days before starting, I had to go back to Sinjuns for a further interview. The old headmaster, Mr Taylor was retiring and I was interviewed by his deputy, Dr Barlow, who was acting as a temporary stand-in, awaiting the arrival of the new headmaster, J. E. Taylor, who was the old headmaster's son. Not surprisingly, when he eventually arrived at the school, he was immediately given the nickname, Jet. As I found out later, most of the masters were given similar nicknames by the boys.

I was very impressed by Dr Barlow. He was a tall, military looking man; most imposing in his mortar board and gown. He had an awesome and inspiring presence. His outstanding feature was his speaking voice, and I'm sure every Sinjun Old Boy remembers it well. He spoke slowly and forcibly, hanging on to the end of every word. He was the epitome of the schoolmaster caricature seen in modern comedy films.

"Now my boy," he boomed, "I hope you realise the tremendous sacrifice your parents are making to send you here, what?" I opened my mouth to reply, but he did not expect an answer and continued with his sermon oblivious of my presence.

"Whilst you are here boy, you will be expected to adhere to the school rules, work hard and uphold the good name of the school. Remember, at all times you are an ambassador of the school, particularly when wearing your school uniform." He continued on in this vein for some considerable time, lecturing me as he had obviously done to many new boys previously. Nevertheless, I was greatly impressed and took every word to heart. At the end of his oration my mother was presented with my school cap and tie, which she had to pay for, and the interview was then deemed to be at an end.

I started the following Monday, setting off to walk the half mile or so, having first been given a farewell hug and kiss by Mum. I was very self-conscious in my new outfit, all of which was that little bit too big, to allow room for growth. For those of you not familiar with Battersea, I had better explain my route. My old school was situated at the T-junction of Musjid Road with Mantua Street, just fifty yards or so from our house. To get to Sinjuns, I had to walk to the other end of our road and turn south along Battersea High Street. This took me through the market, where many of my former classmates now worked.

In those days, at the age of twelve, if you didn't go on to a secondary (grammar), technical or central school, you left and started work. Many of my old friends couldn't wait to get down to the market and earn some money, considering school a complete waste of time. This attitude was encouraged by many parents who had no ambitions for their offspring except to see them contribute to the family income, often by helping out on the family stall.

Now I was obliged to run the gauntlet of their jeers and whistles. I was very apprehensive as I neared the market, but it was all good humoured banter and not half as bad as I had anticipated. As I neared the end of the market on my first morning my eyes fell on an attractive young brunette, about sixteen or seventeen years old, stood at the side of one of the vegetable stalls. She was wearing a red satin blouse and black skirt, protected by a potato sack tied round her middle as an apron. But the most striking thing about her was her face. Although she had dark, crimped hair, her eyes were bright blue. Beneath a small button nose, her mouth had been accentuated by a vivid scarlet lipstick. She instantly reminded me of a beautiful china doll that used to belong to my sister Irene. Even more self-conscious than before, I started to blush as I approached. I didn't know who she was, but she must have recognised me as to my surprise she flashed me a big smile and a cheery, "Hello Buster, you look smart. All dressed up like the dog's dinner." I was too tongue-tied to reply but managed to give her a knowing wink, as I did nearly every morning for the next five years on my way to school. I used to be quite concerned if she wasn't there and hope nothing had happened to her. Being much younger than her, I never did pluck up the courage to ask her out and to this day I'm sure she never suspected how attracted I was to her.

Two years ago, I made one of my regular visits to *Chez Fred's* in Westbourne, Bournemouth, for one of his exquisite fish suppers (an absolute must if you're ever down that way on holiday) when a lady of about my age came up to my table.

"You're Buster Merryfield, aren't you?" she asked. I had no option but to plead guilty, whereupon she continued, "I used to live near you in Battersea." I gazed at her intently, trying to strip off sixty years of aging in the hopes of recognising a familiar face underneath, but to no avail. I made a few wild stabs by mentioning my old school and the names of a few old friends but still couldn't place her. At last she put me out of my misery.

"You're the cheeky one who used to wink at my cousin on the market, aren't you?" They had obviously had a giggle together over my awkward flirtations all those years ago. I felt a bit silly, but managed to exchange a few pleasant reminiscences of school days in Battersea.

"Anyway," she concluded, "You're too late now. She's married with three kids and half a dozen grandchildren." And with a mischievous chuckle, she returned to her cod and chips at the other end of the restaurant.

On arrival at school on that first morning, I anxiously scanned the faces in the school playground, looking for the familiar face of William Bachelor, the only boy from my old school to get a scholarship. He was not to be seen. I wandered round apprehensively trying to appear confident and nonchalant. Eventually I finished up next to a large Howitzer gun, a remnant from the nineteen eighteen war, which dominated one end of the playground. I assume that the school must have been taken over as a barracks, and the gun abandoned at the cessation of hostilities. Whatever the reason, there it was. I wandered over to look at it and got into conversation with another new boy who was doing the same. Before long the caretaker appeared and rang the school bell, whereupon we instinctively followed the older boys into the main building where we were all ushered into the grand hall. I had been through the hall before on the way to my interview the previous week, but the atmosphere was completely different now that it was filled with boys. Sinjuns was only for boys:the girls went to Broomfield Road.

Once inside the hall, we were arranged by rows in ascending ages, youngest boys at the front. We all stood shoulder to shoulder, whilst the masters stood in their gowns and mortar boards down the side of the hall, opposite their forms. At one second to nine, the new headmaster, Jet, mounted the stage and took up his position behind a lectern which bore a huge black bible.

"We will start the day with hymn number seven, *All people that on Earth do dwell*," he announced. With that, the mighty organ, mounted in the gallery behind us, played the opening chords of the introduction. Following the hymn, Jet sent up a prayer thanking God for all the good things He had already given us and would be giving us this day. He delivered the same words every day for the rest of my schooling and I used to wonder why he couldn't thank God for the week and thus save time. Following the prayer, he solemnly read out the school notices for the day before we sang the final hymn, 'Praise my soul the King of Heaven', and filed out to our classrooms.

On seeing that my new playground friend was also in Form 1B, I rushed across the classroom and reserved a desk at the front next to his. During our earlier brief encounter, I had realised that he was a cut above me in background and bearing, and I decided to use him as my role model. I soon discovered his name was Reg Bottomley and we started a friendship that lasted not only throughout our schooldays but on into adult life. He grew up to be a notable citizen, becoming a member of Esher Town Council, a Sinjun School Governor and President of the Sinjuns Old Boy Association. I certainly picked a good'un.

Each form had a Form Master, who for 1B was Mr Lawrenson. Unfortunately, he had difficulty walking. I don't know if this was due to something like rheumatism or arthritis, or whether he had picked up some injury during the first world war. However, most unkindly, the boys called him Kipper Feet, or more usually, just Kipper. This was a pity because when we got to know him he was a very nice man. As our Form Master, he was obliged to give us Religious Instruction twice a week, a ritual that went on in every form, but his subject specialisation was Mathematics. He taught this very well and I suppose it was largely thanks to him that although I was not particularly mathematically-minded, I was able to get a job in a bank later in life, but that's another story.

Having survived the first day, I soon settled into a routine. Every morning I walked through the market delivering my wink, and usually came home again at lunch time. Now I was older, Mum often worked the evening shift as a waitress. This meant she could be at home during the day and provide lunch for me. When she wasn't available, I would either take sandwiches to school or she would give me money to go to the pie and eel shop, Harringtons, which was in Falcon Road and much cheaper than paying for school dinners.

At the pie shop, I couldn't afford the eels that some of the men ate, and had to satisfy myself with pie and mash. The pies were kept piping hot in a heated glass-fronted cabinet and were quite unlike anything sold by supermarkets today. They had rubbery, waterproof pastry holding in the gravy which oozed from the minced beef inside. When cut open, they issued clouds of steam and woe betide anybody who took the first bite without first blowing on it, as it would skin the inside of the mouth. If I had the extra halfpenny to spare, I would have 'liquor' poured on to my pie and mash. This was not alcohol as the name might suggest, but a thin, green, parsley sauce. If I couldn't afford liquor, I would liberally douse everything with what we called 'chilli vinegar'. On each of the bare wooden tables stood a bottle of vinegar containing small red capsicums to add extra spice. It was really provided to add piquancy to the jellied eels, but I used to love it on my pie and mash. Even to this day, I drench all savoury dishes with vinegar, and smother mint sauce over any meat, irrespective of the animal of origin.

After lunch, it was back to school again for more lessons until four o'clock, then home for tea and homework. In the evenings, I would change out of school uniform and go out to play with my old friends as before, although many of them had new interests now that they had a little money in their pockets.

And so I reached the end of the first term at my new school. We were released early on the last day, and not having any homework to do for the next morning, I was in no hurry to get home. I was pleased to meet a couple of my old mates from Mantua Street, who had also been released early from their elementary school. We were wandering aimlessly along the High Street when the opportunity for one of our favourite dares appeared. The dare involved climbing on to the back of a flat bed lorry such as a coal cart and then seeing how long you dared to stay on board as it gathered speed and sped away. Last one off was the hero.

There in front of us was a Charrington's Brewery lorry which had been delivering along the High Street and was now about to return to the brewery with the empties. We waited for the driver and his mate to get into the cab and leapt aboard as the lorry gently pulled away. Having to negotiate the High Street traffic, it did not reach any great speed and we were all three still aboard when it reached the T-junction with Falcon Road where it had to stop for passing traffic. A small queue formed behind it and to my horror, there pulled up behind us was Dr Barlow driving his Austin Seven. I tried to duck but it was too late. I had been seen - and I was in full school uniform. I looked up and our eyes met.

You can imagine the effect this had on my summer holiday. For six weeks or more I worried myself to death, picturing all sorts of scenarios, most of which involved me being called out in front of the assembled school and expelled. I dare not tell my parents what I had done and returned to school the next term full of trepidation. Assembly came and went - nothing happened. Ah, I expect it will be my new Form Master who deals with it. But no - he seemed blissfully unaware of the reason for my lack of concentration. As the day wore on my confidence began to return. Was I going to get away with it? The short answer was 'Yes'. The incident was never mentioned in all the time I was at Sinjuns. Some years later, I returned to the school for an Old Boys reunion day. I was at the reception, glass of lemonade in my hand, watching Dr Barlow going round greeting past pupils. On reaching me he shook my hand and said, "Face is familiar, can't remember the name. Must be getting old. Just remind me will you."

"Merryfield, Sir."

"Ah yes, Merryfield," he sighed, and looking down at my glass, added, "Glad to see you are on the wagon - or should it be off the wagon in your case?" And with a wink and a smile he was gone. He had kept quiet all those years ago, knowing how much my presence at Sinjuns meant to my mother and how hard she had had to struggle to send me there.

I think it was that great comedian Les Dawson who claimed he was such an awful child that his parents moved house whilst he was away at school. Towards the end of my first year at Sinjuns this actually happened to me, although my parents did tell me in advance and gave me the address of the new house.

I mentioned that Mum was now working more and more in the evenings. This enabled her to take on additional work during the day doing housework in the large houses near Wandsworth Common. We used to call it 'charring'. Just as she had saved Billy Waller's rent money to send me to school, she also saved her char money and used it to put down a deposit on a small terraced house in Mallinson Road, which was close to where she went charring. If you know the area, it was one of the side roads leading uphill from Northcote Road, which lies in the valley of the old River Falcon. This alas, was long ago relegated to an underground culvert.

I was not old enough at the time to be included in discussions on family finance, nor did I want to be, so I am a little vague over the cost of the house. However, I seem to recall she had to find £100, which was about a third of the total cost, the rest being on a twenty-five-year mortgage. If only she had bought a dozen more at the same time.

Mum was still paying my school fees out of her earnings and to meet the costs of a mortgage on top of that was virtually impossible. But a combination of determination and a good business sense enabled her to pull it off. What she did was to let the upper part of the house. So we were still sharing with another family, just as we did in Musjid Road, but we owned everything, had greatly improved facilities and were now situated in a much better neighbourhood. The front of the house stood back a yard or two behind a low stone wall backed by a privet hedge. Once again we lived mainly downstairs, having a front room, sitting room, spacious bedroom, a large scullery-come-kitchen and an outside toilet. Having only the one bedroom, once again I had to sleep in the front room. On the upstairs landing there was a bathroom which we shared with our tenants, Mr and Mrs Sealey, who occupied the upstairs rooms. Best of all, behind the house we had a small garden with flowers and a lawn.

I suppose the road was about a hundred yards long with a mixture of houses. Opposite us were much larger, three-storey houses which also boasted basements. From the end of the road there were very convenient bus services for Mum and Dad to get to work on and we were not far from Clapham Junction railway station and bus depot. From there, the Number 37 bus ran to Peckham. Little did I realise at the time the significance that name would have on my life some 50 years later.

I was also pleased to see that once again we were not far from an open market, this time in Northcote Road. I had always found the Battersea High Street market fascinating, but Northcote Road was even better. I would often wander down there on a Saturday afternoon just to absorb the atmosphere which was a strange mixture of rush and bustle but with an underlying sense of warmth and security. It seemed timeless.

My favourite stall sold second-hand books, but also dealt in comics, some of which were third-hand or even fourth-hand. My parents had never had the money for me to have new comics delivered weekly, We were lucky to afford even a newspaper. So I would visit the market and pour over the well-fingered heaps of Magnets and Gems, searching for missing episodes to serials. To this day I still don't know who The Phantom of Cursitor Fields was as I never did find the critical issue of Bullseye.

As Christmas approached, the market became even more colourful and seemed to take on a different feeling. As the weak winter daylight faded away in late afternoon, one by one the stall holders pumped up their acetylene lamps and hung them around the frameworks which supported the striped awnings. They hissed and spluttered in a way that seemed threatening and yet at the same time offered comfort. The light they shed was intensely white, imparting a bluish tinge to all it bathed beneath. It bounced up from the wet pavements casting dancing lights on to the sides of red double-deckers passing by, their tyres zipping out a misty spray.

The marketeers made a special effort at Christmas to decorate their stalls. The fruits were set out in intricately arranged patterns with some carefully wrapped in silver foil or coloured tissue papers for extra effect. Sprigs of holly and mistletoe were placed at strategic points. Most stalls would have coloured streamers and tinsel wound around the uprights, with the occasional balloon bobbing on the breeze stirred up by the passing traffic.

As well as the authorised stalls, whose owners had paid their market dues, there was a myriad of one-man enterprises cashing in on the prevailing Christmas spirit. The Christmas tree man, with trees piled high around him, customers pulling them out of the heap and sizing them in their mind's eye against the space available back home. "How much is this one then?" "To you missus, a shillin'." "I'll take it." And so it went on.

Balloon sellers, tempting children with their gay bunches of multi-coloured balloons floating high above them; round ones, long ones and best of all, some with undulations along their length looking like giant caterpillars or multiple egg timers. Three-card-tricksters, inviting men to find the lady and quickly parting suckers from their money. Fly-by-nights, with open suitcases on the ground in front of them, pressing their wares on the passers by; anything from artificial silk stockings to fluffy dolls and mechanical toys. Amongst them, a woman with a wicker basket selling sprigs of mistletoe and another seeking sympathetic homes for four black-and-white kittens which she held out imploringly hoping their pitiful mews would evoke some reaction.

I stopped in fascination to watch the quack medicine man who, in spite of the inclement weather, was completely bare down to his waist. He was covered in a marvellous collection of tattoos, but was so blue with the cold they almost blended in. He sold various patent medicines including the Elixir of Life, which I suspected was diluted syrup of figs, and what he called 'Pink Pills for Pale People at Popular Prices'. Word had it that he fashioned these from Lifebuoy soap.

Occupying the stall next to him was another favourite who sold metal polish. His stall held a collection of old coal scuttles, kettles and fenders which he used to demonstrate the power of his product. First he tarnished the metal by running a hot blow lamp along it and then showed the ease with which his polish restored a chrome-like gleam. He attracted a large crowd and as he pumped up his blow lamp he cried out, as always, "Run away, Sonny. This is a blow lamp, not a toy." And with that he waved it along the front of the crowd causing me to leap back in mock fear.

But by far the biggest crowd was around the poultry stall, picking out their chickens, ducks and geese for Christmas Day. The birds were strung in rows across the underside of the awning, their crossed feet impaled on butchers' hooks and their wrung necks almost touching the butcher's straw boater. The shoppers stood around the stall, shuffling from foot to foot as the butcher extolled the quality of his fare. But they were reluctant to part with their money, knowing that prices would fall as the afternoon wore on.

Complementing this profusion of sights was an ever-present smell which subtly changed from celery to oranges to leather to fish to roasted chestnuts, as one sauntered around. But above all, it was the sounds that conveyed the spirit of the market. Wandering from stall to stall the vendor's cries would swell and fade.

"Get your bananas here!" from Dave, The Banana King, who sold nothing else.

"Apples and Pears a Pound. Luverly ripe toma'ers." These cries alternated from two sisters who ran a large fruit stall, whilst further on, an unshaven grey haired man in an old army greatcoat shouted, "Don't forget your little dicky bird," as he held out his sprays of millet and groundsel. Outside the Northcote public house stood 'K-legs' shouting, "News, Star an' Standard. News, Star an' Standard. Thank you Sir." His name came from his terrible deformity, a legacy from the war. In between his calls, he took sips from a glass of Guinness which stood on his newsstand, the froth clinging to his straggly moustache.

At one end of the market, a group of non-conformists from the Baptist church bravely competed with the market cries, singing Christmas carols to the accompaniment of the local Salvation Army band. At the other end, stood a smaller group; a trio of ex-servicemen busking a similar selection of carols and hymns, but with a strangely different rhythm. Between the three of them they had a squeeze-box accordion, a cornet and a banjo, but only five legs and five eyes. A large painted sign carried the message, "Gassed on the Somme". Next to this, a smaller temporary sign proclaiming, "Merry Christmas to all" was propped behind an upturned cap containing a few coppers. My eyes misted over at their unique rendering of 'The Old Rugged Cross', played in true evangelical style. Even now, I become very maudlin whenever I hear that tune.

Chapter 6

Hobbies and Activities

Once I had settled in to my new surroundings, I soon discovered there were two other Sinjuns' boys living in the road, brothers, Tom and Colin Lawrence. Later, another local boy called Peter Strowger started at Sinjuns, but he was somewhat younger. We all became very good friends and would walk the mile and a half to and from school together twice a day, except on Wednesdays, which were sports afternoons. On those days we hurried from school straight after lunch to the end of Battersea High Street. Here we caught the bus to the school's sports ground at the 'Surrey Tavern', which was on the south side of Wandsworth Common. So on Wednesday afternoons, we were able to take a very pleasant stroll home across the common. I still see Peter, who now owns an antique shop in Blandford Forum, and we sometimes sit behind his shop taking nostalgic walks back to Mallinson Road.

We have many pleasant memories of the good times we all used to spend on Wandsworth Common, largely centred around two ponds. The larger pond had an island in the centre that was only accessible to the older children, as it involved wading out chest deep across a very uneven pond bottom. We boys considered it quite an adventure in the Summer to put on our bathing costumes and wade out to explore the island. It was completely overgrown and full of wild life. We had to watch out for the swans, who really did get wild if we went too close to their nests.

The other pond was called Two Island Pond, for two very obvious reasons. The smaller island lay in quite shallow water enabling even quite young children to wade out to it. Many people picnicked in the area and even in those days there would be bits of rubbish and broken bottles in the water, resulting in many a child ending up with an injured foot. That didn't stop them from paddling around with small nets fixed to long canes, trying to catch minnows and the red-throated sticklebacks.

The other island was in much deeper water and virtually inaccessible. In that area the pond was edged with spiked metal railings which were supposed to prevent children from falling in, but I managed it. As the water was deep and away from the noise and bustle of children, the larger fish used to congregate at this end of the pond. It would have been perfectly easy to fish for them from the path behind the railings, but boys being boys, we preferred to go inside the railings to reach that extra yard of distance out into the pond. Once inside, there was virtually no bank to stand on and we had to hold on to the railings with one hand behind our backs whilst holding our nets in the other. It must have been obvious to anybody other than small boys that sooner or later the inevitable would happen. Sure enough, in I went. Fortunately I was able to get out again without even letting go of my net. I would like to add that when I got out I had a large fish in it, but I can't. I'm afraid the only thing I caught that day was the wrath of my mother's tongue for coming home wet.

As well as fishing, I would spend a lot of time on Wandsworth Common collecting butterflies and moths. As you can imagine, there were not many butterflies inhabiting the concrete and asphalt of Musjid Road, and in my early days, my only acquaintance with them was through cigarette cards. I was captivated by their beauty and colour and would avidly read about them on the backs of the cards. I could never understand why I didn't see them flitting about, when the cards clearly stated that they inhabited southern England.

However, backing on to our small garden in Mallinson Road was Battersea Rise Cemetery. This had open grassy spaces with lots of flowers, both in beds and on the graves. These attracted a profusion of butterflies which wandered over the fence and into our garden. I instantly recognised all the common varieties from my cigarette cards. Cabbage Whites, Red Admirals, Tortoiseshells, Large Blues, Fritillaries; they were all there.

My interest developed into a hobby which I pursued keenly, visiting first the local library for information and later taking trips to the Kensington Natural History Museum. I bought a butterfly net and carefully mounted the specimens I caught on special pins to add to my growing collection. My enthusiasm infected Colin Lawrence and we spent many hours on the common literally 'pursuing' our hobby. There was a keen but friendly rivalry between us and on first spotting a butterfly which had been unfortunate enough to come our way, there would be loud cries of "Bagsie that Peacock" or whatever. If you got the wrong name, the bagsie didn't count, but if the butterfly was correctly named we would then both join in the pursuit and it didn't matter who finally caught it, ownership had already been established.

Our interest also extended to moths. Most moths only come out at night, so we would make our way to the common in the late evening and hunt along the hedgerows in the increasing gloom, watching for the first flutterings of the awakening moths. Hardly had they stretched their wings and they would be in the net. Sometimes we would get carried away and would still be hunting by torchlight well after my normal nine o'clock curfew. At first my mother worried and I got the occasional reprimand, but later she came to accept it. This proved extremely useful whenever I was out late for other reasons. I only had to say, "Sorry Mum, got carried away mothing" and I would get away with, "I wish you would tell me before you go," her mildest rebuke.

I also used to get some strange glances from our neighbours, who, seeing me cowering in their front hedges, were convinced I was up to no good. It was not easy to convince them I was searching for the elusive Privet Hawk Moth, which I never did manage to find.

I recall one unfortunate butterfly episode that happened on my way home from school. I spotted a magnificent specimen on a Buddleia bush in the garden of one of a row of large detached houses. It was a particularly rare Fritillary that I desperately wanted for my collection. Glancing furtively up and down the road, I decided that it was worth the risk of sneaking into the garden to capture it.

This was not going to be easy as all I had to net it with was my school cap. Gently, I opened the wrought iron gate, praying that it wouldn't squeak. I crunched across the gravel towards the bush which was close to the front of the house.

Just as I got there, the butterfly tantalisingly rose into the air and drifted over the wooden fence into the next garden and began investigating the centre of a rose blossom. Undeterred, I quickly crossed the lawn and without too much difficulty shinned over the fence. Where had it gone? Ah there it was over the other side of the garden now. Once again I began my stalking as it fluttered from bush to bush, only to be thwarted yet again as it cleared the next fence. Over the fence I went and this time I kept my eye on it all the time, managing to corner it in a patch of magnificent multi-coloured lupins. With my cap held poised in front of me I slowly advanced, determined not to let it get away for a third time. Just as I got close it floated up from the plant it was on but quick as a flash I plunged forward to trap it.

Unfortunately, I had been looking at the butterfly and not where I was putting my feet. As I stepped forward I tripped over a wooden stake at the front of the flower bed and crashed headlong into the lupins, bringing down most of them with me. My concentration had been so intense that I also failed to notice the owner of the house who had been watching my escapades with some curiosity.

As he picked me up by my collar and suspended me some three inches clear of the ground, I had the distinct feeling I was in trouble. He was not pleased to see his prize blooms flattened by a delinquent schoolboy. Once again, I had been caught misbehaving whilst in full school uniform and once again, expulsion loomed large in my thoughts. I could feel warm blood running down my leg from where I had tripped and because of this I was extremely frightened. After cursing me loudly for several minutes he eventually put me down, marched me to his gate and cuffed me soundly round the ear as he jettisoned me from the garden. I was extremely thankful to have escaped alive and waited until I was round the corner before stopping to investigate my leg. To my surprise, there was no blood. I had been so frightened, I had wet myself. Back at school I lived in fear for the next few weeks, but as with the brewer's dray incident, I heard no more.

As I grew older, my interests started to change. I become more and more involved with the local Baptist church and its peripheral activities. My mother's side of the family had always had a close connection with the church. Her grandfather, Ralph Stone, had been a lay preacher known all over Buckinghamshire in the mid-nineteenth century for his open air sermons, and every year we all made a pilgrimage to see his grave at Chalfont St Giles. When we lived at Musjid Road, both my mother and father had worshipped regularly at the local Baptist church. I had attended Sunday school and church services as a matter of course, but now I started to develop a teenage fervour for all things religious.

My entire week became absorbed with church activities. There were prayer meetings, Christian Endeavour, Band of Hope and Boys' Brigade. The latter involved parade nights every Tuesday, band practice on Thursdays, football on Saturdays and then a march to church on Sunday mornings in full regalia, drums beating and bugles blaring. This was just the start of a very busy Sunday with afternoon Sunday School following the morning bible class and church service. Then after tea I would join an open air meeting in the market before evening service in the church and a gathering afterwards at the house of one of the worshippers. This often went on until gone ten o'clock.

I was at a very impressionable age and this religious involvement shaped my character and gave me my philosophy for life. However, I was not an instant believer and questioned everything I was told. I was sceptical and argumentative, but found nobody who could give definitive answers to my questions. I eventually had to accept that religious belief could only be based on faith, even if I didn't have very much of it.

The biggest impression made on me was through Christian Endeavour which was run by the Baptist Pastor Newell. On one occasion he asked us each to draw a picture illustrating a biblical text. I chose "Jesus Christ, the same yesterday, today and for ever," and surrounded it with coloured illustrations of flowers, birds and animals which I copied from library books. I was quite proud of it but it paled into insignificance when I saw the work of a boy called Leslie Page. He was a couple of years older than me and quite good at art. He had drawn a scroll tied with a silken ribbon. This was clutched in a gnarled hand which showed every sinew, wrinkle and vein. His text was "Through Christ - I can."

As I gazed at this masterpiece I knew how Saul must have felt on the road to Damascus when God revealed all and changed his life. The hand I saw in front of me was that of my mother. I realised for the first time the determination she had shown to get me to Sinjuns and to build a better life for me, her strength coming through her Christian belief. I made Leslie's text the tenet of my life and although I did modify it many years later, it carried me through many tribulations that I would not otherwise have surmounted. Through Christ - I can - and did.

Although I had this deep religious belief, you mustn't think I was immediately turned into an angelic goody-goody, far from it. Many a night I would be sent home early from Band of Hope or Christian Endeavour for larking about. Sometimes it would be for teasing Gwen Kington, whom I was rather sweet on, and at other times it was for skirmishes with my best friend, Charlie.

I took on a paper round when I was about fourteen and also assisted the milkman on Saturday mornings. This provided me with spending money and I was very proud when I was able to invite Gwen to the local Globe cinema, the shilling from that mornings milk round being sufficient to buy two tickets. The film was 'Rose Marie', and from that day, the song 'Sweetheart' took on a special poignance. We went once or twice more but I kept my heartfelt ardour well hidden and we ended up good friends rather than sweethearts.

Charlie and I were always getting into mischief, with me being the ringleader who led him into trouble. I remember one night we had been ejected from Boys' Brigade for some minor misdemeanour. We were dawdling along Northcote Road, looking for something to occupy us, as an early arrival home might result in embarrassing enquiries. Passing the front of the Baptist church, we could hear Mr Nelson, the organist, practising the hymns for Sunday. We decided to pop in and listen to him play for a while but found the church door locked. Cutting down the side alley we used Charlie's penknife to jiggle open the lock on a side gate which led into a small paved area at the back of the church. Alas, the back door was also locked. By now we were feeling somewhat thwarted and looked round for other means of entry.

"Here we are," I chuckled to Charlie, "let's try this." I was pointing to a manhole cover set in the asphalt, which I knew concealed a chute leading down to the coke store in the basement. I wasn't really serious as I didn't think we would be able to lever up the cover but we eventually managed it using the metal buckle on my Boys' Brigade belt. Once the coal hole was open, I had no option but to lead the way. Sitting on the edge, I eased myself forward down the short slide and dropped on to the top of the coke heap. I was convinced the metallic roar of sliding coke must wake the dead and held my breath in anticipation. After a few seconds silence I whispered up to Charlie.

"Come on then. What are you waiting for?" And with that he slid down and joined me. Although it was pitch black, we knew where we were. The coke store was just one of a number of rooms in the basement of the church hall, which housed the heating system, as well as storage areas for cleaning equipment and musical instruments, and a large room used for band and choir practice. Fumbling our way along darkened corridors we located the stone flight of steps which took us up into the main church hall.

From here, a further staircase led up to a landing behind the church gallery and a way through into the main church. Fearing awkward questions as to how we had got in, we decided not to go through to Mr Nelson in the church, but instead crept silently along the landing to where there was a ladder leading into the loft of the church. This ladder had a big wooden flap padlocked across it to prevent unauthorised persons gaining access, but that was no deterrent to two determined devils intent on mischief. Looking back, it was quite dangerous as the trap door into the loft was quite high up. Undaunted, I gripped the sides of the wooden flap and shinned my way past to the ladder rungs above. From there I was able to help Charlie up to join me. Carrying on up the ladder, I reached up to the trap door which gave access into the loft and gave it a push. Fate decreed that it was not locked. Back it swung to reveal the base of the church tower. Clambering in, we found it surprisingly light with the street lights filtering in through a small coloured glass window. From one side we could hear the strains of the organ wafting through a low, narrow passageway which led into the roof of the church nave. It was quite eerie and exciting. I could hear my heart beating an accompaniment to the music. Crawling on all fours through this passage we soon came to the ceiling of the church nave. At the far end we could see a semi-circular coloured glass panel let into it. As we looked out over the rafters, the lights in the nave below cast a kaleidoscopic pattern of light on to the sloping underside of the roof. This made the roof space look like the inside of an enchanted castle, and drawn by the light we began to edge our way out across the rafters. One slip and we would have crashed through the plaster ceiling on to the hard stone floor some twenty or thirty feet below.

We had to travel like this for about ten yards, through dust and cobwebs, before we found ourselves at the edge of the glass panel. There we discovered an opening where a small piece of glass had been broken at some time. Peering down we could see the balding head of Mr Nelson, oblivious to our presence. My mind went back to the game I used to play in Billy Waller's bread cart, calling out to strangers from my hiding place. I put my mouth to the opening in the ceiling. "Whooooh," I went and then lay still not daring to breathe. Nothing happened. Mr Nelson carried on playing. He obviously hadn't heard me. I tried again and this time Charlie joined in. "WHOOOOOH," we moaned. This time there was no mistake.

"Who's there?" he called. Then after a few seconds, "I know you're there. Come on out." But we remained still and silent. Now he was not so sure and took a hesitant walk around the nave. Finding nothing he eventually came back to the organ and started playing once more. This time I changed my tune. "Too-Wit-Too-Wooooooh" I went, giving my very best owl imitation. Mr Nelson immediately stopped playing, strode to the church door, unlocked it and disappeared into the night.

Charlie and I nearly fell through the roof with laughter. Fancy old Nelson being afraid of a few strange noises. We eased ourselves back across the rafters, through the stone passage and into the loft.

"Shush," I warned Charlie, "What was that?" Below us we could hear voices and they were coming our way. Mr Nelson had been to the flat adjoining the church and was returning with the caretaker. Quickly we descended the ladder back on to the landing behind the gallery, carefully closing the loft door behind us. The voices were getting nearer. They were ascending the stairs up to the gallery. In a few seconds we would be discovered. Where to hide? Looking round I spotted a small storage cupboard let into the wall about three feet off the floor. I quickly opened it up and looked in. All it contained was a dusty print of the Holman Hunt painting, 'Behold, the stranger at the door'. I heaved myself up and crouched in the cupboard. As I pressed back to get the door shut, I could hear the glass in the picture breaking behind me. Charlie tore open the door and tried to come up with me but the cupboard was hardly big enough for one.

"Get off," I hissed. "Find your own hiding place." With that he scurried off down the stairs three at a time into the church hall where, I later discovered, he hid behind a heavy velvet curtain. Unfortunately, the caretaker also discovered this. The curtain stopped a few inches short of the floor and Charlie's shoes were spotted peeking out from below. He was unceremoniously yanked from his sanctuary, and given a good wigging. This was concluded by a clip round the ear to send him on his way.

Charlie didn't split on me and I remained hidden in the cupboard until they had locked up and left. Cautiously I climbed down and made my way back through the church hall to the coke store. Climbing up the chute was much more difficult than coming down but I eventually made it and went home thinking I had had a lucky escape. My confidence was rudely shattered a couple of evenings later when my parents had a visit from the Church Wardens. They had made a few enquiries concerning Charlie's movements that evening and realised he was not alone in his escapade. I was kept under a very strict curfew for many weeks after.

Chapter 7

Sport and Other Distractions

Getting back to life at Sinjuns, the school had a great tradition of sport. On arrival, boys were allocated to one of six houses and inter-house sport was very competitive. I was allocated to Bolingbroke House. The house master and the prefects together selected teams at various levels and arranged matches against the other houses. Back at Mantua Street School, games had been fairly informal but I had developed quite good skills playing lamppost-cricket and street-football, using a tennis ball for both. Keen to support my house, I put my name down for soccer and was delighted to be selected for the junior house team. I played regularly every winter, and eventually became centre forward for the school first eleven. I used to think I was the original model for Roy of the Rovers. My final match for the school was against Sinjuns Old Boys, an annual match played every Christmas morning. I would like to say that like Roy, I went out in a blaze of glory by scoring the winning goal, but as in every other year, we fought valiantly but lost.

I had equal prowess, and definitely more glory, playing cricket. I had a good eye for a ball which helped me to become a rather flamboyant batsman and secure a regular place in the school second eleven. In one house match against perhaps the weakest of the six house teams, we had dismissed the opposition for a very modest score and the result was a foregone conclusion. The bowling was very mediocre and I pulled a succession of powerful shots to the onside boundary. Opposite the sports ground there was a church, with a bell clearly visible in an arch set into the steeple and I was weighing up whether I could hit it with the ball. Seeing what I was up to, Algy, the French Master, who was umpiring the match, came across at the end of the over and whispered in my ear.

"Bet you sixpence you can't hit it." He knew my character and knew I would be unable to resist the challenge. The next over was delivered by their worst bowler. As he sent down the first ball I took a quick step forward and lifted the ball towards the church, but I had not got the timing right and it fell short of the boundary before bouncing over for four runs. Three more times in that over I heaved at the ball but didn't manage to get it out of the ground.

By this time the crowd was beginning to buzz, sensing that I was up to something, but weren't sure what.

I knew if I was going to win my bet, I had to do it that over, as our score was rapidly approaching the required total and I might not get another chance. I prayed that the last ball would be the delivery I was looking for. Slowly the bowler ran up to the crease and flicked his fingers, trying to impart spin to the ball. We will never know if he managed it or not as the ball never touched the ground. Dancing down the pitch to meet it, I gave the ball an almighty smack, 'almighty' being the operative word. Away it soared and was still climbing as it passed over the rope, over the fence, on over the road and with a musical tinkle went straight through the church window. Fortunately I missed not only the bell, but also the large stained glass window which was just above the small plain window I shattered. The match only lasted another over and I got no further chance to win my bet. However, Algy was very generous, and didn't collect his sixpence. I lived on the glory of that moment for a long time.

The other main Summer sport was of course athletics. Although my cricket and soccer training had made me pretty nippy over short distances, I was not able to fully participate in athletics due to my cricket commitments. However, every year, I offered my services to the house for the culmination of the athletics season which was the school sports day. This was a very up-market affair with lots of parents and Old Boys attending. It was held at the sports ground of the Duke of York's Regimental Headquarters in Chelsea Barracks.

I normally went in for either the one hundred or two hundred yards sprint but not surprisingly I was usually beaten by the athletic specialists. On reaching the fourth form, I decided to try something different, and entered the mile. This was the prestige event of the sports and had been dominated for the last three years by Robert Eyres, a tall powerful blonde-haired boy, now a sixth former. Naturally, I was considered to have no chance whatsoever and was repeatedly told so by the other boys, particularly those in the same house as Eyres. By way of retaliation, I gave dark hints of secret training sessions and promised them a sensational race.

On the day, I lined up with about twenty others. The starter called us forward to our marks and without thinking I went straight down into my usual sprinter's position. A murmur went round the crowd. "What was Buster up to this time?" Enjoying the attention and not wishing them to think I had made a mistake, I stayed down. When the gun went I set off down the track at an alarming speed and quickly opened up a large gap over the rest of the field.

The crowd could not believe their eyes and sensed a possible world record. They cheered and urged me on as I sped round the track towards the finishing line. I should add that this was the end of only the first lap of four and by that time the main bunch were closing fast, led inevitably by Eyres. Soon after, the applause died as one by one the field passed me by, until at the finish, I was half a lap adrift. I still raised a few ironic cheers as I finally crossed the line, arms aloft.

I had promised them a sensational race and unbeknown to them, the sensation was still to come. When the South Western Star was published the following Wednesday, there was a large photograph of the school sports dominating the back page. It had been taken and submitted to the paper by one of my friends and bore the caption, "Sir Walter St John's School Sports. Buster Merryfield leads the field in the mile." I discovered the truth of the maxim, 'There's no such thing as bad publicity' and once again was the toast of all the boys in the school - except of course Eyres, who could be clearly seen in the photograph some three yards behind me.

In the Winter, as well as soccer, I also did boxing. The gym master, Mr Broadbent, had always wanted to start a boxing team but had difficulty persuading Jet, the headmaster, to let him do so. However, during my second year, Jet relented and Mr Broadbent put up notices inviting all interested to come to the gym the following Thursday evening. About thirty boys turned up to find the gym had been divided up with ropes to provide four boxing rings. We were paired off by size and age and each pair boxed for three rounds so that he could assess our talents.

My opponent was Reg Cosgrove, a boy I didn't know very well as he was in the form above mine. He had a long, wiry body and I was a little worried when I studied his face and discovered his decidedly bent nose, a sure sign of previous boxing experience. I was right. He had been a member of the Battersea Caius club and within a very few seconds, blood was pouring from my nose as he used my face as a punch ball. Once he had established his superiority, he eased up somewhat and I was able to survive the three rounds. At the end of the bout he put his arm round me and praised me for my courage and told me if I wanted to be a boxer I had a lot to learn.

Despite my humiliation by Reg, or maybe because of it, I came back the next week determined to do better. Numbers were greatly down, with most of the previous week's losers exercising discretion rather than valour. With smaller numbers, Mr Broadbent was able to start teaching the rudiments of ring-craft and when it came to putting them into practice, I always tried to get Reg as my sparring partner, considering I would learn more from him than from any of the others.

Eventually, we were considered good enough to take on the neighbouring Wandsworth County School. We won the contest and I recorded the first of the many wins in my boxing career. Mr Broadbent was an excellent trainer, having been a boxing instructor in the army before coming to the school. The team was very successful, particularly Reg, myself and another boy called Percy Cooper. We became known as the 'terrible trio' and whenever any one of us entered the ring there would be a continuous chant of, "Tree—oh, Tree—oh, Tree—oh."

My speciality punch was a big right-handed cross delivered to the point of the jaw. Many of my fights ended suddenly with a knock out or the towel being thrown in by my opponent's corner. I quickly became the school champion at my weight. Following outstanding local successes, the trio were entered for the London Secondary Schools championships, and after fighting my way through a series of elimination bouts, I became schoolboy champion at the age of 14. I retained my title until I left school nearly four years later, but naturally moved up in weight as I grew older.

Winning the London Secondary Schools championships earned the right to compete in the London ABA All Schools championships, with the winners going on to the Great Britain championship in the Stadium Club, Holborn. Both Reg Cosgrove and I registered wins in three successive years at the London All Schools and I am very proud of the statuette I received one year as the most promising boxer at any weight. The Great Britain championships which followed were tough and I became champion in only one year out of the three, but I was runner-up on the other two occasions. Reg went one better, becoming champion twice.

Not unexpectedly, when it came to inter-house boxing, there was no opposition that could match the prowess of the trio. I used to admire the boys from other houses that went up against me knowing they were on a hiding to nothing. However, one boy, called Don Stirton, nearly gave me my come-uppance. He was a tall, pleasant lad with dark cropped hair that stood on end like iron filings searching for a magnet.

Like me, he was a bit of a clown and used to taunt his opponents into rash moves by dancing round them with his hands down by his sides. Thinking back, he was a forerunner of Cassius Clay, but unfortunately, although he could dance like a butterfly, the bee sting was missing. He scored steady points by flicking in the odd jab as he pranced round and managed to win his way through to the inter-house final, but mostly his punches were open-handed slaps.

I started the first round against him with my usual confidence. I was in no hurry and let him prance round me throwing the occasional point-earning punch, although there were more slaps than punches and his efforts were very ineffective. I watched his pattern carefully and at the right moment unleashed my knock-out punch. The leather whistled through the air and struck nothing. He had seen it coming and rocked back on to his heels, letting it slip past his chin. Right; that was it. Nobody makes a fool of Buster Merryfield. I went after him in earnest but I couldn't catch him. He was like a Will o' the Wisp. He kept that up for three rounds and I didn't manage to land a decent blow throughout. Fortunately, the judges discounted many of his slaps and I emerged a narrow points winner. But it taught me a salutary lesson about over-confidence.

As a result of my deep involvement with sport, my academic work suffered and I soon found myself bottom of the form in most subjects. There were exceptions, most noticeably Art. Sinjuns had, and probably still has, an excellent art studio which formed the top floor of a purpose-built block, the lower floors being taken up with chemistry and physics laboratories. To reach the studio, pupils had to climb an external metal staircase, and there was many a tussle as classes pushed past each other on their way in and out. The art master was 'Aunty' Needham, but there was nothing effeminate about this burly man, who reminded me of a sailor. Children were much less knowing then than they are now and in their youthful innocence had christened him 'Aunty' due to his caring manner rather than any affected mannerisms.

I had good control of a pencil and could readily draw firm bold flowing lines. This enabled me to copy any drawing or cartoon that I saw but I did not appreciate the finer points of art such as composition that were needed for the production of original masterpieces. I suspect that had I developed my skills, I could have had quite a successful career as a draughtsman, but it was not to be.

I still try my hand when there's time and have graduated from pencils to oil paints, but I still produce mainly copies of other people's work. It is one of my ambitions to paint seriously after I retire from entertainment. Who knows, I could be a second Michaelangelo.

Another spin off from my draughtsmanship was Geography. A lot of school work in this subject consisted of copying maps of various parts of the world, putting in major cities or rivers, and then using coloured pencils to indicate coalfields, iron ore deposits or some other commercial assets. People tend to be good at subjects they enjoy, and in my dedication to the production of high-quality maps, I unconsciously learnt all the information on them. I amazed school friends and teachers alike with the amount of detail I could reproduce from memory. One of my party tricks was, and for that matter still is, to name all the principal rivers of England, in clockwise order around the coast. Or I would reel off the ten highest mountains in the world, including their heights to the nearest foot, or the states of Australia and their acreage. I suppose, like many other things I did, this was just part of my egotistical nature.

There were a couple of other subjects areas in which I briefly soared to academic distinction. The first was the third year music examination. During that year we were taught to read music by Dr Hunt, the music master. Unfortunately, crotchets and dotted quavers meant little to me and in the theoretical part of the examination I scored a miserable five marks out of fifty, achieving my accustomed position of bottom. My redemption lay in the second part of the test in which we had to stand in turn next to the piano and warble our way through 'Who is Sylvia?' to Dr Hunt's piano accompaniment. I had a good ear for a note and had received some singing training as an occasional member of the Baptist Chapel choir. Unlike many of the boys, my voice had not yet broken and I was therefore able to give an exquisite rendering which brought tears to the eyes and a lump to the throat. I was awarded the top mark of forty five out of fifty, achieving an honourable overall fifty percent.

The other occasion was in a chemistry examination when in the fifth form. At the end of fifth year we were due to sit the external School Certificate papers which hopefully would also earn us the all-important Matriculation. As part of the preparation, we were set mock examinations which were compilations of questions from old papers. Now I didn't know very much about chemistry, and the few marks I had managed in previous exams were for labelled drawings of apparatus where my artistic skills had once more come to the rescue. This was particularly so in questions on the preparation of various gases. I decided that if I was to have any chance at all, I must concentrate on questions of that type and make them my bankers. So I did just that. By the time the mock examination came round I could draw and label diagrams for the production of oxygen, chlorine, hydrogen, nitrous oxide and many more. Not only that, but I also learnt all the relevant formulae of the chemical reactions which produced them and could write a fair description of the processes.

When it came to examination day and I turned over the paper, I couldn't believe my luck. We were required to answer any five questions out of eight and five questions out of the eight were on the production of gases. My mark was somewhere in the nineties and evoked incredulity from the chemistry master who couldn't believe I could go from bottom to top in a few short months. Fortunately, I was able to convince him of my newly-found prowess and was fully exonerated.

When it came to the real examination, once more I couldn't believe my luck. There wasn't one measly question on gas production. In fact it was worse. There was not one question that I knew anything about. Once I had filled in the formalities at the top of the paper, such as the date and my examination number, I didn't know what to do. I sat staring at the blank paper for five minutes or so and then walked slowly up to the invigilator.

"Please Sir, I've finished. Can I go?" He looked sternly down and took the paper from me. Seeing it was completely blank, he replied in a low menacing voice. "Go back to your seat boy and don't be so silly. Take another look at the questions. Surely you can write something?". But I couldn't. I sat for the full three hours and wrote not a word. Poor as I was at most subjects, I think that was the only time I ever scored zero and I was lucky to get that many.

When the School Certificate results were finally published in the Summer, it was apparent that I had been spending far too much time on sport and other distractions instead of concentrating on academics. I had passed in only three subjects, Art, Mathematics and Geography, and failed to gain matriculation. My parents were quite upset. To make amends I assiduously wrote to several companies seeking employment suitable for an ex-Sinjuns' pupil. I met with little success. I fancied working in a bank but had been dissuaded from applying by my mother, who considered that was above my station. Her horizons extended no further than the Post Office, where an ex-Musjid Road neighbour had once obtained a job, but only as a mail sorter.

Not to be deterred, I wrote off to the Westminster Bank. With my usual over-confidence, I ignored the local branch and wrote directly to their Head Office at Lothbury, behind the Bank of England in the City. Much to my surprise, my cheek paid off. I received a reply inviting me for an interview.

I was nearly seventeen, but had never been to that part of London and caught the underground from Clapham South to The Bank with some trepidation. I arrived hours too early and had time to tour The City before the interview. Off I went along Cheapside to St. Paul's cathedral, coming back past the Mansion House to Lombard Street, Royal Exchange and the Stock Exchange. I was impressed. Already I saw myself as the big city financier. Unfortunately, my interviewer didn't agree. He let me down as gently as he could, but once again it was a matter of qualifications. Clasping at straws, I asked him about the bank's entrance examinations which I had vaguely heard about and extracted a promise that he would contact me when they next decided to hold them. Disappointed, I returned home to break the bad news to my parents.

"Well, there's only one thing for it," said Mum, taking the initiative as usual. "If you have to have qualifications, then qualifications you shall have. We'll send you back to school." And so I found myself a few days later, back with my parents in Jet's office at Sinjuns.

"Is there any hope," they asked, "of him getting matriculation if he came back for another year?"

"Hmm, it's like this," replied Jet, " He has the ability but based on past performance, the only thing he could matriculate in is Time Wasting," which only confirmed what Mr Weatherly had said of me five years before. I adopted my best contrite attitude and after making promises of future devotion to school work, he relented and agreed to take me back. I suspect the additional year's school fees might have had something to do with it.

"I suppose he has it in him," he conceded, "If he's prepared to work, we'll make something of him yet." And work I did. I was extremely diligent and attentive in class and as soon as school was over each day, went straight to the Lavender Hill reference library where I would study and do homework until six o'clock. However, after tea, I considered time was my own and I felt free to continue with my church activities.

I carried on like this all through the Winter. In the Spring I was delighted to receive an unexpected letter from Westminster Bank informing me that they would be holding bank entrance examinations in a few months time and asking if I was still interested. This gave me an additional incentive with my schooling and soon after retaking School Certificate examinations I returned to Lothbury to sit papers in Mathematics, English, Commercial Geography and General Knowledge.

One evening a few weeks later, I came out of the church hall following a social evening, to find both my parents waiting for me. They looked agitated, and my first thoughts were that I was in trouble again. They were bearing a letter addressed to me which had arrived by the last post of the day. Seeing the bank's address on the back, they suspected it would be the examination results and were as anxious as I was to know the outcome. Frantically I tore open the envelope and had to read the letter several times before I could believe it. I had passed and was being offered a job as a Junior Clerk in their main branch in Lombard Street at the princely salary of eighty-four pounds per annum.

It was just as well that I had taken their examinations as my School Certificate results arrived a few days later. I had picked up another couple of subjects but had still not achieved enough to matriculate. If I remember correctly, that required credit level in Maths, English and three other subjects.

This time I left school for good and was taken to the Fifty Shilling Tailors where I was fitted out for my new job. White shirts with stiff starched collars, dark pin-striped suit complete with waistcoat, black shoes with the fashionable pointed toes, and last of all, the traditional banker's furled umbrella. Although I was still only seventeen and three quarters years old, when I put them all on I felt I had come of age. Buster was off to The City!

Chapter 8

The Bank

Monday, the Eleventh of July, 1938 was the big day; my first day at the bank. Setting off down Mallinson Road, briefcase in one hand, umbrella in the other, I felt like the Chancellor of the Exchequer. At the end of the road I turned in the opposite direction to that I had been taking all my school life and headed for the Number 37 bus which would take me to Clapham Common and the underground. It seemed strange sharing the rush hour with all these people, bustling about on their way to work, confident in their familiar routine. I felt very self-conscious, fearing I stood out as a newcomer and yet at the same time looking upon myself as one of them.

There were men of all ages but the women were mostly teenage girls, pre-war society decreeing that the majority of married women looked after their home and children. As we stood waiting for the train to the city I cautiously took in the very pleasant view many of the young ladies presented and breathed in their delightful perfumes. I quickly formed the opinion that I was going to enjoy my daily travels in their company, and who knows, some of them might even work at the same bank.

Arriving at the Bank station in Lombard Street, I had less than a hundred yards to walk before stepping through the impressive double doors and entering the Head Office of the Westminster Bank. It was a few minutes before eight thirty. Inside, was a hive of early morning activity. I was in a large vestibule full of men and girls arriving in their dozens and heading for the lifts and stairs, their feet echoing across the marbled floor. I was most impressed by the bank messengers who all wore smart navy blue uniforms with gold buttons, and were it not for their hats, could have passed for cinema commissionaires. They seemed to be everywhere, pushing trolleys to and fro, piled with ledgers and boxes which presumably had been locked away for safe keeping overnight.

Just inside the door was a small cubicle which can only be described as a sedan chair with no carrying poles. Standing beside it was the Chief Messenger, even more resplendent than the rest. Cautiously I approached him.

"Excuse me sir, I'm starting work here this morning. Can you tell me where I should go?" His eyes scanned slowly down me, taking in the set of my tie, the crease in my trousers, the shine on my shoes, and then travelled slowly up again as if seeking confirmation. Finding nothing amiss, he consulted his clip-board.

"Your name, Sir?"

"Merryfield."

He checked me off on his list, and then after a few seconds pause turned his head and nodded, "Wait there Mr Merryfield." It was then that I noticed two or three other youths of my age standing a few yards away. I exchanged subdued greetings with them and within a very short time there were about ten of us standing in a group. Content that his flock was complete, he signalled to one of the messengers who shepherded us down to the gentlemen's cloakroom which we learned later were always referred to as 'The Dardanelles'.

Having ensured we were all suitably prepared and smartened up for our day's work, the messenger then took us up to the General Office where we waited outside the door of the Chief Clerk. One by one we were called in and after a brief five minute chat, allocated to specific work areas. Together with three others, I was sent to the Clearing Department on the fourth floor.

To get there we had to use the lift and so made our first acquaintance with the Italian lift operator, Lotcho. He was a most remarkable man; large, round faced, and cheerful in disposition, despite having only one arm. As we got to know him better it became apparent that he was one of the bank's characters. Despite his size, the senior staff treated him as part of the lift fittings, and talked openly in front of him. Consequently he knew everything and everybody. Whenever a rumour started the rounds, sooner or later somebody would say, "Well let's ask Lotcho," and his reply usually turned out to be correct. In between operating the lift, he ran a profitable sideline selling anything from cigarettes to sweets and sandwiches which he would buy in from the local shops and resell at a small profit. Everybody in the bank availed themselves of his services and the management either condoned it or were oblivious to his activities.

The Clearing Department was in a very large room which was filled with tables. On each table were a set of horizontal pigeon holes. The clerks sat around them, each with a bundle of cheques which were read one at a time and popped into the appropriate holes. A senior clerk, dressed in a sombre black suit more befitting an undertaker than a banker, directed one of the juniors to show me the ropes and I spent my first morning sorting cheques, relieved only by a ten minute coffee break at ten thirty. At lunchtime, I was taken by my minder to the bank's Luncheon Club over at their Threadneedle Street branch, returning an hour later to continue sorting.

In mid-afternoon I was sent with the other newcomers to 'The Postman'. He was a senior clerk who was responsible for the dispatch of all letters from Head Office out to the branches. This was an activity which had to be done after the bank's normal day's business. We discovered that our duties included working on a roster until 6 pm on three nights a week to fold all the letters, put them in the envelopes and seal them. I can still taste the fish glue. This was not a very popular duty, particularly if one had an evening engagement, and many a half crown changed hands for stand-ins. Having to work on Saturday mornings was even more irksome and cost five shilling to evade, quite a cut from a one pound fifteen shillings weekly wage packet.

As time went on I began to settle in and made many friends at the bank. The work was interesting but rather repetitive and we were constantly seeking ways to enliven the day. There was a good spirit and often there would be communal singing as we sorted our way through the piles of cheques. Our favourites were sea shanties such as 'What shall we do with the drunken sailor' or 'Polly-Wolly-Doodle'. Occasionally we would be in a more sentimental mood and croon our way through 'Carolina Moon' or some other popular song of the times. The senior clerks didn't mind what we did as long as the work got done, but it did raise an eyebrow or two one afternoon when I climbed on to the table to conduct the singing. Will I never learn?

Most of us kept a secret hoard of refreshments under the table and would fish for Lotcho's crisps or sweets as we worked. Some had the occasional bottle of lemonade hidden away, a few of which I suspected contained something a bit stronger than pop, judging by the increasing boldness of the antics as the day wore on.

When the cheques had been sorted they had to be endorsed. This required each one to be stamped on the back and a clerk's authenticating signature adding. During the morning, the signatures would be quite legible but by late afternoon they would deteriorate to scribble. When we were feeling particularly daring, we would try and outdo each other with false signatures. Some of these, such as F. Astaire or G. Rodgers were quite blatant, and I must admit that H. Merryfield looked more like Mickey Mouse on more than one occasion.

Once endorsed, the large bundles of cheques had elastic bands placed round them ready for tallying. This was done on mechanical adding machines which were kept in the basement. The clerks would go down with their bundles in pairs. After each had added up his own bundle, they would swap over and do a second addition. Hopefully, the two figures tallied.

It was while tallying one day, or rather while fooling around, that my career at the bank came into jeopardy. On the afternoon in question, my partner was Charlie Malone. He was quite a keen sportsman and on the way down the stairs to the basement we were throwing the bundles of cheques from one to the other as though they were rugby balls. Once in the basement, we had to pass a small service lift which was used to transport all the ledgers up and down to the general office on the floor above. The lift was raised by a hydraulic ram beneath the basement floor. Consequently, the bottom of the lift well, which was a foot or so below the floor, had a layer of dirty water and hydraulic oil in it. Still larking around, I threw Charlie a particularly tricky pass which he just managed to get his fingers to but couldn't hold. To our dismay, the elastic band broke and the cheques started to flutter to the floor, most of them making their way into the lift shaft where they clung firmly to the oily surface.

Frantically we started to gather up the cheques we could reach and gazed forlornly at those below which were slowly soaking up the oil and water mixture. There was only one thing for it. I quickly removed my shoes and socks, rolled up my trousers and dropped into the well of the lift. One at a time I passed the cheques up to Charlie who laid them out in rows on the stone floor of the basement.

When I was sure we had every last one, Charlie helped me back up again and immediately burst out laughing. I didn't think it was much of a laughing matter, but I wasn't standing where he was. The wet oil had clung to my feet and it looked as though I had black ankle socks on. We looked round for something to clean up with and eventually found some old rags in a cleaner's cupboard. Making our way back to the lift shaft we were horrified to hear voices coming down the stairs. Charlie rapidly gathered up the cheques and I managed to get my socks on but not my shoes. We stood stiffly to attention by the lift as the Chief Clerk and his entourage filed past and went about their business. We got one or two curious glances, particularly from those that noticed the oily footprints and my lack of shoes.

When they had moved on, Charlie and I cleaned up the cheques as best we could. Much of the writing on them was blurred where the ink had run, but fortunately the amounts were shown in figures and words. We did our double tally and much to our amazement, the figures agreed. We placed the more soiled cheques in the centre of the bundle and went reluctantly back upstairs, expecting that by now the incident would have been reported to our department head. Everything seemed normal and we applied ourselves diligently to our work, as if to make amends. As with previous misdemeanours in my life, nothing was ever said and once more Buster got away with it. Mind you, we had to live with the fear of discovery for quite some time, and that was far worse than any possible punishment.

After I had been at the bank for about six months, I was approached by my department head who suggested I should consider studying for the Institute of Banking examinations. These were taken in two parts, each part taking about two years of study over five different subjects. I was quite taken with this idea, particularly the bit where he said my annual salary would increase from £84 to £250 once I had passed them all. And so I started evening classes at Wandsworth Technical College and was surprised to find that the classes were taken by one of the masters from Sinjuns, whom I knew quite well. I was very keen and enthusiastic in my studies, but alas, they were soon to be cut short by a bit of bother on the other side of the English Channel. It was 1939.

Much of my free time was taken up with these evening classes, but I still kept up with activities at the Baptist's chapel. I joined a Monday evening prayer group which was intended for young people leading up to baptism. I should add that I had been forgiven my previous sins by the Church Wardens and was now behaving in a much more responsible manner.

Although it was called a prayer meeting, it was more of a discussion group, which tackled any subject with a bearing on life, usually managing to extract some religious significance from it. I went to my first meeting not really knowing what to expect. It started with unaccompanied singing of a short religious verse which was unknown to me. I therefore had time to study my fellow worshippers as I stood and listened to them singing the words, which eventually became very familiar.

"Blessed be the tie that binds
Our hearts in Christian love.
The fellowship of kindred minds
Is like to that above."

I noticed one boy who sang much louder than the others, determined to be heard above them. He also sang slightly slower so that when the end was reached he was able to sing the word "above" on his own. With that, he smiled at everybody with what I'm sure he considered to be Christian joy, but which seemed to me more like a supercilious grin of self-satisfaction. Surely this wasn't what religion was about?

During the meeting, we were encouraged to give voice to individual, spontaneous prayers. Some present seemed to be seasoned performers and volunteered more than once, deriving some inner pleasure from it. With my usual scepticism, I questioned their motivation. Was this a wish to praise God or a desire to show off? Was it just a performance on their part?

As the evening wore on, it became increasingly apparent that I had not yet made an individual contribution. I was becoming apprehensive. The only praying I had ever said was in private before going to sleep at night and that was hardly suitable for these circumstances. I didn't count the prayers we had all had to endure daily at Sinjuns. But why not? I began to get a buzz of excitement, eager to join in this religious enthusiasm. I would give them the prayer Jet had delivered on my behalf every day for the last six years. I knew it by heart. At the next opportunity I launched forth.

"Oh God, thank you for bringing us this day . . . defending in the same with His mighty power . . . granting that this day we fall into no sin nor run into any kind of danger . . . " on and on I went, carried away by the moment as I imitated the fervour shown by the others. When I finished I almost expected them to applaud. Was I too falling into the trap of self-gratification through religion?

The discussions which came between the prayers seemed no more sincere. I felt that most present were more interested in putting forward clever points of view rather than seeking answers to profound questions. My approach to religious matters was very direct and to the point. I used simple straightforward language and didn't dress up my contentious views. I was dissatisfied that the group seemed to reach no conclusions, apparently happy to have just talked round a subject. I had come to the meeting a firm believer in the maxim 'Seek and ye shall find', but it was beginning to look more as if 'Forever seeking, never finding' was the creed of the Monday night prayer meetings.

Looking back, I suppose I should have made that my first and last meeting, but I enjoyed the fellowship it gave with people of my own age and once I accepted there were going to be no easy answers, I began to enjoy the cut and thrust of the debate and argument. I carefully analyzed all that was said, looking for my own personal religious recipe for life. If belief was a matter of faith, did it matter what one believed? Did one have to declare one's beliefs in public to be a Christian? Which was preferable, a sinful Christian or a good-living non-believer? I eventually came to the conclusion that God came from within. There was no place in the sky called Heaven. Heaven was how you felt within yourself; a clear conscience. 'God be in my mind and in my understanding.' Let conscience be my guide.

My thoughts went back to Leslie Page's beautiful drawing of my mother's hand, and his text, 'Through Christ - I can'. How did this square with my new-found belief of the Christ within? I realised then that it was no use sitting back and waiting for some impersonal God to perform His wonders. I am God, or rather I am a part of God. God is the life force within me. It is the spirit of Christ that will give me the strength and courage to do great things. The text was wrong. Maybe it should read, 'With Christ working through me - I can,' or better still, 'Through me - Christ can'.

Having formed a belief that answered all my previous doubts I felt both at peace and uplifted. I had a philosophy to live by. I saw God as some inner strength I could call on in times of trouble. I didn't have to know where it came from, but could rely on it being there for me to use. I reasoned with myself that it was a bit like a car or some other modern technological innovation. I didn't need to know what powered it or how it worked. All I needed was to know was how to use it. Perhaps this was Faith; faith in the reliability that my inner strength would always be there when I needed it.

I don't know if this is anybody else's view of God, but it doesn't matter. Religion is a personal belief, and this was mine. I am sure others gain just as much comfort and strength from their own entirely different views, and I am glad for them. If I pity anybody, it is those who have no belief. We should all believe in something. Perhaps that is more important than the belief itself.

All this came not as a sudden revelation, but was developed over several months. Once I had got my ideas clearly sorted out, I was ready to be baptised into the church. I considered it to be a serious step, involving a commitment in public to the Christian faith. I knew my religious views were unconventional, but considered they were sufficiently in line with the Church's belief in God for me to become a member. The eventful day took place soon after my eighteenth birthday. I had seen others being baptised and found it a very moving, if somewhat stage-managed, experience.

On that Sunday, I found myself in a small vestibule behind the nave, stripping down to my white underpants before donning a baptismal gown, which was like a large white dress with buttons down the back. Apart from that, I wore nothing except a pair of open-toed sandals. The floor of the church had been opened up to reveal the baptismal pool below and at the appropriate point in the service I walked solemnly down the steps and into the water where the Reverend Nash took me by the shoulders and lowered me in. The water was rather chilly and my thoughts strayed back to childhood. I felt like shouting out, "A drop more hot for Number Five please," as we did at the old Latchmere Road baths. It all felt very unreal, as though it was part of a theatrical production with me in a leading role. Many times since, when on the stage, I have had a feeling not unlike that moment in church. I sense that the Church and the Theatre have a lot in common.

I don't know how I managed to find the time, but I also used to go down to the Battersea Boxing Club two nights a week. Surprisingly, this met at the Latchmere Road baths. One of the pools would be boarded over and two rings set up over it. The changing rooms, baths and other facilities were of course ideal. It was quite a renowned club which boasted no less than three ABA champions. That didn't include Reg Cosgrove and myself, who were both national schoolboy ABA champions. At first I was happy just to be a member and able to train and spar there. After a few months I was selected as a regular member of the club team and felt it a great honour. Most of the matches were in London against other boxing clubs, which were either based around a particular district as ours was, or were run by one of the larger firms.

Soon after joining the club, Reg and I received invitations to take part in a Festival of Sport, to be held in Wembley Stadium. For several weeks we had to go once a week to the Metropolitan Police Boxing club at Peel House for training sessions with Harry Mallin. He was a policeman who had been the Olympic heavyweight champion. We were quite impressed by the large picture of him on the clubhouse wall.

On the day of the festival, there were many hundreds of youths taking part, representing all the different sports. We started by parading around the arena and then broke away to our respective sport. There were four boxing rings set up, with virtually continuous boxing in each throughout the afternoon. This consisted of a series of exhibition sparring bouts rather than serious fights, each lasting about four or five minutes. Naturally, Reg and I were paired up and put on what we considered an entertaining show, without causing each other too much suffering. After about two hours of events, we were once more lined up and all marched past the podium where we all gave a smart 'eyes right' to King George and Queen Elizabeth and the two young princesses, Elizabeth and Margaret. We felt very honoured and were a little peeved the following week when the Sunday papers all carried a large photograph of the march past, but as an advert for Finnon Salts.

I also found time to join the Territorial Army. Everybody was becoming increasingly aware of the political tension that was building in Europe, but it took one particular event to make me take positive action. The newspapers were regularly reporting the activities of the Union of British Fascist, commonly known as the Blackshirts. One Saturday in November, 1938, word went round that Oswald Moseley was to address an open-air evening meeting in Battersea. Judging by previous reports, this would be a lively event to say the least. So just before six o'clock I made my way with a couple of friends to the venue in Comyn Road, which was just off Northcote Road, opposite Arding and Hobbs, the large departmental store.

When we arrived, we couldn't believe it. The road, which was about one hundred yards long, was choc-a-block with people. By the department store were a dozen or so mounted police, and at the other end of the road, a veritable army of blackshirts. Soon after six, a large van turned into the far end of the road and parked behind the wall of blackshirts. After a brief interval, Moseley climbed on to the van roof and began to speak through a loud hailer. Immediately, those at the front of the hostile crowd started to chant.

"Rats, rats, we've gotta get rid of the rats." With that the blackshirts moved into the crowd, knuckledusters flying, trying to suppress the trouble makers. But it was no good. Seeing what was happening, the rest of the crowd took up the chant against them.

"Rats, rats, we've gotta get rid of the rats." At this stage the mounted police decided it was time to move in and break up the spreading conflict. Unfortunately, this was the same time that many who were there just as sightseers decided to leave. People and horses pressed in opposite directions and many fell under foot. Whether it was done deliberately or not I don't know, but something startled one of the horses, causing it to rear and back through the plate glass window of one of the shops. Pandemonium reigned. Fortunately, having arrived late, we were near the end of the road and managed to get away uninjured, but many were not so lucky. It was seeing the brutality of the fascist blackshirts, that stirred the patriotism in me and caused me to join the territorials. I did not want to see England ruled by the likes of them.

Some of the more senior clerks in the bank had already joined an Army reserve unit called the Artist's Rifles. This was a rather elitist organisation for potential officers. For the likes of myself and my fellow junior clerks, the 118th Field Artillery Unit was more appropriate. This had its headquarters by Putney Bridge, and shortly after the Moseley incident, a group of us from the bank went down and enlisted. Amongst those who joined with me were Charlie Malone and Peter Stark, brother of the actor, Graham Stark.

At that time, thousands of others up and down the country were doing the same. As a consequence, uniforms and equipment were in very short supply and we had to go to drill sessions in our everyday clothes. The unit did have one old first world war Howitzer on which we practised firing procedures, but not one shot was ever fired, the only shells being wooden dummies. Just as well really, considering we practised in a drill hall in the middle of Putney! As the summer wore on, there were increasing signs of military activity all around us, with searchlights and anti-aircraft guns being installed on Clapham Common. These were manned by regular soldiers, who were the envy of us all.

The nearest we got to the real army was a week's camp on Tweasledown racecourse at Aldershot. This was a real adventure, being the first time I had ever been away from home without my parents. It was also the first time I had ever slept under canvas, not that we slept very much; we were all far too excited. For the most part we carried out further dummy practices with field guns but did get to fire rifles with real live bullets on the range. I was quite proud to be associated with the Royal Artillery, so much so that I bought a silk handkerchief bearing the regimental crest and sent it home to my mum. She treasured that handkerchief all the time I was away during the war. I found it again when I had to go through her belongings after she died. It is now one of my most treasured possessions.

Back at the bank, I had now progressed on to ledger work, mainly because many of the more experienced clerks had been called up in preparation for war. As a ledger clerk I sat on a wooden stool at a high desk which held a large ledger about three inches thick. Along with about thirty others I spent all day and every day transcribing details from bank transactions into my ledger in my best copperplate script. Although I still had my one and threepenny Platignum pen, for this bank work I was obliged to use ordinary pens with detachable nibs. Depending on the details of the entry, I would write it in either red, green or blue ink, having a separate pen for each. Every morning, one of the messengers would come round with large bottles of ink and top up the three glass inkwells on each of our desks.

As the summer of '39 turned into autumn, more and more desks became empty as different war reserve bodies were called up. Throughout the day we were constantly popping out to the news-stand in front of the bank entrance to see from the stop-press who was next. War now looked inevitable and we knew it was only a matter of time before all who were able bodied would be gone. When our turn came we were relieved. All territorials were to report to their units the next day. We let out a loud cheer and one by one speared our red, green and blue pens into the desk top. Whilst they were still quivering we were on our way home to collect what little kit we had. Buster was off to the War!

Part Two: During The War

Chapter 9

Home Defence

When I meet people in the street today, they often confuse my personal life with that of the character Uncle Albert from 'Only Fools and Horses'. They assume the 'old sea dog' image to be real and I have had many double rums sent over to me in restaurants and public houses which I have to politely refuse, being completely teetotal. By the same token, 'during the war' I was not a seafaring hero, having ship after ship sunk beneath me, and with the exception of a batch of prisoners in transit to Canada which I helped supervise, I never came face to face with the enemy. However, I did have an eventful war, even a dangerous war, coping with the blitz and the doodlebugs, with a notable period abroad in between. Let me tell you of my war.

When I arrived home from the bank, my parents had already heard the news that the territorials were being called up, and they were expecting me. Dad was very serious and gave me fatherly advice as to how to conduct myself whilst away from home. Mum was very tearful, not knowing when she would see her only son again, if ever. Personally, I was quite excited and couldn't wait to get to grips with the Hun. I imagined that I would be on a boat and over to France within the week.

On arrival at the Territorial HQ in Putney, I had to complete various forms, including one for notifying my next-of-kin in case I went missing in action or got killed. This was all very sobering and it came as a bit of an anti-climax when I handed in all my forms and was told to go home and come back again tomorrow. I suppose with the rapid influx of men into the army, there were terrific logistics problems and there were insufficient billets for us all. Every day for the next three weeks, I had to report back to the Putney barracks, and every night I was sent home again to sleep.

One day during that time, I was at the barracks when we heard the famous radio announcement by Neville Chamberlain. "... unless we hear from you by eleven o'clock .... no such undertaking having received, His Majesty's government has no alternative..." War had been declared.

We were all very apprehensive, not knowing what to expect. That very afternoon, the air raid siren went for the first time and we feared the worst. Officers went scurrying around shouting orders, NCOs were blowing whistles and confusion reigned for several minutes before we were all safely ensconced in the newly-built air-raid shelters. These were long, low, brick-built structures with concrete roofs but no windows. There was a steel door at one end, surrounded by a brick blast screen, and a steel trap door in the roof at the other end which was the emergency exit. Inside, there were wooden slatted seats along either side and duck boards down the centre of the floor. There was a single electric light bulb in a shatter-proof cage halfway along the ceiling, which cast barely enough light to reach the ends of the room. We huddled together, talking too much so as not to appear afraid, but we needn't have bothered. It was only a practice.

During those early days, everybody was jittery, military and civilians alike. I remember one evening when I went home, my parents announced they were off to tea with Aunt Daisy and family, so naturally I went with them. When we arrived, they were crowded around the radio, which was the main source of information in those early war days. The programme was giving out public information as to what to do in various circumstances and the announcer was just describing how an imminent gas attack would be signalled by wardens touring the streets with rattles.

One doesn't see this kind of rattle around now, but either side of the war, football supporters had wooden rattles which they took with them to matches. The rattle was made from a round wooden handle with two large cogs fixed to it, over which was a loose frame holding wooden tongues. These pressed on to the cog wheels, and by whirling the rattle above one's head, the tongues would slip from cog to cog making a loud clacking noise. With the outbreak of war, the casual use of rattles was banned and they were used exclusively to signal gas attacks.

Aunt Daisy and Uncle Arthur took the broadcast very seriously. Before we could sit down to tea they insisted on laying rolled blankets along the bottoms of the outside doors as they had been instructed. Looking back, this was rather pathetic, but it was supposed to prevent the ingress of gas into the house.

Eventually, the Army found a place for me and I was sent to

Stanmore. All over the country large houses and stately homes were being commandeered for soldiers' accommodation and I found myself in the erstwhile premises of the British Israel College. This was a very imposing manor house which had previously been the home of Gilbert and Sullivan. It had been turned into a barracks and we slept on the bedroom floors, six to a room.

My companions in the field artillery territorials were a diverse bunch, coming from all walks of life. Army life was a great leveller and it didn't matter what one's background or status was. The man in the next bed might read The Times every day or could equally well be an avid Beano fan. It mattered not. We all shared a great spirit of comradeship which united us in a common cause. Some were extremely talented. In the main drawing room there was a baby grand piano and after obtaining permission, one of the men treated us to evening concerts in the style of Charlie Kunz, whilst another would fill the room with his baritone rendering of 'Marta' or some other concert piece as he did his impersonation of Arthur Tracy, the street singer.

During the day, we still had no real guns to practice with and spent most of the time polishing our kit and laying it out for endless inspections. The NCOs were long-serving territorials but they were pressed to find things for us to do. Consequently, most afternoons were taken up with recreational activities and sports. Once a week we went on a long march of about ten miles. Having kept myself fit through my boxing training, I really took to this healthy active life and it showed. In a very short time I was singled out as a PT Instructor and took groups of thirty or forty men at a time for exercises. I loved every moment.

After the initial panic of the first few weeks, we settled into the anti-climax of the phoney war in which very little appeared to be happening. But behind the scenes, plans for national defence were being devised, and after about a month at Stanmore, I was moved with the battery to Clapham Junction railway station. Although an invasion was not thought likely, there was a fear that enemy infiltrators or sympathetic fifth columnists might try to disrupt the rail network by sabotage.

Twenty four hour guards were mounted on the bridges and along the lines, each of us doing two hours on and four hours off. We were now into December, and sleeping in unheated railway carriages was no joke on a frosty night.

We were relieved when soon after Christmas we were told we

were moving to Richmond and would be billeted in Asgill House. This was a grand-looking lodge set on the bank of the Thames in the corner of the grounds of Queensbury House. I seem to recall a stone plaque set into the wall which claimed that King Henry the Eighth had once kept his mistress there. But it had seen better days and on arrival, our joy was short lived. Our quarters were in the basement which was below the level of the river and over the years water had seeped in through the walls. Consequently, it was extremely damp and overrun with rats. These were so bold that on getting into bed, we had to pull the blankets over our faces for fear of getting bitten. Most nights we would feel them scampering over the blankets in search of anything edible.

Our new duty was to guard the railway bridge that crossed the Thames next to Twickenham Bridge. Two men would patrol along the top, meeting in the middle, whilst two more patrolled the footpath at the base of the bridge. Those up above saw only each other during their two-hour shift, but down below things were a little livelier. In the evenings, courting couples would use the towpath alongside the river as a route from the centre of Richmond through to the Mid-Surrey golf course. Whenever we heard them coming we would merge into the shadows before loudly issuing the challenge.

"Halt! Who goes there?"

"Friend."

"Advance and be recognised." And with that they would cautiously edge forward, holding out some form of identity. At first it was all taken very seriously, but eventually it degenerated into a bit of a farce. The local girls would deliberately come out in ones and twos just for the thrill of being challenged, and then, with a bit of encouragement, would stay and chat to the guards. Many a romance might have blossomed down on the towpath, if it were not for the guards up above. If things started to get too amorous they would hang over the parapet and start singing.

"How would you like to be, down by the Thames with me. Under the bridges of Richmond with you, I'll make your dreams come true."

We stayed at Richmond through the winter and then for no apparent reason I was posted to Baldock in Hertfordshire. Once there it was still no clearer why I had been sent. It was back to the pointless drill and training exercises I had been only too pleased to escape from at Stanmore, but with one difference. Instead of the luxury of a country house, we now lived in a derelict semi. It was a Spartan existence but the harder life got the more I revelled in it. It was not long before I was holding daily PT classes again and taking crocodiles of troops out for runs around the countryside.

Once a month we were given a 48-hour pass. This was just long enough for me to hitch-hike home on the Friday evening and back again late on Sunday. We had to travel in uniform which made it easy to get lifts, but I was so proud to be a soldier, I kept mine on throughout the weekend. I would have been even prouder to wear it over one particular weekend, if only I had checked with the Orderly Room before dashing off home. It wasn't until I returned on Sunday evening that I found out I had been promoted to Lance Bombardier. My spontaneous display of initiative and leadership in running the PT classes had been rewarded.

Promotion meant another posting, this time to Coventry. There, I was put on Regimental Police duties. We had to patrol the streets of town until midnight ensuring there was no trouble, particularly after pub closing time. We worked in pairs, my companion being a six foot hunk called Peter Bridge. Although by comparison I was only five foot six inches tall, it was assumed that my boxing experience would enable me to cope with any trouble, and it did.

Following Coventry, I had a short spell of duty in Wales at Carmarthen. This was the last time I served in an all-territorial unit. During the early part of the war, territorials had their own regiments which were kept separate from the regular army and it was not until after Dunkirk that a policy of integration was introduced. One day, I was told I was being sent to Southampton to a regular artillery unit which was being brought back up to strength following its evacuation from France.

I was not the only one transferred that day and as a Lance Bombardier, I found myself a few days later in charge of a party of half a dozen or so Gunners travelling on the early morning train across the Welsh countryside en route for the south coast of England. We were carrying full kit and between us managed to completely fill a compartment, considering ourselves lucky to do so as the train rapidly filled up as it chugged along the coast from town to town.

At Burry Port, only one passenger entered via our compartment. She was the most beautiful thing I had ever seen. Before we had time to put our eyes back into our heads, she had walked straight through into the corridor beyond and stood gazing out of the window. Immediately, two of the lads gave each other that knowing look and got to their feet ready for the chat-up.

"OK," I said, "you two can sit down again. RHIP," which, as any soldier knows, is army shorthand for 'Rank Has It's Privileges'. Straightening my uniform I slowly got up and taking a deep breath, smiled and offered her my seat.

"Oh no," she lilted in a tinkling Welsh accent, "it's OK, I'm only going as far as Llanelli. It's where I work you see." Despite my gentlemanly protestations she insisted on staying in the corridor and I spent the next few minutes out there with her, gazing into deep blue eyes and desperately trying to keep up a conversation.

"I'm in the Army you know."

"Yes, I can see by your uniform," she smiled.

"I'm posted to Southampton, but I shouldn't really be telling you that," I mumbled.

What I really wanted to tell her was that she was the most adorable girl I had ever met and I longed to sweep her into my arms. But I was acutely aware that the lads in the compartment behind me were listening intently.

I continued with hopelessly banal conversation until the train pulled into Llanelli, managing to elicit from her that she worked in the Bon Stores in the centre of Llanelli where she also lived. Her name was Phyllis and she had just spent the weekend with her grandmother in Burry Port. As she opened the door to alight from the train I plucked up courage and asked if I could write to her.

"Oh I'm not sure, she said, "I don't really know you." But she did not move away, and stood next to the open carriage looking awkwardly down at her shoes. After further cajoling she looked up.

"Hang on, I've an envelope here somewhere that's got my address on." With that she rummaged in her handbag, eventually producing the envelope. Carefully tearing off the front, she handed it to me just as the train was pulling out.

I leaned back against the cool glass of the window, closed my eyes and held the paper to my nose. Yes, it carried that perfumed smell that would always remind me of her. I folded it and carefully put it away in my battle dress pocket before returning to my seat and the ribald remarks of the gunners.

Unfortunately, my posting to a regular army unit meant I had to give up my stripe. It wasn't that I had done anything wrong or had been found wanting. It was just that the regular unit contained many long-serving soldiers with chests full of campaign medals and 'dodgems' half way up their arms. 'Dodgems' was the name given to the upside down long service chevrons worn on the cuff. It would have been incongruous for such men to be overseen by a fresh-faced twenty-year-old who had seen no service. So back I went to being a Gunner. The regiment was spread out all along the south coast, guarding against possible invasion. I was actually stationed at Pagham Bay, helping to keep a twenty-four-hour watch over the Channel from sandbag emplacements and pill-boxes set in the dunes. Apart from enemy planes going over on nightly bombing raids, we didn't see much action. There were always rumours about, of raiding parties being captured further along the coast, but they were never substantiated.

In the Autumn of 1940, I was moved to Southampton and billeted in King Edward's Grammar School next to the Common. I felt quite at home there, being reminded of Sinjuns and Wandsworth Common where I used to hunt for moths with Colin Lawrence. Even though I had lost my stripe I still ran PT classes and would take soldiers out on the common every day past the pond where the local youngsters fished for tiddlers, just as I had done a hundred years before. I hadn't been there long when I was sent to Hendon Police College on a three-week PT Instructors' course. With my veneration of fitness and exercise I did very well on the course, finishing near the top. When I returned to Southampton I lost no time in sewing on my crossed-swords badge and not long after, I had to get the needle out again to reinstate my Lance Bombardier's stripe.

As well as on my working battledress, the new stripe also had to be sewn on to my best uniform, which I hadn't worn since I had travelled down on the train from Carmarthen. Seeing it again reminded me of Phyllis and I went through the pockets looking for the front of the envelope she had given me with her address on. Up until now, I had been very busy settling in to my new unit and I had not really had a chance to write to her. I had also been put off because I would have to tell her I had been demoted. Now I had no excuse.

I still wasn't sure what to write about, and not wanting to frighten her off, I kept the letter very formal and factual, telling her about the daily happenings of a soldier's life and a bit about my home background. I signed off, "Yours sincerely, Buster." Her reply arrived by return of post. Although friendly, she too was formal and described her work in the shop and a bit about her family and interests. Taking her cue from me, she signed herself as "Yours most sincerely."

This was the start of a correspondence that continued for several months and I looked forward to her letters which arrived twice weekly. We gradually became more relaxed in style as we got to know more about each other and developed a real friendship as the weeks went by.

By now the Army was much better equipped and my unit had twelve field guns to tow around the countryside as we prepared ourselves for the forthcoming invasion. Each gun detachment had a Sergeant in charge, a Bombardier gun-layer, a loader and a couple of 'ammunition wallahs' who kept the loader supplied with ammunition from the trailer. Before long I took my NCO proficiency test which got me my second stripe and with it the job of gun-layer.

When Christmas came, I was surprised to receive a parcel from Phyllis. Nothing much, just a few sweets, envelopes and a writing pad. It was Christmas Eve morning and I had nothing for her. In a panic I dashed to the NAAFI families shop where I was able to buy a floral apron. I pinned on to it a Royal Artillery brooch I had secretly bought some time before but had not had the courage to send. I hurriedly wrapped it up and handed it in to the local post office but it must have arrived well after Christmas.

This didn't seem to upset her, quite the opposite, for her letters became more personal, starting, "My Dearest Buster," and ending with an increasing number of paper kisses. I responded with similar terms of endearment but in all that time we were never able to meet again. Our paper romance was all based on that one brief encounter on the train.

In the early months of 1941, the blitz intensified. Each day the radio carried the news of which town or city had been bombed the previous night and on the short waveband, Lord Haw-Haw told us which was the next place to be targeted. However, the information he gave was more often wrong than right and we soon learnt to ignore it, treating it with the disdain it deserved. We did not allow it to prevent us from going out in the evenings and regularly went into Southampton centre for a dance or a night at the cinema. The only problem was that once inside the cinema it was difficult to hear the air-raid siren. So when the siren sounded, the film was topped and an announcement was made, giving people the option to leave for the shelters.

After a series of false alarms, most people ignored the warning, but on one particular night when I was in the Gaumont watching *We Dive at Dawn*, we were forced to pay attention by an almighty bang which brought plaster down from the ceiling. The film was immediately stopped and the lights went up. There was no panic, but people were anxious to get out in case the building was in danger of collapse.

Outside, I could hardly believe my eyes. The entire front of the cinema was missing and the row of shops opposite had been reduced to a smoking ruin. All around, the sky was aglow with the lights of fires started by incendiary bombs. Fire engines and ambulances went wailing past and all around distressed people wandered in a dazed state. I gave what little help I could to restore calm, but knew I couldn't stay. We had strict instructions to get back to the unit as soon as possible in the event of a raid in case we were needed for official rescue work or debris clearance. I soon found out it was impossible to head North along the main Above Bar Road, which was completely blocked by collapsed buildings, and I had to skirt round past the side of the Civic Centre. Although there was a strict black out, it was easy to find one's way from the light of the fires and the flares which hung over the town.

There was a continuous barrage of noise from the anti-aircraft guns which mingled with the roar of the fires all over the city and the sounds of disintegrating buildings. This prevented me from hearing the whistle of the next stick of bombs until it was too late. In rapid succession the ear-shattering bangs traced their path of destruction until the last was so close its blinding flash blew me across the road and into the wall of the Civic Centre. For a few moments I lay recovering, checking that all the parts of my body were still functioning. Gingerly I got to my feet and went to the assistance of a lady who had met a similar fate. Once I had assured myself that she was not seriously hurt, I decided that Southampton was not a healthy place to be in at that moment, and ran the remaining mile or so back to barracks in record-breaking time.

On arrival back at camp, I was met by one of the guards who was checking everybody in, and immediately sent to the air raid shelters. Each troop had its own shelter, so it was easy to see who was there and who was missing. The atmosphere was very tense and there was a loud cheer each time another member of our troop arrived back. After an hour or so, I got permission from the senior NCO to dash across to the billet to collect my accordion. After that the tension eased as we took comfort in the traditional British sing-song as we sat round under the gloomy electric light, drinking mugs of thick cookhouse tea.

We were all aware that we were one missing that night, but early next morning he turned up to a hero's welcome, having spent the night in the thick of the raid helping to pull injured people from the debris. I believe he was later decorated for his efforts. The next morning, although we had had little sleep, we were formed into parties and spent the day clearing the streets and helping to get Southampton back to normal, or at least as normal as possible. This was my first brush with the true horrors of war and like many others who were there it made me all the more determined that Hitler must be made to pay.

It was soon after that Phyllis' letters stopped coming. I was fearful that she might have been killed or seriously injured in a German bomber raid, but I eventually had to admit that in such an event her parents would have written and told me, unless of course they had all been wiped out together. I had not read or heard of any raids on Llanelli and I came to accept a more likely explanation that she had acquired a local boy friend who had come across one of my increasingly passionate letters and threatened her with dire consequences if she wrote to me again. Initially I was heartbroken and daydreamed of going to Wales to challenge this fictitious suitor for her hand. But at nineteen the heart quickly heals and I soon found myself seeking consolation with more attainable girls.

A few weeks later, I was posted as a bombardier to Storrington in Sussex where I became one of the directing staff training conscripts. It was an all-tented camp set on the side of the Downs. By now the Battle of Britain had started and as spring turned to summer, we watched the dog-fights going on overhead and cheered each time we saw a swastika-bearing Heinkel or Meschersmitt plunge to Earth, trailing oily smoke in its wake. At last the newspapers had some good news to report and each day carried ever higher figures of the number of kills. True to character, I organised a daily sweepstake on the totals and remember it reaching a peak of 185.

When not needed for duty we were able to get out into the surrounding area. I loved to go up on to the Downs and gaze out over miles of uninterrupted countryside or just lay in the grass and listen to the skylarks as they soared on the breeze. One day as I lay there, I had a ringside view of an aerial battle between a squadron of German bombers with their fighter escorts, and about a dozen

Spitfires. I watched in fascination, oblivious of any danger until there was a sudden roar of engines close by. Low over the brow of the hill came a Heinkel bomber with smoke and flames pouring from one engine. Giving chase was a Spitfire, guns still blazing. I jumped up and cheered as they passed low over my head and I waved both arms to the pilot in encouragement. Within a very few seconds they had passed and gone, but as the engines died away there was the crump of an explosion as the bomber hit the ground in woods a mile or so away. I was thrilled to have been so close to the action which seemed like retribution for the raid on Southampton. It was not until I looked down again and saw the turf on fire around me that I realised the tracer bullets from the Spitfire had not all hit the German plane. My knees weakened as I appreciated that I had had another brush with death. The next day I went with several others looking for the wreckage but to no avail. Either it was hidden in deep woodland or it had been taken away before we got there.

Later that year, I rejoined my old regiment at Southampton and from there was posted to a field artillery unit at Newbury. One night, whilst on duty as Orderly Bombardier, I got chatting to the Orderly Officer over a cup of cocoa. He was quite an affable young chap of about my age and we chatted about life back home before the war. Surprisingly, I discovered he had a similar background to myself, being an ex-grammar school boy from London. I quizzed him about how he had come to get a commission and he explained in detail, including information on how to apply. The next day I went to the Orderly Room and boldly asked for the necessary forms. There were a few raised eyebrows, but within the week I was interviewed by the Commanding Officer who decided to forward my application. Buster was going to be an officer.

Chapter 10

Iris

On my application form I had to state whether I wanted a commission in the Field Artillery, Light Anti-aircraft Artillery or the Infantry. I selected them in that order. A couple of weeks later I was overjoyed to hear I had been accepted for officer training with my second choice, the LAA. Before going to the Officer Cadet Training Unit, commonly known as OCTU, I had to do a short pre-OCTU course at Deepcut in Surrey. But first I was given a 48-hour pass and was able to go home and tell my parents the good news.

On the Saturday night, I called on an old pal, Stan Gale, and asked him to come out to celebrate my good news. We decided wanted to do something special, something we hadn't done before, but what?

"I know," said Stan at last, "let's go up to Richmond Ice Rink." This was certainly something we hadn't tried before, but it couldn't be much different to roller skating, could it? So off we went to Richmond. Having paid our entrance money, and an extra sixpence for the skate hire, we found it wasn't quite as easy as we thought. Unlike roller skating, it required lateral balance on the thin blade, which put quite a strain on unaccustomed ankles. Before long we were quite content just to hang on to the side rail and watch the real skaters, mostly the charming young ladies who glided graciously along with the minimum of effort.

It was then that I saw her. The most stunning girl I had ever seen. I could hear my heart beating in my ears as she drifted past in her figure-hugging grey jumper and short red skirt which set off those gorgeous long legs that all skaters seem to have. She had jet-black hair and soft brown eyes that gave her a 'Margaret Lockwood' look. As she went past, she spotted me slipping and sliding as I clung precariously to the rail, and gave a friendly smile. My heart turned over. As soon as she had passed, I nudged Stan.

"Wow, did you see that?" I asked him. But he had not noticed and I had to point her out to him as she came round next time with her companion. I persuaded him that we had to get to know these two girls, come what may. Her jumper had the initials I M embroidered on it, so the next time she came past I boldly shouted out,

"Hello, Irene Mary." She just smiled and skated on.

"Hello, Ivy Maureen" and "Hello, Imogene Maud" fared no better, but on the next circuit I couldn't believe my luck when she pulled up beside us and said,

"Actually my name's Iris. And the M stands for my surname, Mountford."

"Iris Mountford," how sweet it sounded. After a few minutes of idle chatter, I managed to persuade her to come for a coffee with Stan and I, but her companion, who turned out to be her sister, declined, stating most pointedly that she already had a boyfriend. However, I must have made a favourable impression on Iris as she willingly left the ice rink long before the session was over and walked with us over Richmond Bridge to the coffee shop. When it was time to leave, I walked her to the bus stop and formally shook hands with her as she boarded the Number 65 bus back to her home at Ham Common.

Whilst I was doing the pre-OCTU course at Deepcut, I was able to see Iris two or three times a week. She worked as the Librarian in Boots, the chemists, on Richmond High Street and thus had Wednesday afternoons free when the shop was closed. We would either stroll round Richmond Park or sometimes walk along the tow path of the canal at Woking which was easier for me to get to from Deepcut. In the course of our conversations, she told me she was twenty-five-years old, and not wishing her to think I was too young for her, I added five years to my age and told her I was the same age. I would have said anything to keep her. I was so smitten. On one Sunday, I took her home to meet my parents but I sensed that my mother was not too keen to encourage the romance. Later she quizzed me about Iris and asked how old she was. When I replied that she was twenty-five, she replied, "I thought so. Far too old for you, son. I would find somebody more your own age if I was you." But she wasn't me, and I was sure that Iris was the greatest thing in my life so far. I had no intention of giving her up.

Just as our romance was beginning to blossom, the date for my OCTU training came round and I had to leave for Llandridnod Wells. We would be apart for seven long months without even a 48-hour pass, but every day Iris sat down and wrote to me and I replied just as often as the course would allow.

I expected the OCTU to be a self-contained unit, but it was spread all over town with just about every hotel and public hall taken over for some function or other. We lived in various hotels and walked every day to classes held in one of the schools. The course was quite intensive but interesting, covering topics ranging from gunnery to aircraft recognition and from dealing with soldiers' welfare problems to using the correct knife and fork at mess dinners.

We were encouraged to participate in communal activities, particularly sports. Soon after arriving I discovered the OCTU ran a boxing gymnasium in the local church hall. So one evening I made enquiries as to how to get there and paid it a visit. I cautiously pushed open the door to see two men sparring in the ring, with about half a dozen officers and a few PT staff standing around shouting encouragement. As he heard the door squeak, one of the officers turned round and looked me up and down.

"Yes, what do you want, Cadet?"

"I just thought I'd come down and watch the boxing, Sir."

"Know anything about it then?" he continued.

"Well, I used to do a bit before I joined the Army, Sir," I replied.

"In that case you'd better come over here where you can see properly." He smiled and beckoned me over. I went in and stood watching the bout. It was obvious that one of the men knew how to box, but the other one was struggling as he succumbed to more and more blows. Eventually he put up his hands to indicate he had had enough and the bout stopped. With that, the officer who had invited me in turned to me and said,

"You're about his weight. Get stripped off and let's see what you're made of." I protested that I had not brought any kit with me, not expecting to box on my first visit, but it was no good. They found a pair of pumps for my feet, and once I had stripped off to the waist, the gloves were fitted. I started defensively, using footwork to circle out of the way of his attacks.

"Come on," they shouted, "I thought you said you could box. Let's see some action." As a new cadet, ever anxious to please, I decided I would have to stand up to my opponent and fight. He was very keen to mix it, and was ardently trying to use me as a punch bag, just as he had done with his previous sparring partner.

"Right," I thought, "Let's see if the old right hand still works." And with that, at the first opportunity I swung my notorious right cross just as he was moving forward into the attack. He was so self-confident he had left himself wide open and the punch caught him squarely on the side of the jaw. He continued to come forward and as I stepped neatly aside, he pitched headlong to the canvas. He was visibly shaken and had no further appetite for boxing.

The officers were quite concerned, firstly over his wellbeing, and then when they saw he was recovering, over his ability as a boxer. It transpired that he was a senior cadet, the best boxer in the OCTU at his weight, and was due to fight in a contest at Ludlow the following Saturday. They had pinned their hopes on him winning but now were not so sure. They came over and quizzed me as I was getting dressed again, Where had I boxed, who for, and how good was I? Having explained my pedigree, they came to a decision. I would be taking his place next Saturday.

Word of my boxing prowess started to spread around the OCTU and people began to point me out as the guy who flattened their champion. I enjoyed the attention it brought me and also the time I was given off to do training in lieu of drill. However, I became a little concerned when I heard a supporters' coach was being laid on; such was the interest.

When the coach arrived at Ludlow and I saw the bill for the evening, I realised it was no small-time event. It was being run under the auspices of the Services Boxing Association and top of the bill was Harry Mizler, the British professional light weight champion. I was billed as Cadet Buster Merryfield, the ex-schoolboy champion of Great Britain. I was down to fight a Flight Sergeant Williams, who didn't seem to be anybody in particular. I was confident I would put up a good show and do my image at OCTU a power of good.

Following the weigh-in I did a little shadow boxing in the changing room and waited for my bout to be called. There were cheers all round as I made my way down the aisle and into the ring and I could see the OCTU crowd away to my right. The referee called us together for the usual instructions on a good clean fight and all that, and then sent us back to our corners to await the bell. I stood facing into my corner looking out at my supporters in the crowd. As the bell went I gave them an arrogant wave before turning to meet my opponent. The next thing I knew, I was coming round in the dressing room. He had obviously been far quicker off the mark than me and was across to my side of the ring as I turned, straight into his blockbuster blow. It was little comfort to find out that he was Harry Mizler's regular sparring partner. The journey back to Llandridnod Wells was a very quiet affair and seemed never-ending. Would I never learn?

Despite that unfortunate start, I must have put up a good performance at the OCTU and managed to avoid the dreaded fate of "RTU", standing for "Return To Unit", that befell some of those around me. About six weeks before the end of the course, the odds on completion were deemed high enough for us to go and be measured for our officer's uniform. We were given a kit allowance and could select one of several military outfitters who frequented the town. Then, for the last month, we were allowed to wear the uniform, complete with Sam Browne and swagger stick, but we still wore the distinctive cadets' white forage cap rather than the officers' peaked cap.

The passing out parade was a big day with parents and high ranking guests invited. It was much like hundreds of other passing out parades that took place during the war and after, so I will not bore you with the detail, except to mention Captain Webb. He was a member of the OCTU Directing Staff who always led the parade and was known throughout the Army for his voice and his mannerisms. He was very loud and the noises he made bore little resemblance to the actual orders he was giving.

"KEEEEY MAAR" meant "Quick March" and "STAAAR HEESE" translated as "Stand at Ease". It didn't matter what he said really as we had rehearsed so often we all knew exactly what to do. His grand finale came as the parade drew to a conclusion and he had been given permission to march us off.

"PARAY ILL MAR CHOFFIN COLNO FREEZE, KEEEEY MAAR AZUWHAAR." And we all knew not to move a muscle until the order was repeated.

At the end of OCTU, we were given ten days leave, but had to report to our new units first. For me this was Windsor and I set off by train from Llandridnod Wells soon after the parade was over. By the time I reached Windsor, it was late at night and after a long, busy day all I wanted was bed and sleep. Next morning I was up with the lark and couldn't wait to get into my carefully-pressed uniform and away on leave. Looking absolutely immaculate, I made a bee-line for Richmond and Iris. I had never been to her house but I knew that by the time I arrived she would be at work. Striding into Boots I went up to the first assistant I saw and asked to see the manager.

"Good morning, Sir," he smiled. "Can I help you?"

I explained that I had come to see the Librarian, Miss Mountford.

"Ah yes," he replied, "She will be upstairs in the library. If you'd like to follow me up." With that he led the way to the upper floor where a couple of assistants were busying themselves tidying the book shelves, but no sign of Iris. He turned and indicated for me to wait and disappeared behind the counter and through a curtain, reappearing a few seconds later with a rather flustered Iris. Before she could say anything I swept her into my arms and held her tight. It had been such a long time without her and so much had happened.

When she could eventually ease herself away from me, she led me behind her curtain where there was a bit more privacy and asked excitedly, "What on Earth are you doing here?"

What could I say, except what was uppermost in my mind. "I've come to ask you to marry me," I gasped out.

"What, just like that?" she asked.

"Why not?" I countered. At least she hadn't said no.

There was no answer to that, and after thinking about it for a few seconds she continued, "This is all a bit of a shock. I think we had better go and sit over a cup of coffee and talk it through." With that she took me by the hand out through the curtain to find the manager. Breathlessly, she explained the situation and he very generously gave her the rest of the day off. Once in the café, Iris took a more down to Earth view.

"Have you taken leave of your senses? How can we get married? We've no money, no house, I haven't even seen you for the last seven months." I continued with my romantic approach, convinced that true love would triumph.

"All that's just detail. Let's get the important things decided first," and going down on one knee I looked up into her eyes with great sincerity. " Will you marry me?" I beseeched her.

What could she say, except, "yes."

With that I made immediate enquiries as to where the nearest Registry Office was. I think I had romantic notions of dashing round there straight away for an instant marriage. I discovered the nearest was in Norbiton and they insisted on forty-eight hours notice. But a newly-commissioned officer couldn't wait that long and persuaded them to cut it to twenty-four.

Having made arrangements for the following morning, we began to get quite excited. There were so many things to do. First we rushed down to the local confectioners and picked out a small iced cake, which they agreed to decorate for us as a wedding cake. Then it was off to the florists for carnation button holes and - oh gosh - we must not forget the ring. I had next to no money, having had to pay for my uniform out of my salary and had not yet got the grant to reimburse me. Iris fished in her purse and managed to find enough for a nine-carat wartime special, costing all of ten and eleven pence.

At the end of the day, Iris decided it was time to take me home and break the news to her mother. I discovered her father worked in Nairobi and normally only came home once a year. Since the war had started, he hadn't even been able to manage that. I suppose in normal circumstances she would have taken me home before she accepted my proposal and I would have asked her father's permission to marry his daughter whilst her mother looked me over. But this was wartime and these were not normal circumstances.

I found the family atmosphere very friendly and casual and completely lacking the formality I had been used to in my own upbringing. Her brother Tommy and younger sister Rosemary made a fuss of me and asked a continual stream of questions about life in the Army. We sat informally round the kitchen table for tea and when one of the neighbours popped in I was introduced as Iris' husband-to-be. The neighbour, Mrs Shadwell, was just as excited as the Mountfords and insisted on being one of my witnesses at the Registry Office.

That night I was given a makeshift bed on the front room floor and after breakfast we set off for Norbiton. There were just four of us; Iris and I, Mrs Shadwell and Iris' brother Tommy. There was only one thing spoiling my complete enjoyment. It had occurred to me as I lay awake in my pre-nuptial bed that I would have to tell Iris that I had lied about my age, and that I was now only twenty-one. I was pondering on how best to break it to her when she looked at me very seriously and said, "Buster, I'm afraid I've a confession to make."

My heart raced. What was she about to tell me? Had she been out with somebody else while I had been away? Did she have some incurable disease? Had she changed her mind about the wedding? All sorts of fears ran through my mind. I could hardly force myself to reply. "What's that then," I croaked.

"You know when we met and you asked how old I was?"

"Yes."

"Well I didn't tell you the truth. I'm not twenty-five, I'm thirty-one."

I was so relieved. Was that all she had to tell me. Now I felt happier, and my confession could only make her feel less guilty.

"I've got a confession to make as well. I'm not twenty-five either. I'm only twenty-one. Now how do you feel?"

"That's funny," she said, "I thought you looked young when we met, so that's why I knocked a few years off my age." With that, we began to see the funny side. When we had got over it and got serious again, we looked straight into each others eyes.

"Will you still marry me then?" I asked.

"Of course I will, you silly old fool, that is, if you still want me." With that we collapsed into a tearful embrace, much to the amusement of the other passengers on the Number 65 bus. Half an hour later we were man and wife and I have not regretted our decision in all the fifty-four years we have spent together since that day.

It wasn't until the following day and we were on our way to Newbury for our honeymoon, that my conscience began to trouble me. I had been so taken up with Iris and her family and all the rush to get ready for the wedding, that I had omitted to tell my parents where I was, let alone that I was getting married. To tell the truth, I had thought about them often during the twenty-four hours since I had proposed, but knowing my mother's attitude towards Iris, I had put off doing anything about it and the longer I left it the worse it had got, so that in the end I didn't want to spoil things. I didn't want my mother waking me up from my dreamlike state and so I had let things slide. The problem was still unresolved. Sooner or later I would have to do something. What I did do only made things worse. At the end of the honeymoon, I took Iris round to see my father's sister-in-law who lived in Tooting. It was partly because I wanted her to meet Iris, and partly because I wanted her advice about how I should make amends with my parents.

"Don't worry," she said, "I'll be going round to see them tomorrow. I'll explain what happened. I'm sure your mum will understand." And so I took the easy way out and let Aunty Em convey the news. When I got back to my billet after the honeymoon, I wrote home and tried to explain, but the reply I got was, to say the least, curt.

When I was first posted to Windsor as a newly-commissioned lieutenant, I was put under the command of a captain, as part of a troop manning four Bofors guns on a trading estate at the edge of town. I must have done a good job as after a few weeks I was given command of my own troop, within the grounds of Windsor Castle. Most of the soldiers on duty there were from the Guards' regiments but there was a small detachment of Royal Artillery looking after four more Bofors which were positioned around the castle.

On arrival, I had to report to the senior Guards' officer, who briefed me on my code of conduct and the etiquette to be observed when the royal family were in residence. The general rule was to salute on sight, no matter how far away the royal personages were. It was quite funny as one could track their whereabouts by the series of shouts of "eyes right" that echoed around the castle grounds all day.

The men slept in old stables in the grounds, but as I said earlier, RHIP, so I slept in the castle, albeit on the library floor. The walls were covered with row after row of huge leather-bound tomes, many with Latin titles which meant little to me despite my grammar school education. Nevertheless, I was impressed by them and often think back on what they must have been worth. I also wonder if they survived the recent fire at the castle.

The duties were not arduous. Each morning I would walk round and inspect the gun emplacements and watch the sergeants putting their crews through their paces. Then, unless I was Orderly Officer, this left my afternoons free for a training run, watching a football match, or sometimes just wandering around the town. Quite often during my morning inspections the sergeant would tip me the wink and I would have to call the crew to attention and salute as royalty passed by in the distance. It was quite a thrill the first time I got an acknowledging nod from the princesses as they went by on their ponies, but after a while it became commonplace.

I was caught unawares one afternoon as I wandered round the grounds, deep in thought, when two small dogs ran out from behind a rhododendron bush and started barking round my ankles. I carried on walking whilst trying to shoo them away and was surprised once I had passed the bush to find the king and queen picnicking on the lawn. Embarrassed in case they thought I was hurting the dogs, I straightened up and gave my best eyes-right salute. I can tell you it is very difficult to maintain a true sense of decorum when one has a corgi hanging on the strap of one's gaiter. The king and queen thought it quite amusing and I found it very difficult to keep a straight face.

I'm not sure why, but we seemed not to stay in one place for very long. After Windsor Castle, my troop travelled around the country for the next few months guarding various airfields. To prevent enemy raids taking out our aircraft while still on the ground, they were moved from one airfield to another and we moved with the aircraft. When we weren't guarding planes, we would be detached on various training courses. I always seemed to be selected for the more physical ones.

I remember one course in particular when I was sent to Battersea for a week's training in street fighting. It was held in a bombed-out area so that we could practice clearing enemy out of the houses. It was quite dangerous with live ammunition being fired over our heads and grenades being let off to add realism. We became quite adept at travelling across the roof tops and then using grappling irons on ropes to cross the alleyways in between. It took quite a lot of courage to swing across feet-first to crash through a window, not knowing if there would be a floor to the room behind.

In the main, the course was made up of large, hairy infantrymen, with me being by far the smallest there and the only Gunner. There were quite a number of injuries sustained and I didn't come out of it unscathed. One day, we had just crossed a flat roof and lying on my belly I peered over the edge to see if it was clear to cross the alley. At the same moment, somebody fired a flame-thrower into the ground floor window immediately below me. Not all the blazing fuel entered the window and a large fire ball shot rapidly up the side of the building taking off my eyebrows and the front of my hair. Fortunately, I was not seriously burnt and the hair soon grew again.

We continued to move from one airfield to another until one day I was told I would be leaving my troop to go on a special posting. I was given a warrant and put on the train for Bracknell. On arrival I found it difficult to find out just why I was there. It was all very secretive and we were not allowed out of barracks at all. Each day more men and equipment arrived and it was obvious that it was leading up to some important mission. It looked as though I might be called upon to use my street-fighting skills for real. The thought of this filled me with excitement rather than fear as I was longing to get into some real action against the enemy. Whilst on airfield duty, I had been putting my name forward every time a notice came round asking for volunteers for any unspecified special service. Now it looked like paying off.

However, it was not to be. With no explanation I was suddenly sent back to my old gun battery up north. A couple of weeks later the reason emerged. I was to go overseas. I was sent down to Woolwich to be kitted out, and judging by the tropical shorts and topee I was given, I was off to somewhere warm. I was given a 48-hour pass to say my goodbyes and soon made the short trip to Richmond where Iris was still living with her mother.

Since the wedding, I had been writing regularly to Iris and less frequently to my mother. Mum was now a nurse and Dad was doing regular Air raid warden duties. Mum's letters gave me all the news of how they were coping with the war, but never mentioned Iris or asked how she was. During that last weekend, I decided I couldn't go abroad without healing the rift and so set off with Iris on the Sunday afternoon for Mallinson Road.

With some trepidation I knocked on the door and waited. After a few seconds I could see my mother through the glass door panels, shuffling down the hall. When she opened the door I just stood there silently.

"You've got a darned cheek," she said in a low voice. And with that shut the door in my face. Undeterred I knocked again. This time she came to the door more purposefully. As she wrenched it open I placed my foot firmly inside to prevent her from closing it again.

"Look Mum," I said, "we've got to talk. I'm being sent abroad and you may never see me again." With that she hesitated and then reluctantly admitted, "You'd better come in then." And so we made our peace. I was able to leave with an easier conscience, and whilst I was away Iris was very good and used to visit my mum regularly. Later that day, Iris and I had a tearful farewell at the station before I returned to Woolwich to collect my kit. From there I caught another train to Greenock where the troop ship, 'Almanzora' was waiting. Buster was off to Africa.

Chapter 11

Journey's End

After travelling through most of the night on the train we arrived at Greenock as dawn was breaking and made our way to where the SS Almanzora was docked. She was a strangely old-fashioned-looking ship with tall, thin funnels which had a pronounced backwards rake to them. Having shown our papers to the rating at the bottom of the gangway, we were directed to the Captain's office. He welcomed us on board and passed us on to the Purser who allocated each of us to our cabin. This was to be my home for the next six weeks.

Each overseas draft was given a code name and I was part of REAGO draft. It contained fifty or so officers and about two thousand soldiers and NCOs. The 'other ranks' slept in hammocks which were slung in tiers in large open areas in the lower parts of the ship. As a junior officer, I shared a small cabin with three others. We had single bunks, two on either side of the cabin, and I found myself on the lower level.

Since I had been in the Army, I had slept in all sorts of surroundings and learned to sleep through all kinds of discomforts and distractions, but I must say I found it difficult to sleep during that first night on board. When the main light was turned out, a small blue safety lamp came on which gave everything a strange glow. Added to that were a myriad of strange sounds that I lay awake trying to recognise. First there was the creak of the beds around me, complaining every time one of my fellow travellers turned over. The lapping of the water against the hull of the ship was soporific but was countered by eerie groans which seemed to emanate from the very fabric of the ship as she strained at her mooring ropes. Most disturbing was a strange whooshing sound which I eventually pinned down to the cabin doors. None of them had handles or locks, but were mounted on double hinges so that they could be pushed open from either side. There were retaining springs to return them to the closed position and air dampers, which were the cause of the whoosh every time a door was pushed.

Eventually I did get to sleep, and on waking next morning took a quick look out of the small porthole at the end of our cabin to see where we were. I should have realised without looking. Of all the noises in the night, the one that was missing was the sound of engines. We were still in dock. We stayed there for two more days taking on men, equipment and provisions, but on the third night I was woken by the sound of the engines starting. As the propellers started to cut through the water there was a rhythmic, pounding, pulsation which seemed to vibrate every metal plate of the old ship as she groaned her way from the harbour and out into the Irish Sea.

We had not been told where we were going and there was great speculation on deck the next morning as we tried to work out from the position of the sun, which direction we were travelling in. We decided it was north-west, and as we could see land on both sides of us, quickly concluded that we were heading up between the Scottish coast and Northern Ireland, en route for the Atlantic. We found this a little puzzling as we expected to be heading down through the Irish Sea which was the main shipping lane for all points south or east. We speculated that we might be on our way to North America, but once we had rounded the top of Ireland, the route gradually swung to a more south westerly direction as we headed towards the Azores.

A few days later, there was a sudden change of direction to south east. After two more changes we began to realise that it was impossible to predict our destination from the ship's movements. We were following this erratic path to avoid enemy submarines. We were not aware of it at the time, but the mathematicians at Bletchley Park had cracked the German Enigma ciphers, and as a result the ship received daily reports on the whereabouts of submarines and altered course accordingly.

Soon, there had been so many changes of direction we did not know where we were, except that the temperatures and the height of the sun told us we must be approaching the Tropics. There was no land anywhere in sight and at night there were a million stars visible in the clear skies above us. Then one morning after two or three weeks at sea, we were amazed to find ourselves surrounded by about twenty other ships who had rendezvoused with us in the night to form a convoy. There was a cruiser and two or three destroyers, but mostly they were troop ships, carrying allied forces from many parts of the British Empire. We were just off the coast of North West Africa and a few days later we pulled into Freetown for a brief refuelling stop, but we were not allowed ashore.

When we set sail again, another troop ship full of Africans sailed alongside us, but we could only surmise where they came from; probably somewhere like The Gold Coast, Sierra Leone or the Gambia, none of which were far away from our present position. Their ship seemed to be terribly overcrowded and we heard rumours of an epidemic of smallpox on board. We certainly saw more than one burial at sea over the side of that vessel, but whether these resulted from the outbreak or were the cause of the rumours was never ascertained.

There was not a lot for us to do on board. Every day we carried out lifeboat drill, which was essential in those hostile waters, and I also started morning PT classes for the officers. Apart from that we mostly sat around chatting or reading with the occasional break to watch one of the escort destroyers peeling off in search of some inquisitive enemy submarine. We would watch them drop their depth charges and wait for debris to rise to the surface, but it never did. Again, we didn't know if they were just practising or whether the submarine had got away.

After eight weeks, soon after dawn one morning, a buzz went round the ship that land was once more in sight. Everybody leapt out of bed and hurriedly made their way on deck. We immediately knew where we were. There was no mistaking Table Mountain. Slowly it grew in size as it came ever closer until we eventually pulled alongside it in Capetown harbour.

As we entered the harbour, a flotilla of colourful, small boats congregated around the ship, each manned by a smiling, upturned face trying to sell us anything from bracelets to oranges, from bananas to sun glasses. They threw balls of twine up to the soldiers hanging over the ships rails or out of the portholes so that they could haul up the goods for inspection before parting with their money. The natives didn't speak much English but still managed to barter with the soldiers, calling them all 'Johnny' whilst assuring them, "Very good bargain, Sir."

As with Freetown, it was just a refuelling stop, but this time we were allowed ashore for the evening. Most of the soldiers headed straight for the nearest bar and had to be herded back to the ship by the regimental police in the early hours. I went ashore for a couple of hours; the first time I had ever set foot on foreign soil. I was fascinated by the mixture of people of different races who promenaded along the streets. There were English, Boers, swarthy-looking Arabs and a variety of different black African natives. I was quite content just to wander along looking in the windows of shops, which, much to my surprise, were still open late into the evening. It was possible to buy things which had become rarities in England such as bananas, oranges and grapes, and best of all, chocolate. I was able to take a little hoard back to the ship with me.

The next day we set sail again, continuing eastward around the coast of South Africa towards Durban. This was nearly a thousand miles from Capetown and took us a further five days to reach. As we eased gently into the harbour we were greeted by a carnival atmosphere. There was a brass band on the quay accompanied by a lady in white who was renowned for greeting all the troop ships. She gave us a stirring rendering of 'Land of Hope and Glory' and was cheered by the troops and the crowds gathered on shore.

We docked about midday, and spent the afternoon preparing to disembark the next morning. First we had to parade and draw our weapons from the hold. This was followed by a pay parade and an issue of mail. We had picked up mail at each of our refuelling stops, where I had collected quite a fat bundle of letters from Iris. Having left Capetown only a few days before, there were only four or five waiting for me this time, but I was able to lie on my bed during the afternoon and savour them.

After tea, we got ourselves ready to go ashore sight-seeing. From the sea, Durban looked much more interesting than Capetown, boasting several tall skyscrapers and a marvellous beach and promenade. I was quite excited at the thoughts of the evening ahead. Two of the other officers who shared the cabin with me were also scurrying round getting ready, but the fourth, a chap called Joe, just lay dispassionately on his bed. I asked him, "Aren't you coming ashore with us, Joe?"

"No," he replied, "I don't really feel like it. I think I'll just lie here quietly and read." I found this rather surprising and suspected he might have had bad news or a 'Dear John' in the mail that we had just received. I tried to persuade him to join me but I could see that he was not interested. He did however accept my offer to bring him back some grapes.

Once more I found the street scenes captivating with their colour and bustle. Most interesting of all were the rickshaws pulled by Zulus, in full tribal costume, with Bird-of-Paradise feathers in their hair. They were obviously for tourists and holiday-makers but being in unfamiliar surroundings I found them a little foreboding and didn't take a ride. Having wandered through the town centre and bought the grapes for my colleague back on the ship, I turned towards the sea front and walked along the promenade breathing in the balmy temperate air. Having a fair skin that burnt all too easily in the intense sun that we had experienced on the voyage, this fresh but warm climate was perfect. I stopped and chatted to some of the white townspeople and was captivated by their clipped accent. As we watched the huge breakers rolling in from the Indian Ocean and crashing noisily on to the golden beach, I decided that Durban must be a very nice place to live.

As dusk fell I found myself outside a cinema and decided to spend a couple of hours watching the show. Seen from the front, the cinema seemed quite normal, no different from cinemas back home. But once inside, I found that I wasn't inside at all. It was an open-air cinema with no roof. In between films, I leaned back and once more wondered at the intensity of the stars in the deep navy-blue sky above.

Wending my way back to the harbour and the SS Almanzora after leaving the cinema was not so easy as there was a partial blackout in operation. Eventually I arrived back to find that my sleeping companions had already returned. I handed over the grapes I had promised Joe and the three of us sat around him excitedly recounting all that we had seen. He listened politely, but didn't seem very interested. Clearly he had other things on his mind.

After we had been in bed for a while, I was disturbed by the main cabin light coming on again. Sleepily opening one eye, I saw Joe stood by his bed wrapping a towel around his naked loins. During our passage through the sweltering Tropics, we had become accustomed to sleeping nude and the habit had persisted.

"Do you have to put the light on?" I complained.

"Sorry," he said, "Didn't mean to disturb you." And with that he turned it out again before whooshing his way out of the cabin, presumably to the toilets which were just along the corridor. Sure enough, a few seconds later I heard the second whoosh as he pushed open the toilet door.

I must have gone back to sleep again, but some time later I was awakened once more. This time I didn't know the reason. I lay there with my eyes closed listening for clues, but all I could hear was the lapping of the water and the groaning of the ship straining at her moorings. I wondered if it had been Joe returning, and dreamily I looked across to his bed. It was still empty.

I had no way of knowing the time without getting up, switching the light on and finding my watch, but in my soporific state that was too much effort. So I just lay back listening, but I sensed that it was the early hours and Joe had been gone some time. It worried me. Had he been taken ill? Had he tripped and fallen and was lying unconscious somewhere? Or maybe he just couldn't sleep and had gone up on deck for some air? I convinced myself that that was it. He had disturbed me by going out again.

I closed my eyes and tried to sleep but couldn't. My doubts were still there. Then I had an idea. If he had just left again, his bed would still be warm. Slipping quietly out, I leaned across and felt. It was cold. An uneasy chill went down my spine. I was becoming convinced something had happened to him. What if he had fallen overboard?

I decided to go and look for him, starting with the toilet, that being his last known whereabouts; I could do with a leak anyway. Wrapping my towel about me I whooshed into the corridor and whooshed again into the toilets. Inside, there was a urinal and four cubicles, the doors to which automatically swung open when the cubicle was not in use. There was no sign of Joe, but one of the cubicle doors was shut.

"Joe, are you there Joe?" I called. There was no answer. I tried the door and found it was not locked, but there seemed to be a heavy weight against the inside of it preventing me from pushing it open. I feared the worst. Joe had probably collapsed and had been lying in the cubicle for God knows how long.

I went into the next cubicle and climbed on to the seat. Taking hold of the dividing wall I was able to pull myself up and peer over. Yes, there he was slumped on the floor; there was blood everywhere. On the floor beside him lay the pistol he had drawn from the hold earlier in the day. He had shot himself through the temple and it must have been the crack of the pistol shot that had woken me the second time. His back had slid down the door leaving a gory trail and his legs were twisted up against the base of the toilet bowl. He had been there long enough for the blood to run down his body into his lap, staining his towel crimson.

I took all this in in just two or three seconds. Dropping back to the floor, I rushed back to the cabin and woke the others.

"Joe's shot himself," I gasped, "What are we going to do?" I decided to wake the Draft Commander, whose cabin was further along our corridor. Once I had appraised him of the situation, he sent one of my cabin-mates to fetch the ship's Medical Officer, while the rest of us hurried back to the toilets. Even with our combined efforts, we still couldn't open the cubicle door. All we were doing was pushing Joe up against the toilet bowl, only for him to fall back again when we stopped pushing. It was eventually decided that somebody would have to go in over the wall and move him.

Being the smallest, and probably the most agile, that horrific task fell to me. Getting over the wall was no problem. Moving him was not so easy, working in such a confined space. I had to first disentangle his legs and then stand him up leaning over my shoulder, before sitting back on to the toilet so that the others could open the door. Once we had him out, he was laid on the toilet floor and the Medical Officer, who had arrived in the meantime, started to examine him. Miraculously, he was still alive, although we could tell by the bloody mucus oozing from his nostrils that he was in a bad way. After no more that a minute or two, the MO stood up and folded his stethoscope.

"I'm afraid we're too late. He's gone. Even if we had found him sooner, I don't think we could have done much for him." Although I was saddened to think he had died, I was relieved to hear the MO's pronouncement as I was beginning to blame myself, thinking that if I had gone looking for him earlier, he might have been saved.

After that the reaction began to set in and I started to shake. I looked down at myself and saw the bloody mess I was in from man-handling poor old Joe. I had never even seen a dead person before and I was feeling very sick and faint. I made my excuses and stumbled out into the corridor and up on to the deck, gulping in the fresh night air. Eventually I began to recover and made my way slowly back below decks to get cleaned up.

First I had to return to the cabin to get my wash things and a clean towel. Whilst I was there, I glanced across at Joe's bed and spotted a folded paper on the pillow that I must have missed when I had leaned over to see if his bed was still warm. I picked it up and opened it. It was a simple farewell note to his mother asking her for forgiveness for what he was about to do. Wearily I refolded it and took it to the Draft Commander before taking my shower. I scrubbed and scrubbed but could not erase the terrible images from my mind.

When I returned to the cabin I was surprised to find it was past four-thirty in the morning. There was no way I would sleep again that night. I dressed and made my way back up on deck where I slowly regained my composure as I watched the sky turn a delicate pale pink as the sun arose from the depths of the Indian Ocean.

When the rest of the ship awoke, news of the previous night's disaster quickly spread. As the other officers became aware of my involvement, they came and offered consolation but invariably tried to extract details of the incident from me. However, this was the one time I did not enjoy being the centre of attention and they soon realised I wanted to be left alone.

I got my wish to a greater extent than I had anticipated. During the morning everybody else disembarked from the ship, but I was told I had to remain behind to give evidence at a Court of Enquiry that would convene the very same afternoon. This turned out to be even more formal than usual. As the ship was tied up in dock at the time of the occurrence, the civilian authorities had to be involved as well as the military. In my evidence I had to go through all the events of the previous night. Then I was quizzed as to Joe's demeanour during the voyage from England and whether or not he had confided in me or the others in the cabin. I explained that although we shared a cabin, during the day we went our separate ways and only met again when it was time for bed. Although we had all got on well together, by the time we reached South Africa we were still no more than acquaintances. By the end of the day the Court of Enquiry came to the only conclusion possible and I was allowed to go. In their report, I was commended for my endeavours for poor old Joe.

The rest of my draft had not gone far and were now at a transit camp about ten or twelve miles out of Durban, called Clairwood Camp. It was readily accessible by commuter train, so later that evening, having collected my rail warrant I shouldered my kitbag and made my way to Durban station. The trains had long open-plan carriages rather like the London Underground trains. Segregation was in force, with some carriages designated 'whites only', but somehow I couldn't find them and I ended up in a carriage full of blacks and coloureds. It wasn't really the 'done thing' for a British Army officer in uniform and I got a few strange glances. I was a little apprehensive but didn't let it worry me too much.

Again like the London Underground, there were route maps above the seats and I noted that there were three stations at Clairwood. There was one just called Clairwood, which I assumed would be in the centre of the town. Then there was Clairwood Camp and finally Clairwood Racecourse. It was as well I had this map to guide me as the stations we stopped at en route were very dimly lit due to the blackout, and unless you stopped immediately opposite the station name plaque, it was impossible to read it.

Eventually the train reached Clairwood, and shortly after, Clairwood Camp. It was a good job I had been carefully following the route as the station was in complete blackness. I surmised that it was used only during the day for troop movements and effectively shut at night, although it did stop to let passengers off.

Pulling my kitbag behind me, I opened the carriage door and stepped out into the dark, considering myself lucky that I saw the large gap between train and platform in time to step over it. Quite dangerous I thought as I shouldered my kitbag and walked on down the platform looking for the exit. As the train began to move past me, a voice called out of the gloom.

"Is this Clairwood Camp, Sir?" Looking round, I saw a fresh-faced young soldier leaning out of a half-opened carriage door.

"Yes, it is," I replied, "but you've left it too late." Ignoring my warning, he flung the door wide open and jumped out, straight into the gap I had fortunately avoided. Jammed between platform and moving train, he was rolled round and round at ever increasing speed as the train gathered pace. His mangled remains were deposited at the end of the platform as the train sped off into the night.

The night air had been filled with his screams but now there was only silence. The station was completely unmanned and in absolute darkness. I waited until my eyes adjusted to the dark and then hurried to the end of the platform. One glance told me he was very dead. Stunned, I walked back to where I had left my kitbag. I sat on it and contemplated my next move. Here I was in the middle of nowhere, all on my own with a dead body. There was no sign of habitation anywhere. All I could see around me in the starlight was thick vegetation. The only thing I could do was to stay put and wait for the next train through.

After what seemed like eternity, I heard the faint sound of an approaching steam train. Throwing caution to the winds, I jumped down on to the track and waited for its arrival. As it came down the track I took off my peaked cap and waved it in the air, all the time being ready to jump out of the way if the train was not due to stop and didn't see me. Much to my relief, the train began to slow and pulled up a few yards in front of me.

I rushed round to the side of the engine and shouted up to the driver, who was as black as the night.

"There's been a terrible accident," I cried, "A man's been killed." The driver looked at his fireman, then back at me and shrugged his shoulders. It was apparent that he didn't speak English. Frantically I raced down the side of the train looking for a white face, but my heart sank. It was an all-black train. By now the passengers were all hanging out of the windows looking at this mad bare-headed English Officer who was prancing up and down the side of the train.

I quickly made my way back to the engine and beckoned the driver and fireman out of the cab. They could see my obvious consternation and although puzzled as to its cause, followed me as I took them to the other end of the platform. It was more than I could do to accompany them all the way, but they continued on down the slope when I pointed them forward. A few seconds later they returned white-eyed and jabbering to each other in Bantu or whatever language it was they spoke. They raised their hands, palms towards me, to indicate that I should stay where I was and then quickly made their way back down to the engine where they climbed aboard and sped off into the night. Once more I was on my own in the dark.

Had I been abandoned, or had they gone for help? I had no way of knowing. It must have been nearly an hour later that I saw a pair of headlights moving through the dense woodland outside the station. At first, I suspected it was just a vehicle passing by in the night, but it gradually got closer as it traced the zig-zag road to the station. Eventually an army pick-up truck pulled up and two medical corps senior NCOs got out. The train driver had apparently phoned the camp from Clairwood main station.

One of the NCOs came over and saluted. "I understand you've had a bit of trouble, Sir." I explained as best I could what had happened. He took a blanket out of the truck and set off with his companion to the end of the platform. A few minutes later they returned carrying the weighted blanket between them and placed it in the back of the truck.

"And would you be on your way to the camp then, Sir?" they asked. When I said I was, they offered me a lift there and then rather than wait for a car to be sent for me. Not wishing to spend a minute more than I had to alone in the dark, I took them up on their offer. I didn't realise until after I had accepted that I would have to travel in the back with the corpse.

When I arrived at the camp, I was shown where the rest of my draft were billeted and I was soon back amongst familiar faces. They were all very inquisitive about the Court of Enquiry and were amazed when I told them of the second death. I was thoroughly drained but they kept me up well into the night talking about it. Eventually, I fell into my bed exhausted. I had witnessed two violent deaths in less than twenty four hours.

Chapter 12

Africa

As I explained in the last chapter, Clairwood was a transit camp which held troops until it could be decided where they were needed. There wasn't much for us to do there except for routine activities such as drill and map reading. Once again, as on the boat, I ran my PT classes and there were many interesting places for our training runs around the camp. In the afternoons we sometimes caught the train into Durban for shopping or the cinema and it was a marvellous place for swimming. The Indian Ocean was home to sharks, but the Durban beach had barrier nets about a hundred yards off-shore to keep them out. Like many others, I hired a surf board and very quickly became quite proficient.

By way of a change, I would sometimes catch a bus along the coast to one of the smaller villages such as Isipingo or Amanzimtoti. These were African settlements set in almost virgin countryside. I would take a packed lunch from the mess and laze all day on the beach although swimming was very restricted without the safety nets. Other days I would go inland and walk through the savannah studying the flora and fauna. It was a marvellous place to pursue my hobby of entomology with the abundance of huge multi-coloured butterflies. I also came across numerous snakes which I observed from a very respectable distance. All in all, life was idyllic and the war seemed a long way away.

One day, after I had been there about two months, I received orders to report to the docks for special duties. I discovered that I was being put in charge of the guards on a prisoner-of-war ship that was due into Durban harbour. It was a Dutch ship called the 'Ruys'. The Allies were at last beginning to win the war in North Africa and had taken many of Rommel's crack Africa Corps troops as prisoners. They had been herded on to the 'Ruys' and transported out of the war zone via the Suez Canal and the Red Sea, down the east coast of Africa and into Durban. From there, they were to be taken by train to Capetown and put on a larger vessel which would eventually transport them to prisoner-of-war camps in Canada. However, there was a delay of two or three days before the train would be available, and I was to be Guard Commander for that period.

The 'Ruys' was just an ordinary cargo ship which had been pressed into war service and hastily converted to carry these prisoners, probably the first taken in any numbers by our troops since the war started. The decks had coils of barbed wire all round the sides to prevent the prisoners jumping ship and there were about four strategically placed machine gun posts covering the deck areas all round the ship's superstructure.

The prisoners spent all their time in the main hold of the ship, sleeping in rows on the bare floor, with just a single blanket each for cover. As part of my duties, I had to go down amongst them every day to ensure that their conditions and treatment complied with the Geneva convention. I had two guards for this, and having descended the companionway, I would step carefully over the bodies and outstretched legs until I was in the middle of the floor area. From there I shouted out, "Any Complaints?", a cry which was immediately repeated in German by their interpreter. He was a corporal who had been educated in southern England and spoke perfect English.

This tour of the hold was a duty I didn't look forward to each day as the acrid smell of body odour was overpowering, but the prisoners seemed to accept all this as part of their lot and there was never any response to my enquiry. They were the elite of Hitler's troops and despite their poor conditions they all seemed very fit and athletic looking. It was very hot down in the hold and they wore nothing on their upper torso except a once-white vest bearing the German swastika. I was quite fit myself but no match for them in size and weight and I felt a little threatened when amongst them. They could have easily overpowered the two escorts and myself, but I was reassured in that they would still have had the problem of getting off the ship past the machine guns.

One surprising aspect was the reaction of the local white residents. The prisoners had to come up on to the deck to reach the single toilet that had been provided for them. As a further security measure, a barbed wire corridor had been constructed from the top of the ladder they used to get out of the hold, and across the deck to the toilet door. There was a constant queue along the route as the men waited for the toilet to become free, and whilst on deck they could be seen by people on the quay. I was taken aback to find that the locals were very sympathetic towards them and would wave and call out to them in quite a friendly fashion.

I also had to make routine calls three times a day on the one and only German officer on the ship. He was a medical officer who was housed in a deck cabin, with two British marines permanently on guard outside the door. Before entering his cabin, I had to leave my pistol outside with one of my escorts. As well as asking if he was satisfied with his treatment as a prisoner, I had to report to him that I had done my inspection below decks and had received no complaints. He understood and spoke English quite well and once the formalities were over we would talk about more general things, but our brief conversations soon developed into a challenge of minds. He warned me that since his initial capture he had already escaped three times, albeit not for long, and he would continue to try to do so. He said this with a smile and I suspect it was deliberately done to unsettle me. By way of retaliation I asked him how a man of his intelligence could possibly fight for the Nazi doctrine. His reply surprised me. He said he had actually met Hitler and found him very charismatic. He summed it up by saying, "What the Fuhrer wants the people do, and what the Fuhrer does, the people want."

On another, more relaxed occasion, he told me he came from Dusseldorf where his wife and children would be waiting for him when the war was over. I hadn't the heart to tell him that just a few nights before, Dusseldorf had been the target of a particularly heavy Allied raid.

On the third day the prisoners were disembarked from the ship and put on a train. This was a particularly harrowing time for me as Guard Commander, as this was the most likely time for any attempted escape. They were brought up in single file and shepherded down the gangway on to the quay where I had stationed guards along the water's edge to prevent the prisoners jumping in.

The event made international news and the cameras were there in force as was a large crowd of South Africans. The latter were restrained some distance away behind barricades, but as before with the toilet queue, there were cheers and whistles in support of the prisoners. This did not go down well with the British guards and only served to harden their feelings towards the prisoners. One prisoner, who stopped at the top of the gangway to acknowledge the cheers, was helped on his way rather too vigorously by one of my men and nearly went over the edge into the harbour. It was a moment that could have had serious repercussions had I not been on hand to calm things down. In the end, we got all the prisoners safely off our hands and I returned to Clairwood Camp with some relief.

Back at camp it was the old routine of training, exercise and boredom. By way of diversion, I entered a services boxing competition that was held in the Durban Civic Hall. This was the first time I had fought competitively since losing so dramatically at OCTU. With little else to do, practically the whole of my draft made the train journey into town and packed into the hall. I just hoped I wouldn't let them down as I had done at Ludlow. Fortunately, my opposition was not of the same standard and I won my contest with an equally dramatic knockout. It made headlines on the sports page of the local paper and did much to restore my self-esteem as well as my reputation as a boxer.

As time went by and we still hadn't been moved on, we became eligible for local leave. Some of the Officers had made friends with local residents and went to stay with them. For others, including myself, holidays were organised by the Women's Voluntary Service. They arranged for a couple of friends and myself to go about a hundred miles or so up the coast to a place called Umvoti. This was a small village not far from the border with what is now Mozambique, but in those days was Portuguese East Africa.

It took us most of the day to get there, firstly on the train and then in the Land Rover which had been sent to the railhead to collect us. The black driver was very respectful, calling us 'Bwana' every time he addressed us. He was obviously a servant of our white host. He took us another twenty or thirty miles along dusty, unmade roads through the Savannah where we saw very little signs of habitation. Eventually he turned in to the entrance of a large sugar farm and pulled up in front of an imposing bungalow. From the door came a white woman of about sixty years of age who was to be our host for the next few days. Although not particularly tall, she was a very impressive figure; the arch-stereotype of the western film ranch-widow. She wore boots, a plaid shirt and denim trousers with a holstered pistol at her waist and a bull whip in her hand. Single-handed, she ruled her gang of fifty-odd natives with a rod of iron. She introduced herself as Mary Bradley.

She made us very welcome and life on the farm was very genteel, much like living in the Officers' Mess. There was no electricity to the bungalow and we ate dinner by the light of oil lamps which cast their light no further than the four of us, sat intimately round the table. The four black African waiters merged perfectly into the gloom beyond, being barely visible except when one of them smiled to reveal a perfect set of teeth.

At night we each had our own room, a luxury I had not had since I slept in the front room at Battersea. The sweet-smelling pure-white cotton sheets were an added bonus. Like most South African buildings, there was a gap between the top of the walls and the ceiling to keep the interior cool. This allowed a myriad of flying insects in, attracted by the oil lamps. With my continuing interest in entomology, I considered this a benefit rather than a nuisance and I was able to identify several species I had not seen before.

After breakfast on the first morning, Mary asked us what we would like to do. Looking round, there didn't seem to be very much we could do and we were quite surprised when she offered us tennis as an option. The bungalow was set on the top of a high cliff overlooking a rocky beach below. One of the servants guided us down a narrow cliff path to the back of the beach where we discovered a full-sized tennis court, complete with a small pavilion containing all the necessary equipment.

We spent a very pleasant morning playing each other in a 'round robin'. At lunchtime, another member of staff brought down a luxurious picnic hamper and a large jug of lemonade made from real lemons. With the lunch came a message from Mary suggesting that we might like to try our hand at fishing in the afternoon. Having agreed, one of the servants disappeared back up the path, returning some time later with a collection of rods and tackle. During his absence we strolled along the beach, clambering over the rocks and gazing down into huge rock pools. These were the size and depth of Olympic swimming pools and we could see large fish swimming round in the crystal clear waters. They had the appearance of sharks but I think they were tope; stranded by the receding tide.

We were exited at the prospect of catching these, but our mentor dismissed them as too easy. He had other ideas. He had brought one very large rod that was almost impossible to lift and three small rods. He baited the smaller rods with small pieces of raw meat and handed us one each, instructing us to cast into the shallow water just a few feet off-shore. We didn't see the point of this as we could see the bottom quite clearly, no more than six feet below, and there was no sign of any fish.

Nevertheless, we did as we were told and dropped our baited hooks into the water. Immediately, as if from nowhere, there was a profusion of silver flashes around each bait and within seconds I was pulling a fish out of the water. I had become rather blasé since coming to Africa over the wonders nature was continually showing me, but I was totally unprepared to deal with my catch.

The fish was about six or eight inches long and as soon as I hauled it out of the water and on to the rocks, it blew itself up into a round ball with a mouth at one end and a tail at the other. It was almost impossible to get hold of it to take the hook out. Our fishing tutor was quite amused at my consternation and came across to assist, explaining that what I had caught was a Puffer Fish. Taking it off the hook he then put it on the hook of the large rod and cast it way out into the ocean. We were merely catching bait for him to use on his shark rod. We continued in this enjoyable fashion for the rest of the afternoon, holding competitions amongst ourselves as to who could catch the most Puffers. By teatime we must have landed at least a hundred between us, but alas, not even a bite from a shark.

And this was how we spent our week at Umvoti. We would either be on the beach or taking trips in the Land Rover into the surrounding countryside looking at the exotic vegetation, chasing butterflies or just lazing round a picnic basket. In the evenings after dinner we would sit around and talk, play cards or walk along the cliff tops as the light slowly faded. In the distance we could just discern Lorenco Marques, over the border in Portuguese East Africa. It was not involved in the war and was lit up like a Christmas tree.

One evening at dinner, there was an excited babble of African voices outside the house. One of the servants was sent to find out what was amiss and returned a few minutes later to say that the boys had trapped a snake. Mary took down a shotgun from the wall and invited us to follow her out to the edge of the sugar cane fields.

Once there, we found a row of thorn trees about fifteen feet tall. The boys pointed excitedly to the top of one of the trees where, perched on the uppermost branch, was the snake. It was a Green Mamba; a particularly venomous type of snake. It had its tail curled around the branch, with the upper part of its body swaying backwards and forwards in the night air above the tree.

"OK," said Mary, "you chaps are supposed to be trained soldiers. Which one of you is going to shoot the snake?" She was aware of my interest in insects and reptiles and was looking directly at me as she spoke. I took the shotgun from her and moved to the foot of the tree. As I took careful aim, the mamba suddenly launched itself through the air, over my head and into the next tree. This was quite unnerving, and I had visions of it leaping down to sink its fangs into my neck before I had time to pull the trigger. Swinging round as though following the flight of a clay pigeon, I fired as the snake landed in the second tree. The blast caught it full on and it fell to the ground in pieces. Excitedly, the native boys rushed forward and once I had inspected what was left of it, they carried it triumphantly away. I don't know whether it ended up as somebody's dinner, but certainly the Africans used to eat some varieties of snake.

Soon after the holiday, my draft moved from Clairwood. This time we were told our destination. We were off to India. It was back to the docks at Durban where we boarded a small troopship bound for Bombay. Although effectively 'next door', this was four thousand miles away from Durban and it took us a month to make the journey. It was an uneventful passage, and once we passed Madagascar we were out of sight of land for the rest of the way and didn't even see any other ships. As with the previous trip on the 'Almanzora', boredom was the main problem and to alleviate this I organised boxing competitions as well as the usual daily PT sessions.

We were relieved when we were told we were nearing our destination and crowded to the side of the ship, anxious to be the first to see the faint purple shadow that would mark landfall. Once spotted, we watched with an increasing tingle of excitement as it gradually grew and took on shape throughout the day. We were transfixed with wonderment as we pulled into Bombay harbour. This was the gateway to the Orient. It heralded a culture that was completely alien to anything we had previously encountered.

Durban had been quite westernised and although unmistakably African, from a casual glance it could easily have been mistaken for a British or American port. It boasted large stone-built buildings not unlike the banks in the City of London and a sea-front that Eastbourne could be proud of. It was a neat and tidy city, with clean tar-macadam roads full of buses and cars, and businessmen in suits hurrying along the pavements as they went about their business.

Bombay was completely different. It was dirty, it was noisy, it was smelly, it was wonderful. Everything seemed to have a yellow light about it, possibly due to the thick dust that pervaded the atmosphere. The buildings were less imposing and mostly made of yellow sandstone. The roads may have been paved but their surface was covered in a permanent thick layer of dirt and decaying manure from the bullock carts which were the main form of transport. Indian cattle freely roamed the streets adding to the squalor, but above all there were people. There were thousands of them. Very few women appeared on the streets but when they did they brought a flash of colour; reds, greens and golds, to contrast with the dull white robes worn by the men.

Poverty was everywhere, with the streets being the only home a large part of the population knew. Many were crippled and diseased with distorted or missing limbs. They were referred to as 'The living dead'. Their deformities were their only livelihood as they sat by the roadside pleading for 'Baksheesh'.

In a strange way, I was reminded of the Northcote Road market and the trio of 'gassed on the Somme' heroes. The plight of these poor devils was infinitely worse and I was full of pity and despair for them. The first time I found myself among them I felt obliged to give what money I had, but I soon learned this was a mistake. Immediately, I was surrounded by every beggar in Bombay and they proved almost impossible to get rid of. For some time after I daren't frequent that area for fear of being mobbed. I learned to harden my heart to their plight and realised it was too big a problem for one junior Officer to solve. Nevertheless, my Christian background would not let me rest easily.

With my fellow Officers, I was billeted in the Taj Mahal Hotel, the best that Bombay had to offer. This was five-star Indian-style. It was built like a temple with huge marble halls and passageways in which large fans constantly turned to recirculate the torpid air. Life there was diametrically opposite to that of the street beggars. I only had to snap my fingers or ring a handbell and my smallest wish would be instantly met by one of the host of uniformed staff. Although I felt uncomfortable to be over-indulged in this way, I took comfort in the thought that their employment in the hotel probably saved them from life on the street and saved their families from starvation.

After four or five days we were on the move again, this time by train. Once again this was an experience completely unlike any train journey I had ever made before. We were heading for a place called Ranchi which was near Jabalpur, about a thousand miles to the north east of Bombay. Fortunately, we had compartments reserved for us as the train was absolutely jam-packed with people, including many who clung to the outside of the carriages or travelled on the roof. For them it was fortunate that the train travelled extremely slowly, taking four days to complete the journey. During that time, we had to sleep sitting up in our seats and to get food by whatever means we could.

Periodically, the train stopped at primitive stations in remote towns and villages where it was instantly surrounded by pedlars selling anything and everything. There were cha-wallahs selling evil-tasting black tea in small glasses. There were chapatti-wallahs who cut open the chapatti to make a kind of purse which they filled with a variety of concoctions, all of which were highly spiced with curry powder. There were fruit sellers with oranges, mangoes and paw-paws, cigarette sellers with English, American and Turkish brands, and trinket sellers with trays of small items ranging from safety pins to silver bangles. There was very little that one couldn't buy on that journey.

Mingled in with the traders were the inevitable crowd of beggars. Some just asked for money, others were prepared to entertain the passengers in exchange for a few coins. I was fascinated at one stop by a conjurer. He had a day-old chick which he stood on his outstretched palm. He would palm it and make it reappear stood on his other hand. He was very adept and it was difficult to see the transfer across. For his finale, he grasped the chick firmly in his right hand so that just its head was showing. He then took hold of it round the neck with his left hand and appeared to pull its head off, only to open his hands and reveal a chick stood on each palm. His arms were bare and there was nowhere the second chick could logically have come from. Needless to say, he was well rewarded for his talents.

Chapter 13

Indian Summer

Ranchi was a very large tented camp which must have housed 2000 or more men. Like Clairwood, it was a troop dispersal centre from which men were dispatched to operational units as required. The Officers of my draft were kept together, four to a tent, next to the marquee which served as the Officers' Mess. We very quickly settled into the usual boring transit-camp routine of drill and PT.

There was very little entertainment in Ranchi village for the troops, but some of the men, and a few of the officers, discovered a small bar where they were entertained by the delights of Sultry Sonia, the local dancer, and her pigeons. I had no need of such titillation, being wrapped up in my new environment where I had a different set of insects and reptiles to study.

The area around Ranchi abounded with snakes. Most of the Indian men carried a forked stick with them as they went about their travels and if they came across a snake, would pin it to the ground in the fork of the stick and stamp on its head. On a walk from the camp to the local village, one would see at least half a dozen in the course of the mile or so journey. I used to stop and study them where they lay at the side of the road.

One day I came across a snake which I recognised as a Black Krait. It was about a foot long and thin as a pencil. Although relatively small compared with some of the other snakes such as Cobras, the Krait is deadly. If bitten by one, the venom quickly travels through the blood stream and paralyses the heart muscles. If not injected with the antidote, a human will die within four minutes of being bitten.

Having made quite sure it was dead, I gingerly picked it up and decided to take it back to camp to study. Two of the other Officers were in the tent and we decided to play a joke on Jock, the fourth occupant. We hid the snake and said nothing about it, although in the course of the evening the conversation got around to snakes and I was able to describe a Black Krait and how deadly it was. There was no lighting in the tent and we sat around illuminated only by our torches. It was quite eerie, almost like telling ghost stories.

We all slept in the nude on our charpoys with just a sheet to cover our modesty. Each bed had a fine net hung over it to keep the mosquitoes out. Once we thought Jock was asleep, we carefully lifted the side of his mosquito net and slid the Krait under the fold of his sheet so that the battered head was hidden but the lower part of it was clearly showing. We then called out to him until we woke him, and told him not to move. We shone our torches through the net on to the snake so that he could see it and he was petrified. He lay rigid, not daring to breathe. He had no idea how to escape from his predicament. After a few minutes in which we found it difficult to contain ourselves, I offered to make a courageous rescue. Moving ever so slowly I slid my hand under his net until I was able to grab the snake by the tail and thrash its head to the floor, thus covering up the evidence of its previous mutilation.

Jock was so relieved and grateful. He just couldn't believe how brave and selfless I had been in my noble act. He assured me that the Camp Commander would be informed of my heroic deed first thing in the morning and he would make sure that I received some award for my bravery. With that we realised the game was up and had to confess to our jape. Jock was not amused. He called us everything under the sun and it took the combined strength of my two fellow conspirators to prevent him from setting about me with his fists. I know I'm a boxer, but he was a big, mean Scotsman about twice my size, and in the mood he was in he could well have achieved all he was threatening to do. I always said Scotsmen have no sense of humour.

When we had calmed him down, we realised our joke had been over the top. If in the future somebody were to get bitten, it would be very serious, probably life-threatening. So we made a pact there and then that where snakes were concerned we would never 'cry wolf', or even 'cry snake', unless it was for real.

With that, we put out our torches, I let down my mosquito net and climbed into bed. I had not been there more that ten or fifteen minutes when there was a plop as something cold and scaly landed on my bare, upturned stomach. I froze and pivoted my eyes down towards it, but with no light I could not make anything out. Like a ventriloquist talking through his dummy, I hissed across to the others.

"Are you awake?"

"What do you want now?"

"I think I've got a snake curled up on my belly."

"Oh go to sleep Buster. We've had enough of your jokes for one night."

"No really. I'm not kidding. We made a pact. Remember?" And so the conversation went on until at last I convinced them enough for them to shine a torch across. They could see nothing, as the fine, white netting threw the light back at them, but inside there was enough light for me to make out that unmistakable reptilian head.

I wanted my heart to stop beating so that it wouldn't annoy my intruder but it only beat faster as the snake started to journey slowly up my body towards my throat. I wondered how long I would be able to lie there as it came closer and closer. Would I be able to just shut my eyes and let it slide right across my face? Fortunately, as it headed north, it veered slightly east and passed over my left shoulder. Once I was sure it was clear of me, I threw myself over the side of the bed and on to the floor. Carefully lifting the netting, the others shone their torches on to my pillow. They were met face to face by the prettiest little lizard you ever saw.

By now, it was nearly a year since I had left England, and I was still in transit. Worse still, India was coming up to the monsoon season and we were all living in tents. The first time it struck was unbelievable. It had been a fairly normal day, perhaps a little more sultry than usual, with short gusts of warm wind stirring up the dust. As the sun descended, there was the most beautiful orange sunset lighting up the clouds which were gathering on the horizon. We were all in bed when the rains came. At first it was just the occasional large drop plopping onto the roof of the tent but within seconds the pace quickened until it became a deafening roar. I have never seen water come out of the sky so fast. It was like standing under Niagara Falls. The force of it was so great that it beat the fly-sheet down on to the inner canvas and a fine spray of rain started to fall on to us inside.

Then came the wind. Howling around at hurricane force, it started by beating the rain in through the tied up front of the tent, soaking everything at that end. Then with an almighty roar it wrenched the pegs from the ground and lifted the tent from its moorings, exposing us to the full fury of the storm. There was nothing we could do except hang on to our possessions to prevent them from being blown away. We were not alone. All around us other capsized tents were cracking like pistol shots as they thrashed about in the wind. As the rain continued to pour down, the water level rose around us until we were flooded to a depth of six inches or more. Chaos reigned.

Twenty minutes later, the storm abated as quickly as it had started and it was all over. Very little sleep was had that night as even though we got the tent together again, nobody wanted to sleep on a soaking wet bed. Next day everything was hung out in the sun to dry and we were quickly back to normal. Next time the monsoon struck we were ready for it with additional tent pegs to secure the tents and water channels cut to divert the floods. The only ones who seemed to enjoy the monsoons were the bull frogs, who drove us crazy with their incessant nocturnal courtship.

After I had been at Ranchi for about six weeks, the camp was visited by Lord Moynihan, the ex-Liberal Party Chairman. He had joined the Army at the outbreak of war and was now Lt. Col. Lord Moynihan. He had been given the task of setting up a new camp to train soldiers coming out from Blighty in jungle warfare and survival. He had come to the transit camp looking for suitable Officers to man this new unit. All fifty Officers in my draft had individual interviews with him, and although I had never set foot in the jungle, I was among those selected. I assumed this was due to my past physical activities and my background as a PT Instructor rather than my gunnery skills.

Shortly after, I found myself back on the train I had arrived on, heading back towards Bombay. This time I was travelling for only two days, getting off at a small town called Nagpur in the Central Province. From there a Land Rover took us along primitive unmade roads to Chhindwara where the first stages of the new training camp were already being constructed, again all under canvas.

I was given a team of NCOs and our first job was to design and build a series of assault courses around the camp. Once I had them organised and getting on with the construction, I was able to concentrate on jungle techniques, reading every book and manual on the subject I could lay my hands on. Each time I read something new, I would take myself off into the jungle and put it into practice as I knew I would have to teach my NCOs before they would be able to instruct the trainees.

I wasn't sure where the people we trained would be deployed but I could make a shrewd guess. The Japanese had overrun most of south east Asia and sooner or later we would have to start pushing them back. Burma seemed a likely starting point. Unfortunately, in the area around Chhindwara, we didn't have the thick bamboo jungle that was typical of the Malayan Peninsula and so I had to make do with the thick tropical forest that was available.

I made lots of trips out into the surrounding countryside, partly to familiarise myself with the terrain and partly because I liked being out there studying the flora and fauna. Sometimes I would build myself a temporary camp and spend a night or two trying to live off the land. Other times I would get one of my men to drop me off about ten miles from camp and I would make my way unaided back to camp, making notes and drawing sketch maps on the way ready for when platoons of trainees would have to do the same. At other times I just reconnoitred an area to see if it would be suitable for a war-games exercise. The only map of the area I had was dated 1918 and I reckoned that was probably the last time any white man set foot in the area. It was so remote I never saw a soul once I had left camp.

One day I had been dropped off close to a river about ten miles from camp. I wanted to explore the river banks and arranged to be collected the next day from a point about six miles downstream. During the monsoon, the river carried quite a lot of water, but now we were back in the dry season and the river was reduced to a shallow trickle down the centre. This was quite convenient as it meant I could walk along the dried up mud of the river bed rather than fight my way through the undergrowth on the banks. I made a note to include this tip in the training notes.

It was a beautiful day and walking quietly over the mud my passage was virtually silent. Consequently, the wild life was undisturbed and I saw many exotic birds with iridescent plumage and several small mammals foraging along the banks. It was exciting not knowing what would be around the next bend in the river. At one time I spotted a small troop of monkeys chattering away in the treetops.

Best of all, I rounded one bend to find the carcass of a buffalo which had come down to the river to drink during the monsoon season and had obviously got stuck in the mud. There must have been about thirty vultures and secretary birds on and around the carcass, tearing pieces off it. I stopped about fifty yards away and concealed myself in the undergrowth where I could watch them through the binoculars without disturbing them.

After about half an hour I decided I had better get on. Coming out of my hiding place, I stood in the river bed and clapped my hands together to frighten them away. They made a glorious sight as they rose as one into the air and began to circle over my head. With them out of the way I continued on down the river. Now I don't know if they thought I was some sort of rival who was about to steal their kill, but they began to attack me, flying down across my path and trying to claw at me. This was quite a frightening experience and I decided discretion was called for.

I made a beeline for the bank which was quite high at that point, but I managed to scramble up and into the cover of the trees. There was nothing for it, I would just have to push my way through the undergrowth until I was past the buffalo. At this time, the river was on my left. Looking to my right, I could see that the forest thinned out on that side which would make my travel much easier. Pushing myself in that direction, I soon found myself stood on the bank of a small 'nullah', a tributary of the main river, running through the trees. Ideal I thought; far easier to travel down the nullah than fight my way through the jungle.

With that I jumped the six foot or so off the bank down onto the dried mud below. There was just one small problem. Being in the shade of the trees, the mud had not dried out to anything like the same extent that it had in the main river. I went straight through the thin crust and sank immediately up to my knees in the slimy ooze underneath. Like the buffalo I had just witnessed, I was trapped.

It was so ridiculous. I was less than a yard from the bank but it might just as well have been a hundred miles away. There was no way I could reach it. I tried to pull one foot out but only succeeded in driving the other one deeper into the mud. The more I struggled the deeper I sank. I was now in it up to my thighs. I told myself I must keep calm, but all I could think of was that Iris would never know what had happened to me. I was sure I would slowly sink until the mud closed over my head without a trace of my whereabouts.

Totally illogically, I began to shout for help, at the same time knowing that it was pointless, but there was nothing else I could do. If I moved I sank deeper, and if I kept still I would never get out. Again I shouted for help and thought about the two men I had seen killed in Africa. I wondered if their families knew what had happened to them. I thought about writing a note. I could put it in my hat and throw it up on to the bank. My team knew roughly where I was and might find it. They might even guess what had happened to me and recover my body. I didn't want to be left here to be eaten by the vultures. I would shoot myself first. But by now my pistol was under the mud and I was not sure if I would be able to reach it. Was it worth making the effort to get it now, knowing it would cause me to sink a few more inches.

I was debating this in my head when I heard the crack of a dead branch in the forest. Was it some carnivorous animal that had sensed a possible meal? On the other hand it could be somebody coming to rescue me. I thought it worthwhile to shout for help again, at least if it were an animal my shouts might frighten it away. There it was again, only closer this time. I shouted louder and out of the undergrowth appeared a young Indian girl dressed in a sari.

She stood on the far bank and gazed down at me with a puzzled look on her face. The thought crossed my mind that I could well be the first white man she had ever seen. How I loved that girl and how I wished I could speak to her in Urdu, her native tongue. I had learnt one or two words that had a military context but none of them seemed appropriate to this situation. I must make a note to include the Urdu for 'Help' in the training manual.

"Jaldi" I cried, which was all I could think of, "Jaldi hai". And with that she obeyed my instruction and went away. It was what we used to get rid of the beggars. I hope I hadn't offended her, I needed her help. After that I kept very still not wanting to sink any further into the mud. It seemed a very long time, but was probably no more than a few minutes before she returned with several men and the all important rope. A few minutes later I was stood on the bank beside them.

None of them spoke any English and I didn't speak Urdu, but words were unnecessary to convey my gratitude to them. They led me through the forest to a clearing about two hundred yards away where they had a small settlement. As I approached the mud huts, young children peeped curiously around corners to see this strange apparition that their menfolk had captured. When I turned and waved to them, they fled into the huts and peered out over the tops of the walls.

I was given an old oil drum full of water and was able to clean most of the mud off me and my equipment. The rest of it flaked off later as it dried. My rations had been ruined but through sign language I was able to indicate to them that I was hungry and they produced a very palatable meal of curry and fresh fruit. The only animals that I could see around, apart from their dogs, were goats. I just hoped that it was curried goat that I was eating.

At nightfall, I was taken in to one of the huts and offered a bed on a pile of forest litter. After my ordeal I could have slept anywhere and was most grateful. The next morning, they escorted me back to the river and walked with me the rest of the way to my rendezvous. It was quite an emotional farewell when my transport eventually came. On the way back in the Land Rover I made further notes for my training manual. "Rule One: Make friends with the local natives."

Back at Chhindwara, we continued with our preparations for the jungle warfare course, but we were still many months away from being ready. I was now busy reading up on tropical diseases and finding out which plants and insects were harmful and which could be eaten. All over camp people knew of my studies and would bring things for me to study or identify. The strangest was a young faun that has probably been left in the undergrowth for safety by its mother, but the soldiers who found it didn't appreciate that and brought it back to camp. I tethered it outside my tent overnight, intending to take it back the next day so that its mother could look after it, but unfortunately, it died during the night.

On another occasion one of the soldiers brought me a large black scorpion which I put in a glass jar so that I could study it. I concluded that I should start a collection of jungle insects that could be used for instructional purposes. I would mount them on a large card and label them all. But first I would have to kill the scorpion without any external damage if it was to be of any use. I recalled the method I used to kill the butterflies and moths that Colin

Lawrence and I used to collect on Wandsworth Common. I got some cotton wool from the Medical Officer and placed this in the bottom of the jar. Over this I poured some neat ammonia from the same source and then placed a perforated cardboard platform above it with the scorpion on top. The idea with the butterflies was that the fumes would kill them without them coming into direct contact with the ammonia which would damage the delicate colours of their wings.

I suspected that the scorpion might be a little tougher than the butterflies, so I put plenty of ammonia in the jar and left it overnight. To my amazement, he was still alive the next morning and seemed to have suffered no ill effects whatsoever. In desperation, I removed the cotton wool and cardboard and half filled the jar with liquid ammonia. It nearly knocked me out so I was sure it would finish off the scorpion.

Sure enough, when I came back to it later in the day it was floating completely inert. I fished it out of the jar with forceps just in case but I needn't have bothered. I got a needle and thread from my housewife and neatly looped him on to the white card I had got as a mount. I then labelled it 'Arachnid Scorpaenid', varnished it and left it to dry.

Next morning when I went to see if the varnish was dry I was confronted with a blank card. The scorpion had gone. I couldn't believe that anybody would take it and couldn't understand what had happened to it. I found out a few days later when I discovered it lurking under my bed. It had gone into suspended animation when threatened by the ammonia and had remained doggo all the time I had been handling it and sewing it on to the card. In the still of the night it had cut itself free. After that I considered it had earned its freedom and I let it go, ensuring that it was well clear of my tent.

Another time, I was given a chameleon. I knew what it was, but had never seen one before and decided to keep it as a pet so that I could study its habits. It had most peculiar feet which had only two toes so that it could grip round a branch. It could remain still in one position for hours as it waited for insects to come within range of its long darting tongue. It would keep watch all the time with eyes that swivelled independently. It could change colour to suit its surroundings but its range was limited to a deep red through to a pale green. I supposed that would be the natural range of leaf colour that it might find itself on. There is no truth in the tale that they can match themselves to a tartan kilt.

One night we had a formal dinner in the mess in honour of a visiting Brigadier. After the meal was over and a few glasses of wine had been supped by him and Lord Moynihan, I was asked to fetch my chameleon from the tent and show it to the Brigadier. He was quite intrigued by it but couldn't understand why it didn't turn white when placed on the table cloth.

I explained about the range of colour it could achieve whereupon the Brigadier picked it up and placed it on top of Lord Moynahan's auburn hair. The chameleon sat motionless on top of his head for a few seconds, its tail dangling down by the colonel's ear. Then without warning it did its business all down the side of his face, much to the amusement of the Brigadier and the assembled officers. Needless to say, Lord Moynihan didn't ask me to bring it to the mess again.

That was not the only dinner night on which I earned the colonel's displeasure. A few weeks after, the officers were all assembled in the marquee waiting for the colonel and his guest to arrive when a large Swallowtail butterfly flew in and made its way up to the apex of the roof. Knowing my interest, there was an immediate shout of, "There's one for your collection Buster. Don't let it get away." After a few more similar taunts I started to climb up the wooden pole that supported the centre of the marquee. On my way up somebody handed me a Flit gun and once at the top I proceeded to squirt away every time the butterfly came within range much to the delight of the Officers below who cheered every time I got a direct hit.

In the middle of the excitement there was a shout of "Attention" as the colonel and his guest walked in. Now its not very easy to salute whilst sliding down a pole and it didn't help when a crazy butterfly crash landed at the colonel's feet. However, his guest saw the funny side of it and I was forgiven. The colonel just accepted it as being part of the nature of this eccentric extrovert he had as his Jungle Warfare Officer.

I managed to get myself a motorbike, which was very handy when doing my 'recces' as I could get to places on it which were not accessible by Land Rover. One day when I was out riding on it, I started to get a pain in my eyes whenever I looked to either side. At first I dismissed it, but it rapidly got worse and it was all I could do to get back to camp. I went to the Medical Officer who examined me and immediately sent me to the local military hospital. I had contracted malaria.

I thought it ironic that this should happen to a jungle warfare instructor, who was supposed to know how to protect himself against such things. But then I did spend more time than anybody else out in the jungle where the mosquitoes were. I was in hospital for quite some time with rhythmic period of shivering alternating with high temperatures and profuse sweating. I was regularly dosed with quinine but at the end of it all I was considerably weakened.

Even after I returned to work, I had reoccurrences which sapped my strength still further. As a result, I was not able to fight off the other tropical bugs and soon after, I went down with dysentery. This put me back into hospital again for several weeks. I eventually got back to work again but I was rapidly loosing my enthusiasm for India. In Africa, it had been a dry, temperate heat that suited me fine, but in India it was much hotter and the humidity was very high.

Then one morning, after I had been out in the jungle all day, I woke to find my face so swollen that my eyes would not open without manual assistance. For the third time in as many months I was back in hospital. This time they could not diagnose the cause of my illness. The doctors suspected that I had developed an allergy, probably to one of the jungle plants. I was now thoroughly debilitated and when I saw a specialist he recommended that I be sent to Poona to recuperate where the climate was a little kinder. I was there for many months undergoing treatment and convalescing. Eventually, they decided there was no more they could do for me. I was put on a train back to Bombay to await a hospital ship. Buster was going back to Blighty.

Chapter 14

Back to Blighty

The hospital ship was the SS Wanganella; an Australian vessel with an all-Australian crew. She was painted completely white with a large red cross on either side, that being the international standard for hospital ships. At night, flood-lights, mounted on long booms protruding from the ship, were turned on to illuminate the sides so that there could be no mistake by trigger-happy submarine captains. Nevertheless, it was quite nerve-wracking, as on both my previous sea voyages we had observed strict blackouts.

I shared a cabin with Major Angel, who was suffering from sprue, a particularly nasty complaint which causes chronic inflammation of the entire alimentary canal and was very debilitating. He was so weak that I had to help him up on to the deck each the day. I was allergic to the direct rays of the sun, so we would sit in the shade on a couple of deck-chairs and read or chat to pass the time away. He told me that before the war he had been connected with the Windmill theatre in London, his wife being the sister of Sheila Van Damm, whose husband, Vivian, ran the theatre.

It was a pleasant, uneventful journey home, much shorter than the journey out had been as we were now able to use the Suez Canal. The Australian crew were very kind and considerate towards their sick passengers and would often stop for a chat. They were hoping that they would be with us all the way back to the United Kingdom as they were very keen to visit 'The Motherland'. However, it was not to be. Once we had passed through the canal, we disembarked at Port Tufik opposite Port Said and the Wanganella headed south again back down the Red Sea.

We were kept under canvas for a few weeks whilst another ship was found to take us the rest of the way home. During that time I had to stay out of the sun, but I did manage to cover myself up sufficiently to join a trip to the Sphinx and the pyramids near Cairo. Shortly after, we embarked on an old, grey tub called the Alcantara which slowly rolled its way along the North African coast, past Gibraltar, through the Bay of Biscay and eventually up the Irish Sea to Greenock. I had left there barely a year before but it seemed like a lifetime. I had to remind myself that I was still not yet twenty-three years old.

Everybody was anxious to disembark and get back on British soil but formalities dictated that we were kept on board a little longer. I managed to talk my way ashore for a few minutes to make a brief telephone call to Iris, who was still working as the librarian at Boots in Richmond. She was overjoyed to hear me again after such a long time apart, but we still had a few more days to wait before we could be together again. From the ship, I was sent direct to a military hospital at Peebles for an initial check up.

Once these tests were over, I was given a week's leave and naturally made a bee-line for Richmond. Iris' understanding boss once more allowed her time off, as he had done when I had come to propose, and off we went to her home. It was a very emotional reunion and we used the time getting to know each other again. We had so much to say to each other and so many tales to tell. Iris had made regular visits to my parents during my absence and after a couple of days we went to stay with them in Battersea. After the initial greetings were over, I was surprised when my mother said,

"Hang on a minute Son, I've a letter here for you somewhere." As soon as she handed it to me and I caught the whiff of the familiar perfume, I knew who it was from. After a gap of two and a half years, it was a letter from Phyllis. My heart missed a beat as I slowly opened the envelope. At last the mystery would be solved. I had surmised correctly. She had fallen for a fellow from the Royal Air force who had objected to our correspondence. She had been engaged to him but had since broken it off. She was now unattached and keen to renew our friendship but would quite understand if I was married or anything, in which case she would not expect a reply.

I had never told Iris about Phyllis as I thought it was all in the past and of no further concern. Although the friendship had been entirely innocent, I now felt guilty at having to explain. I was not making a very good job of it, so finally I handed the letter to Iris, who read it through, first with puzzlement and then with increasing apprehension. The letter said it all for me and she handed it back in silence. I looked into her eyes and slowly tore it up. We fell into each others arms and that was the end of my brief encounter with Phyllis.

All this was the Autumn of 1943 after the start of the German V1 flying bomb campaign against London. The V1s were unmanned, jet-propelled aircraft, filled with high explosives. The note of their engine was quite distinctive, sounding not unlike that of an outboard motorboat. It was this that gave them their nickname of 'doodlebugs'. They were launched from ramps along the French coast and given enough fuel to take them as far as London, the idea being that when the fuel ran out they would quickly glide to the ground and explode, causing widespread devastation and panic among the civilian population.

At first this worked, but the people of London were very adaptable and knew that as long as they could hear the motor, they were safe, and that particular V1 was not destined for them. Only when the motor stopped would they dive for cover.

During the time Iris and I were staying with my parents in Mallinson Road, Iris decided to take a bath. She had hardly had time to get wet when the siren went to signify a doodlebug raid. We decided that she could stay where she was, but I would go outside and listen for the distinctive engine sound. If I heard it, I was to rush in and warn her, hopefully in time for us to reach the air raid shelter, just in case it decided to cut out in our vicinity.

The first part of the plan worked fine. I stood outside the house watching the cautious few hurrying along to the shelter. Meanwhile I was straining my ears for the tell-tale sound. In such circumstances, the imagination can play tricks and at first I didn't believe it, but eventually I had to accept that there was a V1 and it was getting nearer. Hurriedly I dashed up the stairs and hammered on the bathroom door.

"Get out Iris," I yelled, "I think I can hear a doodlebug." Without waiting for a reply I bounded down the stairs and out into the street again. Had I been mistaken? I couldn't hear it now. I looked at the people dashing past and suddenly realised. In the few seconds I had been inside, the motor had stopped and the doodlebug was on its way down. Frantically, I raced back up the stairs and tore open the bathroom door. Iris, who was busily drying herself, instinctively clasped the towel around her.

"Quick," I gasped, "You've no time for modesty. Stick this on." With that, I threw her dressing gown around her shoulders and practically dragged her down the stairs. But it was too late. As we reached the front door there was an almighty bang that made our heads reel and set our ears singing. Fortunately for us, the flying bomb had landed several hundred yards away in Honeywell Road and we were unharmed. The 'All Clear' sounded a few minutes later and I went with some of the other men from the street to see if there was anything we could do to help. However, it was all under control and our services were not needed. The ARP Wardens and the Fire Brigade were doing a marvellous job and we went back out of their way.

Returning home, I could see a crowd of people around our door and wondered what was amiss. My first thoughts were that Iris had suffered some after-reaction to the shock of the explosion. Rushing inside, I found her perfectly all right and seemingly quite amused as she came to greet me.

"Guess what," she said, "We've got a barrage balloon in the garden." I was puzzled. I was fully aware of the large, silver, blimps that were deployed over south London to deter low-flying enemy aircraft, but we didn't have one in our garden. However, I was

*Buster and sisters
- already the scene stealer.*

*Some of my boxing trophies, most
of which I unfortunately sold.*

On holiday with my parents at Clacton.

War-time wedding day - 8th April, 1942.

Taking the job seriously as Branch Manager at Thames Ditton.

*Leading the troupe in the dance routine
from Joseph and his Technicolor Dreamcoat.*

On stage at the Connaught Theatre, Worthing, with Nyree Dawn Porter.

*On set for my first episode as
Uncle Albert in 'Only Fools and Horses'.*
Picture courtesy of Radio Times.

wrong. When I went through to the back, I couldn't even see out of the kitchen window. It was covered by a huge, half-inflated balloon that was lying in the garden like a stranded whale. It had presumably been hit by a piece of shrapnel from the doodlebug and had made a graceful descent into our garden.

There were plenty of volunteers to assist in its removal. Our garden was surrounded by the neighbouring gardens and the only way out was through the house. If you have ever tried to deflate and roll up a beach Lilo at the end of the day when it's time to go home, you will know that it's impossible to get all the air out and it ends up filling a much bigger space in the beach bag than it did on the way there. We had the same problem multiplied a thousand times over. They squeezed and they squashed and then tried to feed it in through the back door, some pushing while others pulled. The balloon expanded to fill every available inch of space in the hall and as it was heaved slowly along, managed to pull the pictures from the wall, tear down the light fittings and smear the distempered walls with mud from the garden. By the time it emerged from the front door, the house looked as though a bomb had hit it.

That was my first encounter with a doodlebug, but I was to have many more. At the end of my leave, I took up my posting on the Kent coast. I was put in charge of four Bofors guns on the cliff top near Capel le Ferne. We were part of the defence against the V1s. By now, we had a very good home-defence radar-system which could detect each wave of missiles as they were launched from the French coast. They would then track them and issue alerts to the appropriate areas. First the heavy ack-ack guns would have a go at them whilst they were still at long range. Then, as they got closer, our light anti-aircraft guns came into play, engaging them until they crossed the English coast. Once they had passed us, it was up to the RAF fighters to stop them reaching London where the barrage balloons formed the last line of defence.

All in all, the system worked very well and I believe about eight out of every ten were destroyed before they could do any damage. They would reach us in waves of thirty or forty at a time and there were mid-air explosions every few seconds as the guns scored direct hits. The fighters fired at them in an attempt to blow them up, and when they ran out of ammunition it was rumoured they would fly alongside and tip the doodlebug's wing up, causing it to circle back out to sea again. I don't doubt this did happen, but I don't recall ever seeing any flying in that direction.

We were kept very busy night and day and had to live with our guns. I had a tent positioned just behind the centre of my troop and I worked, ate and slept there. In with me I had a telephone operator to receive the alerts from the Area HQ, and a plotting table on which we marked the radar sightings. The gun crews lived in tents on either side of mine and if the V1s were heading our way I would issue the 'Take Post' command ready for action.

I was worried each time a wave of V1s went through in case Iris might be at risk. There was a truck on site to enable the crew to go backward and forwards to the main camp to collect mail and rations; to enable me to report to camp for briefings, I was issued with a motor bike. One day, when there had been a particularly large number of V1s, I stopped at a little hamlet about a mile or so inland from the battery and found a bungalow with tell-tale telephone wires leading to it. I then knocked on the door, explained where I was from and asked if I could use their telephone to check if my wife in London was alright.

The gentleman who answered the door was very sympathetic and immediately invited me in and put his telephone at my disposal. When I had finished the call and ascertained that Iris was safe, he refused to take any payment. Instead he said,

"I couldn't help overhearing you on the telephone. Did I hear you asking for Mrs Merryfield?"

"Yes," I confirmed, " I'm Lieutenant Merryfield."

"Would that be Buster Merryfield?" he asked. I was amazed. How could he possibly know my Christian name. He saw the look on my face and knew he was right.

"Wait here," he said, "I've just been reading about you." And with that he disappeared into the other room, reappearing a few seconds later clutching an old Sinjuns' school magazine.

"My son was a Sinjuns' pupil and I've still got all his old school magazines" he explained. "Whilst he's away in the war, I like to get them out and read through them as a reminder of happier days. I've just been reading about your boxing exploits." He saw this link with his son through Sinjuns as a bond between us and he made it clear that I could visit any time to use the phone. I made good use of his offer, but on future visits I insisted on paying him for the calls.

The radar warning system we had along the south coast wasn't infallible. I recall on one occasion, sitting in my tent completing a report, when I thought I could hear that faint throbbing note that signified an approaching doodlebug, but there had been no telephone call. Sticking my head out of the tent into the miserable, wet, windy weather outside, I called to the guards to see if they had heard anything, but they hadn't. If there was any sounds out there it was masked by the noise of the wind and rain.

Pulling myself back inside, I listened again. I was sure I could hear something, but perhaps it was just the weather playing tricks inside the tent. As a check I phoned through to HQ. No, they had nothing on the radar screens for my area although there was a raid on further along the coast, but way out of my earshot. I put the phone down and listened again. I was convinced I could here something. I threw a groundsheet over my head and went out into the gloom. With the help of the guards, I scanned every inch of the sky, and then I saw it. Low down over the water I could make out the distinctive orange flame issuing from the rear of the jet engine. No wonder the radar hadn't picked it up; it seemed to be skimming along just above the waves and what was more, it was heading in our direction.

I quickly gave the order to take post and within seconds the gun aimers had picked it up and locked on the predictor computer. There was just one problem. The angle of elevation was so low that the guns were unable to depress far enough to engage it. Now what? I took another look through the binoculars. It looked as though it might crash into the cliff face immediately below us, which would be all right if it was near the bottom, but if it was anywhere near the top we would be in mortal danger. It could even cause a cliff fall, pitching us all on to the beach below.

It was still half a mile or so away and I watched carefully, trying to judge its height as it came ever nearer. I checked the elevation angle with the predictors. It was five mils positive. Thank goodness for that. It meant that the doodlebug would pass above us, but not by much. I just hoped the predictor was accurate. We waited and sure enough the angle slowly increased as the missile closed in. Soon it came within the elevation arc of the guns but I dare not give the order to fire as it was now so close that we would have been hit by the blast of the explosion and debris would have rained down on us in the gun pits.

Eventually, it passed directly above with about fifteen feet to spare. We said a silent prayer of relief and turned to watch it make its way inland. It was then that we realised with horror that there was no way it would clear the rising foothills of the North Downs.

It was heading straight for the hamlet from where I made my phone calls to Iris. There was nothing we could do except watch helplessly as it disappeared into the darkening gloom. Seconds later came the flash, followed by an ear-shattering bang and a great rush of air as the shock wave of the explosion passed over us.

Next day, I got on my motor bike and made the short journey to the hamlet. I was relieved to find my friends were safe and their bungalow undamaged apart from having all its windows blown out. The V1 had come down in a field just outside the hamlet, causing damage to the church roof and demolishing two cows who were unfortunate enough to be in the field at the time.

A few weeks after the incident, the doodlebug attacks suddenly ceased. The allied forces in France had overrun the launch pads, forcing the Germans to hastily build new sites in Holland. The V1s were now coming in over East Anglia and soon after, we received movement orders ready to counter this new attack. The gun sites were dismantled and re-established at Southwold in Suffolk.

The attacks were only a token gesture by Hitler as the V1s were at the limit of their range by the time they reached England and mostly landed in open farmland. I'm not sure if it was because the Germans realised this, or whether it was due to the swift Allied advance which quickly overran the Dutch sites, but by the time we had got our guns set up, the raids had ceased and we didn't see one doodlebug.

It was clear we were rapidly winning the war and with no enemy raids to contend with, we were able to relax a little more. I decided to get myself fit again, having had little time for any organised exercise since I had left Peebles. There were a lot of American servicemen in the area and while chatting to visiting US Air Force officers in the Mess, I got an invitation to use their gymnasium. This was in a hangar at the USAF airbase at Ellough, about five miles away between Southwold and Beccles.

At first I concentrated on running and basic exercises to build up my strength and stamina again. There was a boxing ring in the hangar and inevitably before very long I became drawn to it. The American airmen were a very sociable bunch and soon made me welcome. It was not long before I found myself in the ring and sparring again. It was good to be back.

One evening, the Officer who ran their boxing told me they were arranging an inter-services tournament and would I like to take part. I think the invitation was made more out of politeness than anything else, but I took him up on it, providing he agreed to find me an opponent who would not be too taxing. I explained that I hadn't boxed since leaving Durban two years before and that I was still recovering from malaria. I was secretly pleased when he still wanted me in the tournament as it gave my training some purpose and I took to it with renewed vigour.

The tournament took place two or three weeks later in the hangar on the base. I had been billed early in the programme for a preliminary contest against a merchant seaman, the main contest at my weight coming later on in the evening. There was quite a large crowd from the base and I was impressed by the 'razzmatazz' of the event organisers. I was given a big build up by the announcer and even greater acclaim when I won by a knockout just 38 seconds into the fight.

I was still in the dressing room changing out of my boxing gear when the main bout at my weight took place. It too was all over in the first round, this time in 41 seconds. When the winner and his entourage came through into the dressing room, they came over and congratulated me on my victory and expressed their regrets that I hadn't been matched against their boy. As they put it, "It would have been one hell of a fight."

After the conversation had continued in this vein for some time, the suggestion was made that we should be matched against each other in the near future, and at the end of the tournament it was announced to the crowd that the match would be top of the bill in two weeks time. Now I really had something to train for.

I hadn't seen my opponent fight but that didn't worry me as I preferred it that way. However, I did make a few enquiries about him. I discovered he was of Cuban extraction and I was surprised to hear he was lightweight champion of the US Navy. It was hoped that he would get a crack at the United States national title when he returned home after the war. I had certainly picked an opponent this time.

Word of the contest soon spread and a dozen or so of the Officers from my Mess decided to come and watch. I had visions of Ludlow all over again, but I was determined that I would put up a good fight and give it my all. I sat in my corner during the fight preliminaries, weighing up my opponent. He appeared to be a fit, slim, bronzed, mean-looking fighter.

When the bell went for the first round he lived up to his appearance. He rained blows in from all directions and I spent most of the round on the defensive. I was not unduly worried by this as

I was managing to anticipate most of the punches and I was not getting hurt. I was prepared to bide my time and wait for an opportunity to use my big right hand.

At the end of the round my seconds were very encouraging. They too realised that I was holding my own, despite the cheers and whistles for my opponent from the partisan crowd. As the bell went for the second round they optimistically bid me, "Go finish him off, Buster." Easier said than done I thought, but I was beginning to get the measure of him. I watched carefully, trying to pick the moment when his left was coming in low to the body so that I could deliver my killer right over the top of it. His left didn't carry a hard punch and I knew I could afford to take it in order to deliver the winning blow. Yes, there it was again and once more he had signalled it by leaning over to his right just before the punch went in. I waited for him to do it again, whilst at the same time staying out of range of his strength sapping right jabs to the heart.

Half way through the round, there was that imperceptible lean to the right as he went in with his left, but I got no chance to deliver my right cross. His blow landed way below the belt, right in the middle of my belly and I had no option but to sink to one knee to recover. I don't think it was a deliberate foul but without hesitation the referee moved between us and disqualified him.

As the MC made his announcement, the arena erupted in pandemonium. There were boos and catcalls and seat cushions came flying into the ring. I was very glad to get away to the dressing room. I suspected that there may have been quite large bets laid on the fight with most of the money on my opponent. It transpired that this was the first time he had ever lost a fight and they were infuriated that it should end with what they considered a dubious decision. His supporters followed us into the dressing room and were keen for a re-match in the next tournament, but I was not having any. The lessons of Mantua Street playground had been well learnt. Never get into a fight you are not sure of winning. Buster was a survivor.

Chapter 15

Victory

The Americans did not take kindly to my lack of cooperation over the re-match and the reception I got next time I visited their gymnasium was decidedly frosty. It was of little account, as shortly after it was considered there was no longer any reason for us to stay in East Anglia now that the doodlebug raids were over. I was posted to Braunton in North Devon. Although victory over the Germans was in sight, the inertia of the war machine trundled on and I found myself training newly enlisted men in field warfare. We ran exercises on Exmoor and conducted firing practices on the ranges at Braunton Burrows.

I had not been there many weeks when victory in Europe was announced. We were all relieved and joined in the celebrations and street parties with the local population. However, there was a feeling of anticlimax as nothing much seemed to change. We continued with the training although it was unlikely that the trainees would ever see combat. Sure enough, a few months later, atom bombs were dropped on Hiroshima and Nagasaki, causing the Japanese to surrender. The war was over.

The Army found itself with a large number of bored men waiting for demobilisation. Something had to be done to keep them occupied whilst they waited their turn to collect their civilian 'demob' suit. We were each given a number depending on age and circumstances. Mine was 27, which meant I would not return to 'civvy street' for quite a few months, older men being demobbed first. The new conscripts would be kept in much longer than me and had to be amused.

The Colonel in charge of the training depot sent for me one day and told me he was appointing me Sports and Entertainments Officer. As a start, I put up notices on the camp announcing that soccer and rugby trials would be held. I was overwhelmed by the response. Until then, I hadn't appreciated how much sporting talent there was in the services. I was able to raise six or seven very respectable soccer teams and our first eleven had no less that seven professional league players in it, including one from Sunderland, a First Division side.

I found myself fully occupied as trainer, manager, fixture

arranger and outside right for the first eleven. I'm not sure my skills warranted the latter role, but there was great comradeship amongst the players and they insisted that I be part of the team. We mostly played against other service units in the area such as RAF Wrafton and the air base at Chivenor, but we did have more ambitious matches against Barnstable Town and home and away fixtures against Plymouth Argyle.

I thought I had done a very good job for the Colonel and I was a little put out when he sent for me again and rebuked me, albeit rather tongue in cheek.

"You are doing a grand job with the sports, Buster," he announced, "but I appointed you Sports and Entertainments Officer. We haven't seen much of the entertainments yet, have we?" He went on to say that the garrison had a theatre standing empty and he would like to see some sort of show put on there during the run up to Christmas. To hear was to obey, but my only encounters with the theatre were one or two variety shows that I had seen at the Clapham Grand before the war. So variety it would have to be.

Once more the notices went up on the boards asking for volunteers for auditions, and once again they produced a wealth of talent. There were singers, comedians, jugglers and even a ballet dancer who had performed at Covent Garden before the war. As with the football teams, I found myself with multiple roles. First I was producer, auditioning the acts and selecting those I thought suitable for the show. Then I had to write scripts for sketches, similar to those I had seen at the Grand. Having selected the performers, I then directed rehearsals and even helped construct scenery. I decided to call the show 'Plain Nuts' and I think I must have been, to take on such a mammoth task. Fortunately, one of the volunteers, Captain Teddy Law, was an experienced dance band leader. He took charge of the music and put together a very commendable theatre orchestra. I was also able to off-load the tasks of publicity and ticket sales to other people.

I had lots of acts to choose from for the show but was left with the problem of finding a compere to link them all together. Eventually I decided to lead from the front and take that role upon myself. As an officer, I had become used to addressing men, although I had found that a bit of a nervous ordeal when I was first commissioned. I considered that being compere was not much different, except that one would be expected to crack a few jokes while making the announcements. Thorough to the last, I went into town and purchased a Razzle joke book and a Beano Christmas annual as sources of material.

The show played to a packed house and was a rip-roaring success. The star of the show was a Captain from the Welsh Fusiliers called George Groome, who did an excellent comedy routine. We became firm friends during rehearsals and acted together in some of the sketches and comedy routines. I lost touch with him after we were demobbed, but nearly fifty years later he rang me up after hearing me talk on the show *Wogan* about our comedy routine. His wife rang a few weeks later to say, sadly, he had died, but I still carry fond memories of him from those early post-war days.

Another very successful act in our show was Doctor Wesoski, the Polish tight rope walker. This was a ruse which I thought up to fill a ten-minute gap in the programme. As far as the audience were concerned, they saw a genuine tight rope walker doing some amazing feats including handstands and back flips along the rope. The reality was somewhat different. We had got a long, stout builder's plank and painted it the same colour as the backdrop. Then a thick hawser was painted white and nailed along the front edge. The plank was then raised on trestles up to the audience's eye level and the side curtains drawn across to hide the trestles. The acrobatics were done on the plank which could not be seen from the front. The illusion was quite effective.

Doctor Wesoski was a very strange, secretive character. He made his entrance in the middle of the concert from the back of the hall. He was heavily cloaked, carried an umbrella, wore sun glasses and sported a large white beard. It wasn't until the act was nearly over that some wag in the audience shouted out, "Pull the other one, Buster". I don't know how he recognised me as in those days I didn't have a beard.

Whilst at Braunton, I also had time to continue with my fitness programme and to participate in boxing matches which I arranged on the unit. Early in 1946, a circular came round inviting entries for the annual Army boxing championships, and I decided to enter. They were based on regional heats and my first match was to decide the South West District champion. There only one other entrant at lightweight. He was the brother of Eddie Thomas, who was a British professional champion and I did not rate my chance of success as being very high, particularly as he was fighting on his home territory at Plymouth. It was a comparatively small affair with not much atmosphere. Unlike the larger tournaments, which were attended by all the senior officers, this was witnessed only by the few boxing enthusiasts from his unit. Quite naturally, they all supported him, but their cheers of support for him only made me more determined. It was not a fight for purists, being a dour, toe-to-toe slugging match which I just managed to shade on points.

Winning that match made me a contender for the Southern Command championships where I would have to compete against the Southern and South Eastern District champions for the title. These were to be held in the Territorial Hall on Holdenhurst Road, Bournemouth. This was quite some distance from Braunton and as it was mid-winter, I convinced my CO that I should be allowed to stay down there overnight and travel back to camp the next day. He happily agreed and off I went on the train.

It occurred to me on the way there, that if my contest finished at a reasonable time, it might just be possible for me to catch a train to London and spend the night with Iris. So when I got to Bournemouth station I made enquiries, only to find that the last train left at a quarter past eight. As the event wasn't scheduled to start until seven-thirty, I didn't hold out much hope of getting away on time. My hopes were dashed even further when I got to the hall and saw the programme. My semi-final wasn't due until midway through the evening. Having only just made it through the District eliminator, I didn't bother too much about the final, which wasn't due until gone ten o'clock.

I was disappointed, but didn't given up hope altogether. I was the only Officer in the contest so I had a word with the Master of Ceremonies. I managed to convince him that I needed to get away as soon as possible as I was required back at camp the next day. He agreed to pull my semi-final forward and put it on as the first event.

My opponent was a soldier from the Paratroop Regiment and as soon as we started exchanging punches I knew I could take him. At the first opportunity, the big right came over and bid him 'Goodnight Vienna'. The fight had lasted less than two minutes.

But it was a hollow victory. I had done myself a disservice. I would now have to wait for the final and would miss my train to Iris. Still full of bright ideas, I sought out the MC again.

"Look," I explained to him, "The other finalist had a bye, and my fight hasn't taken anything out of me. How about putting the final on next?" He was somewhat taken aback but couldn't fault my logic. The second bout had started, but he found my opponent who agreed to pull the final forward. He too was from the

Parachute Regiment and couldn't wait to get revenge for his comrade's swift defeat.

So at the end of the second bout, the further change of programme was announced and back into the ring I went. It was still only ten minutes to eight, and if the fight didn't last too long, I might still just make that train. As soon as the bell went I was off my stool and punching. This was in complete contrast to my usual boxing style of watch and wait, but it worked. He had no answer to my onslaught which culminated in a knockout blow before the end of the first round.

As soon as the formal announcement of my victory had been made I hastily thanked the MC for his cooperation and prepared to leave.

"Hang on a minute, Sir," he said, "What about the prize-giving? Now you have won you will have to stay to collect your cup." I was having none of that. There was no way I was going to be thwarted at the last minute.

"Can't you just give it to me now?" I asked, "You can still make the announcement later but explain I had to leave on urgent business." He reluctantly agreed it was possible, but he wasn't sure which of the trophies was mine as none of the individual trophies which the winners kept permanently had been engraved.

"I'll tell you what," I said, "I'll take this small one here, then nobody will be disappointed if I've got the wrong one." And with that I picked up the smallest trophy there and hurried away whilst he was still thinking about it.

As soon as I got to the dressing room I looked at the clock. Arguing with him had cost me valuable time and it was now five past eight. If I was to stand any chance of getting the train, there was no time to change. I stuffed my uniform into my holdall, threw my greatcoat over my shoulders and left the hall wearing nothing else but my boxing boots and shorts. It was a frosty mid-February night with snow on the ground, but that didn't worry me. I set off running along Holdenhurst Road, holdall in one hand and trophy in the other. I covered the mile to the station in under five minutes, thankfully sinking into my seat seconds before the train pulled out. I attracted some strange glances from my fellow passengers, but as soon as I had recovered my breath, I disappeared into the toilet and changed.

It was gone eleven by the time I reached Ham Common, but Iris was delighted to see me which made my journey worthwhile.

The next day, before getting the train back to camp, I bought the early edition of the evening papers. Turning to the sports page I was delighted to see the headline, "Army Officer's two knock outs in five minutes". I wondered if that constituted some kind of record. One of these days I might contact *The Guinness Book of Records* and find out.

A few weeks later I had to go to Aldershot for the Southern England championships. I always used to read the sports pages of the newspapers, especially for boxing news, and was flattered when I read Jimmy Wilde's column in one of the Sundays. He was one of my boxing heroes and had written that he was looking forward to these championships as he was particularly interested to see how the ex-schoolboy champion, Lieutenant Merryfield, would fare following his recent double knock-out.

On the night, I got Iris to attend, which was quite an achievement as she hated boxing and wanted me to give it up. Much to our surprise, she found she was sat next to Jimmy Wilde. Like the Southern Command finals, there were semi-finals and finals at each weight. My first opponent was the Canadian Army champion, whom I managed to beat on points. Usually, I try not to see my opponents before I fight them, but the lure of being able to talk to Jimmy Wilde made me take a seat with Iris after my semi-final was over and watch the other two contenders. It was a very one-sided affair won by a soldier who was extremely tall for his weight. He was able to stand back and pick off his opponent with a succession of piston-like left jabs and the result was in no doubt. He was just the kind of fighter I don't like meeting as I needed to get in close to stand any chance of delivering the famous right hand.

Whilst waiting for the final, I got to worrying more and more about this and completely psyched myself into defeat. I was mesmerised as soon as I went into the ring and by the middle of the second round, my face was a swollen pulp, causing the referee to stop the fight. Iris was most upset to see me in such a state and between her and Jimmy Wilde, I was persuaded that my boxing days were over. After all I was now an old man of twenty-five: well, old in boxing terms anyway.

I kept up with the training as a means of keeping fit and still do the warm-up exercises every morning even though I am now nearly seventy-six years old. I also go swimming regularly, finding it both pleasurable and a good way of getting all over exercise in a comparatively short time. I find half an hour is ample.

After the fight, I returned to camp a chastened man and devoted my energies increasingly to entertainments with less emphasis on sports. Ever since I had returned to England, my mother had regularly sent me the South Western Star, which was the local paper from back home. One week I saw that the Clapham Grand was putting on a talent contest. Following the success of the first variety show, I had put on a couple more and George and I had polished up our double act to the extent that I felt we could enter the contest.

I rang up the theatre and was disappointed to learn that the heats of the competition would be held every night of the following week after the main show, with the final on Saturday night. There was no way we could get away other than at weekends, but after explaining our circumstances and a lot of pleading, the organiser agreed that as servicemen, we could have a dispensation and go directly into the Saturday night final.

Delighted at the news, we explained to the CO who promptly wished us well as he signed our 36-hour pass. We were also able to get a warrant and rushed down to Braunton station as soon as work was over on Saturday morning. By the time we got to Clapham, time was getting on and we had to go straight to the theatre. It was all rather rushed as when we got there the organisers decided that as we were an additional act, we would have to go on before the genuine finalists. We hastily applied our make up and got into our costumes as quickly as we could, being chivvied along all the time by the manager who was anxious to get the show started.

Ours was what was known as a crosstalk act. George was the straight man, immaculately dressed in dinner jacket and bow tie, whilst I was the clown, wearing a bowler hat, red nose, hunting jacket, plus fours, white plimsolls, but no socks. It normally took some time to get myself fully attired, and in my haste I managed to put my foot through the seam of the crutch of my trousers. However, there was no time for repairs and we were hustled out of the dressing room. We were given a brief introduction by the MC, who explained to the audience about this being an additional act put on by servicemen.

We had carefully rehearsed our script which started with us coming on from opposite sides of the stage to meet in the centre. As we turned to face the audience we both talked together.

"Good evening, Ladies and Gentlemen." (Pause) "Look, are you going to address the audience or am I going to address the audience?" (Pause) "I don't want to undress the audience." (Pause for laughter)

But the laughs had come as soon as we turned towards the

audience and our words were lost in loud guffaws and shrieks as they curled up helplessly. What on Earth was going on? Why were they pointing in our direction? Self-consciously we looked around and then at each other.

"It's your trousers they're laughing at, Buster," George hissed out of the side of his mouth. "I don't know what they can see, but I know what they think they can see." I had underpants on but I instinctively crossed my knees and pulled the torn trousers around me, which immediately invoked further gales of laughter. Well, we were here to get laughs, so let's make the most of it. We continued with the act, playing to the audience as much as possible. I held my hands strategically in front of me and moved them round whenever I had to turn and George pretended to cover me as best he could with the tails of his dinner jacket.

We came off stage knowing that whatever else, we had entertained the crowd, and I found it exhilarating. After all the acts were completed, we each had to go back on stage and the result was decided by the volume of the applause. It was no contest. We took our bow to a cacophony of cheers and whistles that went on for wave after wave until the MC had to hold up his hands to get the audience to stop. First prize was all of two guineas but we felt we had won by default and insisted it went to the next best act which was a young girl acrobat. I felt more than rewarded by the buzz I got from the adrenaline that coursed through my veins as the audience cheered. Buster was hooked on the theatre.

Part Three: After The War

Chapter 16

Civvy Street

At long last, on the sixteenth of March, 1946, the Army decided it could get along without my further services and I was summonsed to Aldershot for demobilisation. It was a surprisingly efficient, well-automated process. On arrival, there was the inevitable form filling, after which I joined a queue which shuffled slowly along from storekeeper to storekeeper, each handing over a separate item of civilian clothing. At the end of the line we were confronted by half a dozen shop dummies, each dressed in a different pattern of demob suit. A corporal, armed with a tape measure, took a swift measurement of waist and inside leg before handing over a suit in the pattern of one's choice. There were cubicles available for a quick fitting, after which one signed for everything before it was all bundled into a hold-all. Items of Army kit such as webbing had to be handed in whilst my uniform, which I had bought when I was commissioned, could be retained. I still occasionally wear my Officers' khaki tie and like many others, I had my greatcoat died black and wore it for many years after. Iris found that much more acceptable than the demob suit I had chosen, which sported a loud check pattern. Looking back, it was the sort of thing Max Miller might have worn on stage. Perhaps when I chose it, I already had thoughts of a stage career in mind.

Back at Braunton, I had followed up my success in the Clapham Grand talent contest with a number of local stage appearances for charity. The act I developed came about almost by accident. The Officers' Mess owned a rather grand radiogram and a collection of records. At that time, Al Jolson was very popular and his renderings of 'Mammy' and 'Sonny Boy' were the two most played records of all. We would often sing along with the record, competing with each other's exaggerated actions and going through the full gamut of emotions. With my in-born talent for showing off, I usually won, but my singing voice was not always appreciated by my fellow officers. So on one occasion I went through all the motions but just mimed the words.

"Gosh, that's good, Buster," remarked on of my friends, "From a distance it looks just as though you are singing it." And so my solo act was born. Years later, many people went on stage doing similar acts, but at that time I believed I was unique.

Following my metamorphosis from soldier to civilian, I was given ninety days leave to enable me to adapt to civilian life and find a job. I tried to convince Iris that my future lay on the stage, but she was having none of it.

"Are you crazy?" she asked, "You've a perfectly good job waiting for you at the bank. It's about time you got your feet back on the ground and remembered your responsibilities. All the applause you claim you got on stage in the Army was probably just the soldiers taking the mickey out of an officer who was making a fool of himself." If the truth was known, she may well have been right, but I had ninety days before I had to start work and I was in no hurry to contact the bank.

One day I made up my mind. I had to give it a go, otherwise I would wonder all my life. That afternoon I announced to Iris that I was off to the West End to prove once and for all whether or not I was any good. What I didn't tell her was what I planned to do. About four o'clock I set off on the train dressed in my stage costume which consisted of a tattered jacket and trousers, dirty raincoat and the bowler hat I used to wear at the bank. Under my arm I had an old mechanical wind-up gramophone that I had bought at a second-hand shop.

An hour or so later I was stood in Piccadilly. However, I was not there to look for theatrical agents. I had my sights set on the cinema queues. I had previously been round to the local police station and made enquiries concerning the law and the police attitude towards busking. They told me that whilst strictly speaking it was against the law, they generally turned a blind eye, providing there was no obstruction of the highway or breach of the peace. That had been good enough for me and I was here now to test my ability in front of the most critical audience I could find. It was a wild, wet, windy, March night and the faces in the queues looked far from happy as they waited for the first house to finish. I would have to be good to make any sort of impression on them.

The cinema was showing the film *The Jolson Story*, starring Larry Parkes in the key role. Just after the war, film-going was at its height and there were long queues leading away in both directions from the foyer. It was my intention to try out my Al Jolson act on these unsuspecting people. At that moment, both queues were already being entertained, one by a violinist and the other by a blind accordionist. That was OK, it would give me time to get ready.

I didn't have any make-up, but I knew I needed to black my face if I was to be at all convincing. I slipped quietly round the corner and scraped up some of the mud from the wet gutter, smearing it over my face as best I could. I had been a bit apprehensive when I first arrived, fearing I might meet somebody I knew. Reason told me the possibility of that was remote, but officially I was still in the Army until the end of my leave period, and it would not do for an officer to be caught busking on the streets of London, particularly attired as a tramp. Somehow the mud gave me anonymity and restored my confidence.

Returning to the front of the cinema, I noted that the violinist had finished his recital and was now down at the far end of the queue soliciting tips. This was my opportunity. Placing my gramophone on the pavement I started my spiel.

"Good evening, Ladies and Gentlemen. What a dreadful night you've chosen. You must be really keen Al Jolson fans to stand out here in the wind and the rain - and look at the length of the queue! Are you sure you're going to get in? Fortunately for you, I'm here tonight to make sure you're not disappointed. I can't guarantee you a seat, but I can guarantee you entertainment. Ladies and Gentlemen, my impression of Al Jolson!"

At that point I started the gramophone and launched into my version of 'Mammy'. I gave my all, but it was not easy. The gramophone was not loud at the best of times and in the large, open space the wind carried away what little sound there was.

"I'd walk a million miles for one of your smiles, My Ma-a-a-ammy," I sang, sinking down on one knee, with arms outstretched for effect. Strangely, I thought of my Mum and her determination to fit me for a decent career. If she could see me now. Somehow I don't think she would have approved.

As the last strains from the gramophone faded away, I could feel water from the puddle soaking through the knee of my trousers and the rain was already washing the mud from my upturned face. Had I passed the test? How would my efforts be received?

All through the song the people in the queue had maintained a respectful silence and I had noted out of the corner of my eye that one or two passers-by had stopped out of curiosity. Now was the moment of truth. A young man close by started to clap, waking my audience from their reverie. The applause quickly spread along the queue as far as my act had carried on the wind. At the insistence of her children, a lady reached into her purse. Her two children came forward and each pressed a florin into my hand. They felt sorry for this poor, bedraggled down-and-out who was no doubt trying to scrape up enough for a crust and a bed for the night. Of course, I didn't make this analysis until later, and at the time was convinced I was a success. I thanked the children profusely. Getting to my feet, I removed my bowler hat and holding it out in front of me, shuffled down the queue muttering, "Thank you, sir. Very kind of you, Ma'am," as they dropped in the occasional coin.

The first-house showing of the film was still not over. I considered I had time to repeat my act to the queue on the other side. Making my way across, I replaced my gramophone on the pavement.

"If you don't want that broken, I suggest you pick it up again, pronto." I straightened up to find myself face-to-face with two tough-looking characters who were standing rather too close for comfort.

"I'm not trying to muscle in or anything. I just thought I'd entertain the queue for a few minutes," I replied lamely.

"Well you can just think again, Mate. This pitch is booked." I wondered if I might bring one of them down with a surprise right cross before taking on the other, but mindful of the police warning about causing a breach of the peace, I humbly withdrew. I retired to a nearby café for a well-earned cup of tea, where I was served with obvious reluctance. Once at the table, I tipped out my bowler and counted the night's takings. Twenty-four and sixpence for three minutes work. Just wait until I tell Iris.

After finishing my tea, I went out into the night and washed my face as best I could in a puddle before walking back to Waterloo for the train. When I arrived back home, Iris looked at my sorry appearance with condescension.

"I saved your dinner in the oven. and after that you'd better get those wet clothes off if you don't want to catch pneumonia. I'm just off to bed." Not a word from her asking where I had been. I ate my dinner and gave myself a good towelling down before getting in to bed. At last Iris spoke.

"By the way," she said. Ah, now I would be able to tell her of my adventure. She continued, "did you enjoy your liver and bacon?" I couldn't believe it, and could only mumble an affirmative reply.

She never did ask about my West End trip although I believe she knew what I had been up to. But she had made her views on show business known earlier and there was nothing more to be said. Next morning I arranged for an interview with the bank to confirm I would be coming back to my old job.

Initially, I restarted at the Lombard Street Branch in the City and hadn't been there long when there was a bank inspection. Normally, these were carried out annually, but because of the war, there had been no inspection for many years. Consequently, the inspectors had to do a thorough job and were there for several months. They got to know the staff quite well, which was all to the good as one of their other roles was to spot potential talent for employment in the London area branches. I must have given a good impression while they were there as shortly after, I was promoted to teller and moved to the Westminster's branch at King's Cross.

One other pressing thing I had to attend to when I was first demobbed was to find somewhere permanent for Iris and I to live. Initially we were in with Iris' parents, but it was not a very satisfactory arrangement. Iris was still working in the library at Richmond and I went out daily knocking on doors all the way from Richmond to Kingston, but the reply was always the same. What with the blitz and the sudden increase in ex-servicemen trying to set up home, accommodation was at a premium.

As a temporary measure, we moved in with one of Iris' married sisters but she was shortly due to move out of the area so I had to carry on looking. Eventually I managed to find a single room in Whitton. The house was run by an old lady called Edie who let off most of her house, one room at a time, to old people. We were not allowed to do any cooking in our room, and as she only provided bed and breakfast, we had to go out every evening to eat, which proved rather expensive. When we came back each night, we had the choice of going straight to bed or sitting in the lounge with the rest of her lodgers where we were expected to play cards or board games to entertain them.

At first we found this amusing, but after a week or two it became tiresome and we started staying out later and later, hoping to get home after they had all gone to bed. The only problem was Spot, the dog. He slept in the back kitchen, but had ears like a bat. We would be on tiptoe all the way from the front gate and gently ease the key into the lock so as not to disturb him. Taking our shoes off, we would cautiously creep up the stairs, but invariably there would be a creak or a bump that would start him off.

"Wow - wow - wow," he went, with a tone that was both accusation and condemnation. Having been shopped by Spot, we would then be rebuked next morning by Edie with a disapproving, "You were in late last night", even though it might have been not much later than nine-thirty.

We stuck with this arrangement for the rest of my leave, but as soon as I restarted at the bank, I applied for a bank loan, and I put down a deposit on a semi-detached house in Hounslow. This was near the rugby stadium and the Kneller Military School of Music, not far from where we were lodging in Whitton. I remembered my mother's strategy before the war and took in a lodger to help with the cash flow. She was a charming girl called Beryl Shelton. She was a tall, attractive brunette who worked for BOAC as an Air Hostess. We got on very well together and were quite proud to see her trip off each day in her neat, navy blue uniform. She lived with us for over four years and we still keep in touch with her, fifty years on.

Having used the bank loan to pay the deposit on the house, we had very little money left for furniture. We scrounged what we could from relatives and managed to get a second-hand three-piece suite for thirty pounds. We did buy a new bed and bedroom suite but it was all 'utility' furniture, flimsily made from plywood. Unfortunately, money would not run to a cooker and we had to manage with a single gas ring which sat in the corner of the kitchen floor.

We made good friends with our neighbours, Basil and Muriel Pounds, and with several of the other young couples who lived in the area. None of us were particularly well-off, and we mainly met socially in each others houses, where we would spend the evenings chatting and drinking endless cups of coffee. On Sunday mornings we invariably all went swimming in the local baths.

One week about a dozen of us decided to go to a dance together. We had not been to the place before and found it quite small and intimate. Towards the end of the evening, the MC came up to me as I was dancing with Iris, put his hand on my shoulder, and whispered, "One Three Seven" into my ear. I found this somewhat puzzling and kept my eye on him. Sure enough, a few moments later, after scanning intently over the dancers, he approached another couple and again whispered something to them. By the end of the number (no pun intended), he had approached about eight or nine couples, including my friend Basil. As we sat down again, I asked Basil what he had said.

"Well, it sounds strange, but all he said was 'One Three Seven'," replied Basil, "I haven't a clue what he was talking about."

"Yes, it's funny," I continued, "He said exactly the same to me. We must find out what it means." By then the others in our group had joined us and we were all intrigued by this mysterious message, but no one could come up with any sensible explanation.

Shortly after, we went to the cloakroom to pick up our coats. As she handed them to us, the girl behind the counter asked, "Are you off to One Three Seven then?" At last the mystery was solved. It was nothing more than the MC's house number. He lived nearby and was in the habit of selecting couples to come back for further entertainment at his house after the dance. We were a bit suspicious as to what form this entertainment might take, but as we didn't take up the offer, we never did find out. It could all have been completely innocent.

However, I was intrigued by the way everybody had become engrossed by this cryptic message and got to wondering how others might react to it. The following day at the bank, as we were sat on our stools behind the counter, waiting for the bank to open, I leaned across to Fred Marvel at the next window and tapped him on the shoulder. When he turned, I gave him a knowing look and said, "One three Seven", just to see his reaction. Needless to say he was puzzled, but before he could question me further, I turned to my other side and repeated the message to Dennis Griff, one of the other tellers. Before he could react, the bank doors were opened and we had to attend to the customers.

Throughout the morning, I watched as first Fred and then Dennis conversed with other bank staff in low whispers, with strange glances in my direction. This was proving to be an interesting psychological exercise. During the lunch break, several people asked me about it but I did not let on and continued with the plot.

We were half way through the afternoon when Fred suddenly gave a yell.

"Good God. One Three Seven," he cried, "Look, it's One Three Seven". Immediately, the Head Cashier went over to Fred to see what the fuss was about.

"This customer has just paid in One Hundred and Thirty Seven

Pounds. But how did Buster know it was going to happen?" It was an amazing coincidence that had resulted in a completely unexpected result to my experiment. More was to come. The customer was not at all pleased to have his business confidentiality broken by Fred shouting it all over the bank, and immediately demanded to see the manager. Fred was summoned into the office and shortly after, I was sent for. It was not an easy thing to explain and I felt rather stupid. However, I hadn't done anything against bank rules, and it was Fred who took most of the blame. He was sent along to the customer's premises to apologise but they refused to see him. Fortunately, we didn't lose the firm's business and no long term harm was done. That was the end of my psychological experimentation period.

Shortly after, I got another lesson in human psychology. I had a friend called Leslie, who had been in the Merchant Navy during the war. He had spent a lot of time in Hull, where he had been befriended by a couple who helped out in the Seamen's Mission. Now that the war was over, he wanted to show his gratitude by bringing them down for a holiday in London, but he didn't have anywhere for them to stay. He knew we had a spare room in our semi, and we agreed to put Mr and Mrs Hiley up for a week's bed and breakfast.

It was mid-Summer and extremely hot on the Saturday they arrived. I first spotted them some way off peering up at front doors in the search for our house number. Struggling along under the weight of their suitcases, they were the personification of the seaside couple on a McGill postcard. She was an extremely large lady, dressed in a red, polka dot dress and wearing a straw hat. He was as small and thin as she was large and fat. He sported a bookie's tweed suit with trousers held up by bright red braces. On top of his head was a large cloth cap. As they staggered down the street, sweating profusely, the only thing missing was the whippet.

They turned out to be a very jolly couple and we spent several happy evenings playing cards with them. At the end of the week, we had great difficulty persuading them that Leslie had already paid us for their accommodation. Even then, they persisted in trying to give us extra. In the end, when we would not take any money from them, Harry Hiley said, "I'll tell thee what. Keep thee's eyes open fort' 'orse called 'The Student'. Next time thee sees it running, back it. It's a winner."

I had never had the slightest interest in horse racing, but Iris had the occasional flutter on the Derby and the Grand National. She kept her eye on the papers and sure enough, a few weeks later, saw 'The Student' was running in the Eclipse Stakes. Reading the tipsters, it transpired that it was one of two horses from the same stable and was only being run as pacemaker for the other horse, which was the favourite and ridden by Gordon Richards.

On reading this, there was no way I was going to waste good money backing it, but gullible Iris put a straight bet on of five shillings to win. You can imagine how I felt when it won at ten-to-one. Things weren't made any better when we received a letter from Hull a few days later hoping we had taken full advantage of his tip. When I wrote back explaining that I had not had enough faith to back it, Harry's reply was full of commiseration and offered another tip. The horse this time was a two-year old called 'Straight Jane'.

I watched the papers with interest and when I saw it was running in a twenty-horse race at Redcar, I not only put ten shillings on it at twelve-to-one, but also told all the people at the bank to back it. It lost of course. I wrote and told Harry who wrote back with some very plausible reasons for its lack of success. "Next time," he said, "Sure thing." Next time, the odds were much shorter and I had to put a pound on to try and recoup my previous losses. Once again it lost.

"Ah yes," said Harry, "I think the owner is trying to lull the bookies into a false sense of security before he takes them to the cleaners. Stick with it" So stick with it I did, again and again, each time doubling my stake in an attempt to recoup my losses. Finally, the letter came from Harry. "The horse and jockey had been incompatible, but now they had engaged a new jockey. This is the big one. Put your shirt on it." I managed to raise ten pounds which was two-weeks wages at the bank and put it all on a straight win.

On the day of the race I found it difficult to concentrate on my work. As soon as the race was over, I nipped out for the afternoon paper and frantically turned to the stop press. It was not even in the first three. Dejectedly, I returned to the bank, but on the way home a bought another paper, seeking confirmation. I think I was hoping for a miracle, like the disqualification of first, second and third. As it happened, there was some late news on the race. A short paragraph at the bottom of the stop press announced, "In today's 3.30 at Catterick, Straight Jane fell and broke a leg and had to be shot". I experienced a feeling of relief. Fate had got me off the mad merry-go-round in an unexpected way. I have never placed a bet on anything from that day to this. It was the perfect cure for gambling.

Chapter 17

Karen

Since my demob, Iris and I had never seriously discussed raising a family. Our minds had been more concerned with re-establishing life after the war and getting used to living together as a married couple. Most of my time was taken up with my job at the bank and Iris was busy getting our house in Hounslow the way she wanted it. It was therefore something of a shock when she told me one day that she thought she was pregnant. She went round to our local doctor and we were delighted when he confirmed her suspicions. In his estimation we would become proud parents sometime in January 1948.

All through the pregnancy, Iris regularly attended the pre-natal clinic, which was just as well, as in early December the doctor was concerned to find traces of albumen in her urine. I'm not sure if she had any treatment or medicine for it, but by mid-December things had not improved and it was decided that she would be better off in hospital where she could be kept under observation.

I did not relish life on my own, but five and a half years in the Army had taught me to be self-sufficient and I survived, even though dinner some nights was not much more than bread and butter and a tin of baked beans. I would come home from work, hurriedly prepare and eat whatever I could manage in the time, and then dash off to the hospital to sit with Iris for a couple of hours in the evening. I was pleased and relieved when they said she was well enough to come home for Christmas, which that year fell over a weekend.

The bank was quite busy during Christmas week, with customers drawing money out for last minute shopping. Consequently we were all expected to work right up to the normal half-past-three closing time on the Friday, which was Christmas Eve. I had arranged with the hospital the previous evening that I would go directly from work to collect Iris. Knowing the situation I was in, the branch manager was very kind and let me leave at lunch time so that I could collect Iris early.

After thanking him most profusely and wishing him a merry Christmas, I dashed out and took the tube to Waterloo where I would catch the train out to Twickenham. On the way it occurred to me that the hospital was not expecting me until later, and they would not have Iris ready. Undaunted, I decided I just had time to give them a quick phone call from Waterloo station.

Fortunately, I had two pennies in my pocket and knew the number. I was put through to the ward and explained who I was and gave my message.

"Just hold on while I check," came the reply from the duty nurse and then silence. I began to get frustrated, not knowing whether my tuppence would run out before she returned or whether I would have to abandon the call in order not to miss the train. Eventually she came back on.

"Hello, are you still there?" I confirmed that I was. "I'm sorry," she continued, "I think you must have the wrong ward. There's no Mrs Merryfield here." I remonstrated with her, explaining that I had been there less than twenty-four hours before. She stuck to her story and I had no option but to cut her off in mid-sentence and dash for the train.

I was quite worried for the rest of the journey and even more worried when I got to the ward to find an empty bed where Iris had been the night before. Fortunately, the women in the neighbouring beds recognised me and explained that Iris had been moved to the labour ward. This did little to alleviate my worry, as the baby was not due for another four weeks. I found the Ward Sister who directed me to the labour ward and I was relieved to find Iris sat up in bed completely calm and unruffled. She explained that the hospital doctors had become concerned for the baby and had decided to induce the birth, even though it would be premature. She had been given an injection, but as yet it had not taken effect.

At four o'clock I was thrown out with all the other visitors and walked the mile or so home full of excitement. After a hurried bite I was back again for the evening visitors' hour but still no change. I discussed with Iris the arrangements for the following day which was Christmas Day. When we thought Iris would be coming home for Christmas, some friends at Kew had very kindly agreed to cook Christmas dinner for us. Iris insisted I should phone them up to explain her unavailability, but that I should still go so as not to let them down completely. I agreed with her. After all, who wants to be left with half a turkey.

All through Christmas Day I phoned the hospital almost hourly from Kew, but still no change. On Boxing Day morning I phoned again. Yes, they thought the labour had started but it was still in its early stages. I could hardly wait for visiting time so that I could get there and check the situation. I spent the afternoon holding hands with Iris, with her squeezing mine more and more frequently as the spasms gripped her. Eventually I had to call for the nurse whose first action when she arrived was to ask me to leave. The birth was imminent and in those days fathers were considered a hindrance to proceedings and were not encouraged to hang around.

I went home and rang in at six o'clock. There was no news. There was still no news when I rang again at seven o'clock, eight o'clock, nine o'clock and ten o'clock. After that I gave up and went to bed. At seven o'clock the next morning I was back on the phone.

"Just hold on one minute while I make enquiries," came the reply. "Are you a relative?" I explained that I was more than a relative, I was the father. After a while the nurse returned to the phone.

"Congratulations, Mr Merryfield. You're the father of a girl weighing four pounds seven ounces, born at three o'clock this morning." I was so relieved, but the significance of the low weight did not dawn on me until later. Even allowing for the premature birth, that was quite small and probably accounted for the concern of the doctors.

When I arrived at the hospital later in the day, Iris had been moved yet again, this time to the recovery ward. Here, each bed had a cot at its foot and I was able to catch glimpses of tiny pink hands and noses as I walked down the centre of the ward. Arriving at Iris' bed I peeped coyly into the cot only to find it empty. For a moment my heart stopped, but Iris quickly explained that as the baby was under-weight, she had to be kept in an incubator in a special premature baby room. I was taken there by one of the nurses, and she was gorgeous - I'm referring to the baby of course, but the nurse was not bad either.

As I gazed fondly down on her tiny face she looked like a china doll, so small and fragile. A feeling of love welled up in me mingled with relief that it was all over. Iris and the baby had come safely through their ordeal. I suppose my tiredness and the tension of the past few days had something to do with it, but as I stood there I couldn't stop the tears from rolling down my cheeks.

We decided to call her Karen Hannah. Karen was an unusual name in the fifties, but it had appealed to me ever since I had collected photographs of film stars in my youth. At the age of fourteen I had been secretly in love with a picture of a dark-haired Nordic actress called Karen Morley. Now I would have my very own Karen. The second name, Hannah, was in honour of Iris' best friend. It was Hannah who gave us the pram and Hannah who came round and polished the house some weeks later when it was eventually time for Iris and Karen to come home.

Karen was not allowed out of hospital until her weight reached five pounds and at first I was quite worried when she went down to less than her birth weight. However, I was assured that this was normal and eventually she recovered and reached the magic figure. As you can imagine, she was the centre of attention, with all our friends and relations calling round to see her. Soon after she came home, I arranged the Christening and was delighted when we heard Iris' father would be home from Kenya at the time. Unfortunately, my own father's poor health prevented him from coming. February is not the best of months for somebody with bronchitis to stand about in a draughty church. However, Mum was able to make it as were many other friends and relatives.

Meanwhile, I was slowly establishing myself as a reliable teller at the bank and was pleased when I was promoted to Foreign Clerk and transferred to the Notting Hill Gate branch. It was a bit of a mixed blessing as it was much more difficult to get to than King's Cross, and meant I had to get up earlier in the mornings to catch the train. It had been difficult enough before, and then Iris had nothing else to do except get my breakfast and see me out of the door. Now, with the earlier start and the baby to cope with, things were a bit of a rush and most mornings saw a bowler-hatted figure sprinting down the road in a last minute attempt to catch the train. It did help me to keep fit and fortunately I was only at Notting Hill Gate for about nine months.

It was quite interesting work which brought me into contact with people who were going abroad, something that was nowhere near as common then, as it is today. I got to meet many interesting characters including one called William Russell-Flint. He was a very renowned artist and a member of the Royal Academy, who specialised in semi-draped Spanish beauties. His studios were not far from the bank and on one occasion when I told him I was interested in painting, he invited me round. He was just off to an artist's convention in Prague or somewhere and had called in for his foreign currency. That made it difficult to take him up on his offer immediately and I let the opportunity pass. I regretted this later when I became very interested in painting, but that's another story.

From Notting Hill Gate, I was transferred to the West Kensington branch, right opposite Olympia. The bank had decided that this attracted a lot of foreigners, making it worthwhile opening a foreign currency till. I was given the job of setting it up from scratch. I had only the nine months experience at Notting Hill Gate to rely on and had to put in many hours of evening work before I had got things set up to my satisfaction. Once again it was a very interesting post. Whenever there were exhibitions on at Olympia, they would attract continentals from all over Europe who would call in to exchange money. Most winters, a foreign circus performed there for several weeks and some of the performers would come in to send their wages home. They were paid in English pounds from the box office takings. We would convert them to roubles or whatever and arrange the transfers to their home countries. All told, I was at the West Kensington branch for five years and in some respects sorry when it was time to move on.

Each branch of the bank had its own messenger who did everything from running errands to keeping the bank clean; at West Kensington ours was called Mac. Like Lotcho back at Lombard Street, he was rather a bossy character and although he was never impolite, he liked to keep everybody in their place.

One afternoon, just before closing time I had to go out with a query to one of the nearby shops. It was a filthy winter's afternoon with mud and slush everywhere. By the time I arrived back the bank was closed and I had to ring the bell to get in. The door was opened by Mac who took one look at me and announced, "You're not coming in here with those feet, Mr Merryfield. I've just mopped the floor. You will have to wait until it dries before you can come in."

I had no intention of waiting. I wanted to get my cash reconciliation done so that I could go home on time, but it was a brave man who defied the gaze of big Mac. It was then that the idea came to me.

"Stand aside, my man!" I cried, and with that executed a neat handstand and proceeded to walk across his precious floor on my hands.

I suppose in all I had about eight or ten yards to go from the front door to the doorway that would take me through to behind the tills. Before I had gone very far there were cheers of support from my colleagues who were all busy cashing up. I have always prided myself on being athletic and it proved no task at all to cover the distance, except that when I got to the doorway, my passage was blocked by a pair of neat, shiny, black toecaps that I instantly recognised as belonging to Mr Bucklow, the Branch Manager. He was not amused and not for the first time in my life I found myself lamely trying to give an explanation for my silly behaviour.

Word of my escapade travelled throughout the banking world. Years later, I had cause to visit a Westminster branch up north, I think it was either Workington or Warrington. Whilst we were having some repair work done at West Kensington, some old blown-up photographs of various branches, from the beginning of the century, were discovered tucked away in an attic. It was thought they might be of interest to the branches concerned and I agreed to drop some off when I had to go up on other business. Imagine my surprise when I introduced myself, only to receive the reply, "Not the Buster Merryfield who bumped into his manager whilst doing cartwheels across the bank?"

In the course of time I managed to live the incident down and got on better terms with Mr Bucklow. One day he invited Iris and I over to his house at Harrow for dinner. I felt very honoured and found his house fascinating. He was a renowned rifle shot and his house was full of trophies he had won at Bisley and other places. The evening was not without purpose, and all through the meal he questioned Iris and I on our backgrounds and quizzed me on my ambitions and attitude towards banking. I wondered if he thought I was perhaps not suitable for that kind of career and I tried to reassure him that I was conscientious and would take on any job he cared to give me. I told him I would even be prepared to mop the floor if necessary, at which he gave me a rather sour look. I think he thought I was taking the mickey over my hand walking escapade.

Two weeks later, my worse fears were realised when he summonsed me into his office and told me I had to go for an interview at Head Office. Forearmed is forewarned, so I boldly asked him what it was about. What had I done wrong? He laughed.

"Don't look so worried Buster. I've mentioned you in my report and they just want to put a face to the name." I wasn't fully reassured. Why would he want to put me in his report? Surely my escapades hadn't been that bad. I had only recently bought my first car and I had visions of having to sell it again if I got down-graded. I did not dare entertain the thought that I might get the sack.

On the day of the interview I drove up to Lothbury in my new Ford Classic. Well it was new to me, although it had had several previous owners. I was shown in to the office of one of the senior managers who proceeded to review my performance at the various branches. Eventually he looked up from the folder in front of him.

"What do you see as the next step then, Merryfield, Branch Accountant?" he queried.

"Branch Accountant?" I echoed. What was the man talking about. That would mean promotion. I couldn't believe it. Branch Accountant was the last step before becoming sub-Manager and then Manager of a branch. He could see I was lost for words and did not wait for an answer.

"We've been keeping an eye on you and feel you have earned promotion. We have a post that needs filling but there is a snag," he continued. "The Sub-Manager at Twickenham has had a heart attack and is now only able to work part time. If we appointed you, you would also have to assist in the branch management, taking his place for a couple of days a week when he wasn't there. What do you think?"

What did I think? Not only was he offering me promotion and a half, the Twickenham branch was just round the corner from where I lived. I couldn't believe my luck. I thanked him most profusely and couldn't wait to get home to tell Iris the good news. I was so elated I felt we just had to celebrate in some way. Iris was just as excited and I could tell she was pleased for me. We decided that we should go off on a second honeymoon, somewhere a bit more romantic than wartime Newbury.

Iris persuaded her sister Lily to look after Karen for a couple of days and by six o'clock the following Friday evening we were heading west out of London in the new car. By nightfall we had crossed the Severn and pulled in for the night at a small farmhouse somewhere near Monmouth. We were very much in love and happy to be alone together for the first time since our marriage. The next morning we awoke to a beautiful Spring morning and revelled in the crisp clean air.

After breakfast we continued westwards through Abergavenny and Merthyr Tydfil, skirting round the edge of the Black Mountains heading for the west coast. It must have been as we were passing through Ammanford that I saw the sign. It was just a metal finger pointing south saying 'Llanelli 19', but it brought back all the old memories of my wartime correspondence. I felt I had to see Phyllis and find out what had become of her since that last poignant letter. In it she had sounded alone and forlorn and I had wondered several times since whether she had found somebody to care for her. She was a nice girl and deserved to have a happy life.

It took some time for me to explain to Iris that it was curiosity and nostalgia and not passion that was drawing me back, but eventually, being the kind sweet person she was and confident in the strength of our love for one other, she reluctantly agreed to a diversion to seek out Phyllis.

After a few enquiries, I eventually found the house I had written to so many times. It was a typical Welsh miner's cottage in a terraced row. I left Iris in the car and nervously knocked on the door. It was opened promptly by a middle aged lady who clearly was not Phyllis. When I explained my mission, she was most helpful. Yes, she knew Phyllis and somehow even knew of her correspondence with me. Most importantly, she was able to give me the address to which Phyllis had moved some years before.

Alas, I drew a complete blank at the new address, but was directed further along the road to an old lady who had lived there all her life and claimed to know everybody. This time I was in luck and she was able to direct me to a house on the other side of town where Phyllis' brother lived. By this time Iris was beginning to lose patience and was anxious to continue with our journey. However, having got this far I was not going to give up now.

The door was answered by Phyllis' sister-in-law who was aware that Phyllis had a wartime pen-pal and was quite excited that I should have shown up after all these years. She insisted on telephoning her husband at work and he in turn told me of Phyllis' whereabouts. She was now married and was running a fashion shop in Hove with her husband. I returned to the car and we continued with our weekend. At least I now knew Phyllis had found somebody to care for her. The ghost was laid.

We had a delightful weekend but were pleased to get back to Karen, this being the first time we had ever left her. I still had a week or two to do at West Kensington teaching my replacement the intricacies of foreign currency, after which I moved to the Twickenham Branch as the Branch Accountant. They had not been wrong when they said I was urgently needed. It was not really the sub-manager's fault as he had been off ill for some months, but during that time the bank's affairs had got into a bit of a mess. It was just as well that I was close to home as I found myself having to put in a lot of overtime during the evenings and weekends to get it sorted.

Within a few months, I had things organised the way I wanted them and I enjoyed my new-found responsibilities without too much worry. I was then able to devote my spare time to other outside interest as I will explain in due course. The only event of note at the bank was the loss of my car. Together with the other bank employees, I used to park my car on a piece of waste ground next to the river. One winter we had very heavy rain coupled with spring tides and an easterly wind. This unfortunate combination resulted in the River Thames bursting its banks and flooding the car park.

The police had been touring the streets earlier in the day issuing warnings over the police-car loud-hailer, but inside the bank I had not heard them. It wouldn't have mattered much if I had as there was nowhere else I could move the car to. I don't think even the police anticipated it would be quite as bad as it was. When I came out of the bank in the late afternoon to go home, the water was half way up the windows and I had to leave car where it was. I went back during the evening after the river had receded, but the water had got into the engine and it would not start. In the end I had to call out a tow truck from the local garage, whom I then asked to fix the car. What I hadn't realised was that it wasn't just a case of cleaning the engine and drying things out. The mud had got everywhere and as it dried it began to smell. The seats, the carpet, the upholstery, it was all ruined. The sludge had even got down into the door panels where it was impossible to shift. In the end, I had to add hard-earned cash to the insurance money and buy another car.

I stayed at the Twickenham branch for five years until I was eventually given my own branch to manage, as I shall explain later, but there's lots more to tell you before then.

Chapter 18

Tour de France

By 1949, I had been out of the Army for three years and had not had a proper holiday in all that time. What with setting up house and then the birth of Karen, there hadn't been time, and now, with a young child, it would be far too difficult. At least, that was what we said to our friends. In reality, we just didn't have the money to spare. However, that didn't stop me from dreaming of faraway places and one day I had an idea.

At the time, there was a series on the radio called, 'The Hard Way' in which the narrator recounted his adventures as he walked the length of the south coast, existing on only five shillings a day. Well if he could do it on five, I could do it on four, thought I, and if he can walk across England, I can walk across France. On second thoughts, I might be able to do it for nothing once I'm over the Channel. That's it, I'll hitch-hike from the Channel to Marseilles and back, spending no money whatsoever.

From the outset, Iris made it quite clear that whatever plans I had in mind, I should include her out. She didn't mind me going but at the same time she was apprehensive about me travelling alone in case I had an accident or something. I asked around the bank to see if anyone there would care to accompany me over the Whitsun break. One or two were interested until I explained the bit about taking no money. Then it was quite amusing to see them hastily thinking up excuses. In the end, I persuaded Iris' younger brother, Tommy, to come with me.

Although I intended taking no money, I realised it would be difficult to carry a week's food and it was my intention to barter. France was still recovering from the war and I knew that there were two things I could take with me that would be worth their weight in gold. These were English cigarettes and coffee. So I bought two pounds of coffee beans in quarter pound packets and one hundred Capstan in packets of ten.

Apart from these we each carried small quantities of sugar, butter, margarine and jam as well as tins of condensed milk, beans and spaghetti. The rest of my kit consisted of a small primus, knife, fork and spoon, mess tins, a map, a diary and two blankets. These were all packed into a large rucksack, with my ex-army groundsheet rolled up and tied on the top. Although we would be abroad and not likely to meet anybody I knew, as a bank employee I felt uncomfortable to be hitch-hiking. As when busking, I again found anonymity in my tramp's outfit, but this time without the bowler hat.

Quite by chance, we left Victoria for Dover on Friday, the thirteenth of May. On the station we were stopped and questioned by two patrolling policemen, who could not believe that two itinerants had legitimate reasons to board the boat train. It took a few words of explanation and sight of our tickets to convince them. Even then they were shaking their heads and muttering as we went through the barrier.

We found ourselves seats in a third-class compartment which we were obliged to share with six Frenchmen. I listened to them intently, but despite my French lessons at Sinjuns, was unable to follow their conversation. If only they wouldn't talk so fast. At exactly ten o'clock in the evening, the train pulled out and two hours later we were in Dover. We had a bit of explaining to do at customs, but the cigarettes and coffee were within legal limits and we passed smoothly through to the ferry.

By the time we boarded, all the free couchettes were taken and we had to content ourselves with armchairs in the passenger lounge. Most of the other passengers seemed to be holiday-makers dressed in their best going-away clothes and carrying smart luggage. We tended to stand out and were the subject of many curious glances.

It was a smooth, uneventful crossing, but we were far too excited to sleep. Long before we reached the other side we went on deck and watched the approaching lights of France, making the steward's cry of "Dunkerque" superfluous. Once down the gangplank, all the other passengers disappeared on to the waiting Paris train, leaving us alone on the quay. It was 5 am. It was dark. It was cold. It was raining. It was alien. Suddenly, our adventure didn't seem such a good idea.

"Well, Tommy," I said, as cheerfully as I could, "We'd better get going. It's a long way to Marseilles." With that we hitched up our rucksacks, draped our groundsheets over our shoulders and set off through the silent town.

I had already planned the route we would take, the first objective being Cassel, a small town about thirty kilometres to the south. At that time of day the roads were empty and it was an hour or so before I was able to deliver my first 'Bonjour', to a peasant pushing a small handcart laden with goods for the morning market. He returned my greeting with a smile and a courteous nod as he passed, leaving us alone on the open road.

Soon after, we heard the welcome sound of an approaching vehicle, but it too was heading back towards Dunkerque. This seemed to be the pattern of early morning traffic and it was some time before a lorry-driver travelling in our direction pulled up and offered a lift.

"Bonjour Monsieur. Voulez-vous donner moi un passage au Cassel, s'il vous plait?" I asked in my best schoolboy French.

"Certainement," he replied, "Entrez vous". Needing no more bidding, we joyfully climbed up next to him in the warm cab.

"Voulez vous désirer un cigarette Anglais?" I asked, offering him one of the Capstans.

"Merci, Monsieur. Vous êtes trop genereux. Les cigarettes Anglais sont très magnifiques," he replied as he gratefully reached across and pulled one out. He was so delighted with it that I gave him the rest of the packet. We spent a pleasant journey with him and were sorry to leave him when he set us down in Cassel half an hour or so later.

The town was still shrouded in morning mist, but we were in no mood for sight-seeing and pressed on down the road towards Bethune, our next destination. It took six hours, eight lifts and ten more cigarettes to cover the forty-kilometre journey and by the time we arrived we were very hungry. Iris had packed us a few sandwiches, half of which we had eaten on the ferry. We now sat in the cobbled square and ate what was left, washing them down with cooling water from the fountain.

During the afternoon we travelled on through Arras, passing row upon row of crosses marking the first world war military cemeteries, and by evening had reached Bapaume twenty kilometres beyond. Here we decided to call it a day and made our way to a farmhouse where we negotiated the exchange of six eggs and the promise of a night in a hay barn in return for a packet of our coffee beans.

However, soon after our arrival at the farm, a visiting truck-driver offered to take us on to Ham, over forty kilometres away. Not wishing to look a gift-horse in the mouth, we quickly stowed the eggs with the rest of our rations and carried on with our journey. It soon began to look as if we were going to make it to Marseilles non-stop, for no sooner had we been dropped off in Ham when a car driver offered a lift to Compiegne. This was not on the planned route, but roughly in the right direction. However, we were in two minds as to whether we should accept as we were both becoming very weary and had eaten nothing in the last twenty-four hours except Iris' sandwiches. Nonetheless, we hopped on board and were dropped off in Compiegne at ten o'clock at night.

Not wishing to spend the night in the open, I engaged several of the townspeople in conversation, hoping one of them might take pity on us and offer shelter for the night, but it was not to be. As time went by, we became more and more despondent. We had been on the road for 17 hours and covered not much more than 100 miles out of a total round trip of 1400 miles. There was no way we would reach Marseilles at this rate of progress. After a fruitless hour, feeling low, tired and hungry, we headed for the railway station, intending to get the next train to Paris and home.

On making enquiries at the station, we found there were no more trains that night. We would have to come back next morning. Wearily we trudged out of town hoping to find a farmer that might let us sleep in his barn. By now Tommy was nearing total collapse and I was carrying his pack as well as my own. I soon realised we would have to find somewhere for food and sleep very soon. Finding a convenient hedgerow, we sank down beneath it and chewed on a bar of chocolate before falling into an exhausted sleep.

Fate was not on our side. No sooner had we wrapped ourselves up in our blankets than the rain started. It came down in torrents and in a very few minutes we were soaked. There was no option but to head back to town and more substantial shelter. I decided the most likely place was the station waiting-room. The night-porter was a stickler for rules and would only allow us to wait there if we were bona-fide passengers catching the next train, which was due out at four-thirty in the morning. There was no need to bend the rules. We were desperately tired and fully intended being on that train. We had had enough.

The next thing we knew, it was daylight. My watch told me the train had left two hours ago. As I got to my feet, I felt as though I had been kicked all over by a horse and a quick consultation with Tommy confirmed he was just as stiff. Stepping out on to the platform, we found the sun was quickly dispelling the overnight dampness. Feeling infinitely brighter, we decided to take a walk to get our legs working and at the same time get ourselves some breakfast. If need be, we had all day to catch a train back to the ferry.

Cautiously we crept out of the station and made our way through the town, only pausing for a quick drink from a convenient fountain. Once clear of the town we stopped in a small park to make breakfast. Three of our eggs had somehow been broken and everything in my rucksack was covered in a gooey mess. We scraped up what we could and added it to the others in a large omelette which we shared between us along with a tin of baked beans. The park had a public toilet where we were able to get a wash and tidy ourselves up. Our spirits were rising as fast as the sun and over a cup of thick coffee, full of condensed milk, we decided to press on as far south as we could get.

What we had not taken into account was that Frenchmen are slow to rise on a Sunday. We were unable to get any lifts and ended up walking over thirty kilometres to Soissons, just to get back on to my original route. It took us all day but by now we had abandoned any sense of urgency and were just enjoying the pleasure of walking through France. However, we did not refuse the kind offer of a lorry-driver who took us to Chateau-Thierry, a further forty kilometres along our route.

After the difficulties we had in getting accommodation the previous night, we thought it better to leave the town and continued on foot for another kilometre or two until we reached a small village. This time, I made sure my quest for food and a bed would be successful by offering the coffee and cigarettes from the outset. The enthusiasm of the villagers was boundless with one man immediately offering to give us his daughter's bed, minus daughter I should add. We thanked him for his kindness, but settled for a sweet-smelling pile of hay in his stable, where, after another meal of scrambled eggs and beans, we fell into a deep, deep sleep.

Next morning, we found ourselves the centre of attention as more and more neighbours came to see the mad Englishmen who lived on nothing but eggs. They were all very friendly and readily agreed to a group photograph before waving us on our way to Montmirail, some twenty kilometres away. Once again, we had to walk most of the way, but when we did get a lift, the driver was extremely helpful.

He took us to a baker's shop, run by an ex-patriot Englishwoman who used to live in Chiswick. She was delighted to be able to converse with us in her native tongue and to talk about her pre-war life in London. When we insisted we had to get on, she filled a large bag with cakes for us and despite our protestations refused to take any coffee or cigarettes in exchange.

Once clear of the town, we found a pleasant grassy bank on

which to lie and eat the eclairs and meringues for lunch. No sooner had we finished and got to our feet than a lorry pulled up and we were offered a lift to Esternay; not on our route but still to the south. Soon after we were dropped off, the inevitable rain started again, dampening our spirits as much as it did our bodies. Once again we began to doubt the wisdom of carrying on. We had been travelling nearly three days and tomorrow at the latest, time would force us to turn for home. We convinced ourselves that we might as well start back now. Who knows, with a bit of luck and a couple of good lifts, we might make it back to the friendly village near Chateau-Thierry before nightfall.

It was not to be. We trudged north through the rain, but the road was little used and there were no lifts. After about twelve kilometres we were soaking wet and could walk no further. Seeing an isolated farmhouse we approached and knocked hopefully on the door. It was late at night and all was in darkness, but eventually the farmer answered our knocking. He was not too pleased to have been woken from his bed, but on seeing our bedraggled state his attitude softened. Once more the coffee beans did the trick and soon after, we were cooking the inevitable omelette in one of his barns. We even had the luxury of half a loaf of dark granary bread to go with it.

We slept soundly, but at crack of dawn there was no mistaking where we were, with the cockerel competing with the lowing cattle in the next barn. By way of a change, we fried our breakfast eggs and were delighted when the farmer's daughter brought us a small pail of fresh milk, straight from the cows. In daylight, we found we were in an idyllic spot and were reluctant to leave, but we had to press on if we were to get back to England.

There was no more traffic on the isolated country road than there had been the day before and once more progress was slow. At one time we were overtaken by a violent thunderstorm and we had no option but to stop and shelter. We had walked right through Montmirail and to within ten kilometres of Chateau-Thierry before we were picked up and taken the rest of the way. It was still daylight, so we thought it best to press on into the countryside where we seemed to have more success at finding shelter than we did in the towns.

We had no trouble getting a lift out of town along the Soissons road but that was the end of our good fortune. Down came the rain again and as darkness fell we had to put the groundsheets on over the tops of our packs to try and keep the contents dry. In the gloom we must have looked like the hunchback of Notre Dame and his twin brother out for an evening stroll, but there was nobody to see us as we trudged along the country lane, all alone in the world with not a glimmer of light to be seen. It was gone midnight before we staggered into a small hamlet which we later discovered went under the grand title of Racourt Saint Martin par Coincy. The name was longer than the village.

Following our successful routine of the previous evening, we selected a likely-looking house and pounded on the door. The poor Madame who opened it was frightened out of her wits. She gave one shriek and disappeared back inside. Within seconds her place was taken by her husband, shotgun in hand. Once his eyes had got used to the dark and I had explained our predicament as best I could, he lowered the gun and beckoned us inside. He was an ex-Air Force pilot who now ran a garage. His family couldn't have been kinder to us and after filling our bellies with a magnificent supper of cold meats, showed us to a large double bed for the night.

Next morning, I insisted they accepted a packet of our coffee beans and some cigarettes before we bade them goodbye and once more headed north. It was a lovely fresh morning after the overnight rain and before long we got a lift into Soisson, immediately followed by another to Ham, a good forty kilometres away. The Gods were feeling benevolent that morning as within minutes of being set down in Ham we were once more on our way, this time with an English school-teacher who was touring France by car. We wondered if he might be going all the way to the coast, but that was too much to hope for. However, having told him our tale, when he dropped us off outside Perrone, he insisted on giving us part of his food supply. We thanked him profusely for the tin of sardines and - wait for it - two hard-boiled eggs!

We were making extremely good progress and our luck was still holding. From Perrone we were taken by lorry to Bethune, over seventy kilometres away, easily our best lift yet. It was midnight by the time we arrived, but we had covered over 150 kilometres since breakfast.

We thought it too late to start knocking on doors and wondered if there might be a late-night train we could take to Dunkerque. We spotted a patrolling gendarme who was extremely helpful. No, there wasn't a train until morning, but if we wished we could spend the night in a cell back at the police station. Next morning we were woken at six with the news that a lift had been arranged to take us all the way to the ferry. Overjoyed at the news we off-loaded the rest of our 'cigarettes Anglais' on to a grateful French police force before climbing aboard the lorry.

By half-past-ten we were in Dunkerque. Having made such good progress back, we were in no hurry to depart. Having ascertained the time of the ferry we spent the next two hours sight-seeing in the town. By now I was getting quite proud of my French, but in asking the ferry times I confused my 'moins quarte' with my 'plus quarte' which meant we had half an hour less than I had calculated. In the end it was only a quick dash in a Citroên with a coffee-loving Anglophile that got us to the quay on time.

We felt a sense of real achievement as we relaxed on the ferry back to Dover. It was all over. All we had to do now was sit back until we reached our destination. No more anxiety over lifts. No more worry over getting a bed for the night. By the time we had completed the train journey back to London, it was approaching midnight again and we were ready for our beds. Iris was very pleased to see me and was full of questions, but they would have to wait until morning. After a mug of hot sweet tea I sank thankfully between the cool white sheets.

By the time I awoke next morning, Iris was already up and about. Hearing me stir she called up for me to stay where I was and she would bring me breakfast in bed - what a treat after the hardships of the previous week. I lay reflecting on our adventure. It had been tough but it had been worthwhile. I was glad we had done it but not sure if I wanted to do it again, at least not for a while. I was roused from my musings by Iris with the promised breakfast.

"You're lucky," she said, "I've saved you a real treat from the rations." What was it? I'm sure you have already guessed. It was a large plate of scrambled eggs - with coffee, of course.

Chapter 19

The Calling

After my busking experiment, when I was first demobbed, I complied with Iris' wishes and put my banking career firmly in front of my show business aspirations and was quite successful.

However, I did not completely give up thoughts of the stage and continued to develop my miming act. I looked through the rest of my record collection seeking other performers that I could imitate. I used to take my gramophone into our bedroom and practice in front of the large mirror on the wardrobe door. With Al Jolson, I had a ready-made character to imitate and it was easy to copy all the actions and gestures that I had seen him do in his films. With my other records it was not so easy as the singers didn't have the same visual presence. I experimented with Bing Crosby, but his style was so laid back he was difficult to parody. I have never smoked but I managed to get hold of a large pipe as a prop, but it didn't seem very effective.

I had a bit more success with Nelson Eddy and Jeanette McDonald. I got one of Iris' old dresses and cut it down the middle, and did the same with an old suit. I then sewed the left half of one to the right half of the other. By standing sideways and then quickly turning round, I could present either half to the front, switching from one to the other as they sang their duet. It looked quite effective in the mirror and I thought an audience would find it funny. The only trouble was that on the record they quite often sang together in harmony and I then didn't know which way to turn.

It eventually dawned on me that I would be better off inventing my own character - the mad music professor. To be effective I needed to dress the part and although Iris didn't approve of me spending the money, I went out and bought a suitable attire. Not that I spent a fortune on it. I toured the pawn shops looking for the tattiest dinner-jacket or frock-coat I could find. Eventually I came up with something suitable for only ten shillings. It was a long-tailed dinner-jacket similar to those worn by concert pianists and came complete with black trousers. It had seen better days and looked as though it had provided many a breakfast for hungry moths. I took it home, patched it up and tried it on. The fact that it was about ten sizes too big for me only added to the effect I was trying to create. It was perfect.

As the mad professor, I would be able to sing to my classical opera records and in between the arias I could take out a baton and conduct the orchestra. Reading this, you are probably thinking this was a commonplace act, as many have done similar things since. But as I explained when I went busking, I believe that in the late forties I was unique.

When I was ready, I offered my act to a local charity who were putting on a concert in aid of homeless ex-servicemen. On the night of the concert, I got them to announce me as a serious singer. The curtain went up to reveal me stood under a spotlight behind a large column microphone, looking very dignified in my dress-suit, which from a distance looked reasonably respectable. Music for the show was provided by a lone pianist but the audience quite accepted that as a serious opera singer I should be accompanied by pre-recorded music from a gramophone. I gave them Figaro's aria from 'The Barber of Seville'.

It took some time before they realised I was miming. After a couple of minutes, I left them in no doubt as I started to add exaggerated actions to the words and in no time they were in tears of laughter. It was all the funnier in that as soon as I started to move about, the excessive size of my outfit became apparent. Every few bars I would stop and hoist my trousers up in time with the music.

"Figaro here" (Jerk), "Figaro there" (Jerk), "Figaro here" (Jerk), "Figaro there" (Jerk), . . . they were loving it. When it came to an orchestral interlude, I started conducting an imaginary orchestra and at the same time wandered slowly away from the microphone, only to dash back just in time for the next bit of singing. This too was greeted with howls of laughter. I was in my element but all too soon it came to an end as the curtain came down. The applause was thunderous and as I took my bow there were stamps and whistles and cries of 'More' from the audience. I was in heaven.

As a result of this success, I was asked to perform in several similar events and was also asked if I would be prepared to be an after-dinner entertainer at a firm's annual Christmas dinner. I eagerly accepted this invitation, particularly as the deal included a free dinner. It wasn't until after I had accepted, that I realised a five-minute stage act would not keep a room full of salesmen entertained for long enough. I needed more material.

The only thing I could fall back on were my Army variety shows. Doctor Wesoski's tightrope act was obviously unsuitable, but I might be able to resurrect some of my Master of Ceremonies patter. I still had the old Razzle magazine, but I went out and bought the latest issue. Using jokes from these and some I remembered from Braunton days, I put together a stand-up comedy routine to supplement my miming, which would come as the finale to my act.

During the dinner, I ate very little. This was the first time I had ever performed for reward, albeit only the cost of a dinner. I was nervous and unsure. The routine I had put together was new and untried and I began to wish I hadn't been quite so keen to accept the invitation. My hosts could tell I was uneasy and tried to ply me with table-wine to restore my flagging spirits. However, I had stuck with the advice given me by Mr Broadbent, my boxing coach at Sinjuns, and never smoked or drunk alcohol in my life, and I didn't intend starting now. I would just have to rely on my inner strength and fortitude.

My abstinence was not followed by the rest of the diners and the wine flowed freely throughout the meal. As soon as it was over, the brandy and port came round and after the Loyal Toast, the cigars were lit. Very soon, it was difficult to see across the room and my eyes were beginning to water profusely. My moment of truth was drawing ever closer.

The Managing-Director rose to his feet to deliver the customary end-of-year pat on the back to his sales force and was greeted with ironic cheers. His speech was interspersed with groans and 'Oohs' and 'Aahs' from his audience and cries of 'Get on with it'. They were obviously anxious to get to the entertainment. At last he came to the conclusion of his message and introduced me as, "The man you've all been waiting to hear, Buster Merryfield!" I rose nervously from my chair and began.

"Did I ever tell you about my mother-in-law?" I asked rhetorically. Quick as a flash, the reply came back.

"No, we've never met you before." Whereupon there were guffaws of drunken laughter, but they were laughing at me rather than with me. I continued with the joke but the effect had been lost. Perhaps the next one would be better.

"I've invented the ideal thing for bald-headed men," I quipped, brushing my hand across my thinning brow.

"Didn't work on you, did it?" came the reply from the same quarter and once again the cruel laughter. I ignored the heckling and continued into the punch line.

"Its bald-headed women," I added, but it was too late, the timing had been ruined. I pressed on as best I could, wishing the floor would open up and swallow me. The majority of the diners were attentive and wanted to hear what I had to say, but I was unable to give them my best, being in constant fear of the next interruption.

Eventually I got to the end of the jokes and started my *Figaro* routine. I had done that many times before and knew it would go down well. However, even that was spoiled. There was no microphone for me to wander away from and dash back to and the gramophone was down the end of the room, some distance from the top table where I was stood. This completely destroyed the illusion that I was doing the singing. They listened and I got lots of applause and whistles at the end, but I knew in my heart of hearts that I had not been at my best.

It was a sobering experience and I gave it much thought when I got home. I realised that at this type of function I was dealing with a totally different audience to that at a charity concert. Furthermore, the setting was different. I was not isolated on a stage where I had command but down amongst them where it was more difficult to make my presence felt. I managed to suitably amend my act and was more successful on future occasions. I even developed a routine to put down drunken wise-guys. This earned their displeasure but brought cheers from their colleagues. Even so, this was not what I wanted. There was something missing.

It was not entirely what the after-dinner audiences wanted either. At one event, there was a succession of acts, including a straight stand-up comic. His routine wouldn't raise a hair today but for the post-war era it was very suggestive. People didn't actually laugh at his material but he got lots of sniggers and lewd comments, and it seemed that this was what they wanted. However, I was determined that if I was going to make it in variety, it would be with a clean act. If I had to resort to risqué jokes then I would have failed.

Meanwhile, it was a case of 'don't give up your day job' and every morning I would leave the house at Hounslow and dutifully take the train to the City. It was always a rush to get to the station on time but I always had a seat waiting for me on the train. I used to travel with a colleague called Irene Simmons who worked in the same office at the bank and got on the train two stops before me at Hampton. As we travelled up each day, we would discuss the theatre, me telling her about my evening engagements and she telling me about her amateur dramatics.

She was a member of a charitable theatrical company run by her local church. They put on plays for institutions rather than for the general public. They called themselves The Liberty Players which I found rather amusing, presuming they performed for the prisoners in Wandsworth Prison and Wormwood Scrubs. To be fair, they played to hospitals and old-folks homes in the area.

One day Irene confessed they were having trouble with their next production, a comedy called *Painted Sparrows*. They always chose plays to suit their limited cast, but having selected this one, the potential leading man had just announced he was moving out of the area. Now they were stuck for a replacement. The character he was supposed to play was described as 'a short Cockney' and she wondered if I might be interested in joining the company and taking his place.

Disregarding the sketches I did in the Braunton variety shows, I had never done any acting, but I was willing to give anything a go. Besides, she was quite a little charmer and I was sure I would enjoy being in her company, both theatrical and personal. The following Thursday evening, I took the train out to Hampton for the initial reading of the play. It took part in the local school, a most depressing place. It was a gloomy, Victorian building, smelling of wet rain-macs and disinfectant.

Irene introduced me to Joan Groves, the producer, who explained the part they would like me to read for. The story line was centred around a country inn where all the staff and guests had problems of one sort or another. These are eventually sorted out by the main character, Syd Fish, and everybody lives happily ever after. It wasn't a terribly riveting plot, but was typical of the productions that hundreds of amateur dramatic societies were putting on in village halls up and down the country. Nevertheless, I was flattered that they should want me to play the lead as Syd.

The first act of the play set the scene in the inn before Syd arrives. Whilst this was being read I was able to look around at my fellow performers. They looked kind, sincere people and seemed to have a genuine regard for each other. I was also able to read ahead and think about the character I was going to play and how I would portray him. When it was time for him to make his entrance, I gave it full expression.

"Good evening, Madam, I'm afraid my motor bike has broken down. I'm hoping you can put me up for the night." I declared in my best Cockney accent. For some reason the rest of the cast thought this was extremely funny. I suppose it must have been something to do with the way I said it. We continued to the end of the scene, at which point Joan turned to me.

"Buster, that was perfect. You really must take the part." What more could I say except, "Yes". I was now a member of the Hampton Liberty Players.

The first presentation of *Painted Sparrows* was at the Star and Garter hospital for disabled servicemen in Richmond. There was no theatre as such but they had a large community room with a raised platform at one end that served as a stage. It didn't have any curtains and we had no scenery or proper stage props. When we arrived, we roughly explained the setting of the play and the staff went off and found things, such as tables and chairs, that we could use to create the set. Once this was done, we were ready for the audience.

So far, the patients I had seen in the Star and Garter were what one might call the 'walking wounded'. Some had arms in slings, some swung themselves along on crutches, while others hopped about on artificial limbs. I was impressed and at the same time humbled by their bright, cheerful dispositions. Chairs were set out in rows and give or take the odd leg stuck out in the gangway or perched up on a stool, they were all able to fit in comfortably.

It came as rather a shock when the nurses started to bring in some of the other patients. First came those in wheel-chairs. As the first was pushed into position in the side-aisle, it was apparent that he had no legs, just two bandaged stumps protruding from the gap in his dressing gown. Behind him was another who had been terribly burnt. He had both hands swathed in bandages and seemed to have very little flesh left on his badly-disfigured face. I was appalled by these horrible injuries that had been inflicted by the war; a war far more terrible than that I had experienced. I wanted to look away and put it all out of my mind but I couldn't help but watch as each one was brought in. I felt most upset by those that were brain-damaged and had lost control of both their minds and bodies. Heads lolling, eyes rolling, mouths open, chins dribbling, limbs twitching backwards and forwards to some unheard, internal rhythm, they uttered strange plaintive cries as they tried to communicate their frustrated needs to those around them.

Finally, to complete our audience, four or five beds were wheeled in and placed along the front just below the stage. In them were the most-seriously ill patients, some with tubes inserted into their bodies, carrying life-preserving drugs and fluids. They were propped up on piles of pillows so that their heads pointed roughly in the direction of the stage.

In all, patients and nurses, we had an audience of nearly 100 people. One of the male nurses explained to everybody that they were going to see a play called *Painted Sparrows* and those in the first scene climbed on to the stage. It was not a very long play which was just as well considering the nature of the audience. When it was over, each performer walked to the front of the stage to take a bow. The nurses clapped enthusiastically, but there was very little response from the patients. Being the main character in the play, I was the last one to come forward. I was amazed at the ensuing response. As well as the claps from the nurses, each patient did his best to show some sort of appreciation. Crutches were banged on the floor to add to the cheers and whistles from the more able. Even the badly afflicted managed to raise a meandering arm into the air and utter joyous cries and moans.

I had never before witnessed such emotion. I telepathically sensed the feelings of gratitude that came flooding towards me. I was completely overcome and could do nothing except stand and look out at my new-found friends. Gradually their faces blurred as the tears welled in my eyes and slowly trickled down my cheeks. I had never felt so emotionally naked, but it didn't matter. I was among friends and wept from absolute happiness. It was a strange joy that came not from self-satisfaction but from an inner feeling that I had able to give something, no matter how small, to these unfortunate people.

I walked off the stage literally dumb-struck. The other actors congratulated me but I acknowledged them as if in a dream. I felt dazed and deflated and wanted to be alone with my emotions. The small reception that had been laid on seemed trite and of no consequence by comparison with the emotional experience I had been through. I just wanted to go home.

When I did get home I tried to explain it all to Iris. Knowing me as she does, I think she thought I was over-dramatising, and I'm not sure that she fully understood how I felt. I lay awake that night trying to rationalise all I had been through and the feelings I now had.

Up until now, my life had followed whatever route had been dictated by events and other people. My mother had sent me to Sinjuns and steered me towards the bank. The same with religion - I had not consciously chosen to join the Baptist church. I had gone out of custom and habit. I was a follower of family convention. And the war - I had made the decision to join the territorials as a result of seeing Moseley, but after that the next six or seven years of my life had been decided for me. I was nearly thirty years old and I needed to think more about the purpose of my life.

My thoughts turned back to show business. Ever since the yo-yo contest and the funny face competition I had felt an excitement from being on stage, from being the centre of attention. Having found I could amuse people, I deliberately played the clown. When obliged to participate in Army entertainments, I had chosen variety and comedy, but I had gained no deep satisfaction from it. I likened it to going out with girls. It was a pleasurable thing to do but until one fell in love with the right person, one didn't know what deep emotion was. I had flirted with show business, but now I was in love with the theatre. I had discovered what it was like to stir peoples emotions by acting. This was what I wanted to do. This would be my vocation, my purpose in life. I was being called just as surely as a missionary is called.

I knew I had to be realistic. I had a wife, a daughter and a mortgage. I could not throw everything away and seek my fortune on the stage. Circumstances dictated that I continued to work in the bank, but once work was over, my time would be my own and I would devote it to acting. I would get there one way or another. I thought back to my earlier vows to myself and my philosophy for life. 'Through Christ I can' - and I would.

Chapter 20

Drama

The Liberty Players put *Painted Sparrows* on at several other locations and I took part in these and other of their productions. However, I did not find Syd Fish very challenging. Having been bitten by the drama bug, I wanted something stronger in the way of parts. On the other hand I didn't want to let the group down and so I continued with them until I changed banks to the West Kensington branch and no longer worked with Irene. This gave me the opportunity and excuse to move on to something a little different.

I realised my best bet was to join an established amateur dramatics club. I made a few enquiries and discovered that the Richmond and Twickenham Arts Club had the best reputation in the area and made them my choice. They met in the Oddfellows Hall, Richmond which was quite close to the professional Richmond Theatre.

It was quite an unusual set-up. The club was very eclectic, catering for a wide variety of arts activities. They ran painting classes, poetry-reading groups, sculpture, pottery; in fact anything that was remotely art could claim affiliation. Some activities used the Oddfellows Hall whereas others hired rooms at other locations such as the Community Centre.

By far the biggest group was the drama club, which put on two or three productions a year, usually in Saint Mary's Hall, Twickenham. They would get audiences of over 200 for the right play, and if they were lucky, make a few pounds profit to subsidise the subscriptions paid by the Arts Club members. It all helped to pay the rental on the Oddfellows Hall and the other hired rooms.

Tuesday nights at the club were considered special evenings at which members of all the groups met socially, and it was to one of these evenings that I first went. There would be lots of social interchange over biscuits and endless cups of coffee in between artistic presentations. Usually, one person would be made responsible for the evening and would invite other members, or outsiders, to be their 'guest performers'.

Between them they would put on a genteel variety show, with singers, monologues, instrumentalists, play-readings, poets, ventriloquists, magicians or whatever other talents were available. The main thing was that it was a testing ground. Anybody who fancied having a go could get up and perform, and nobody would think any the worse if they dried in the middle of a speech or missed the top note of their recital. Like the Olympic games, the taking part was more important than achieving success.

I had gone to the club hoping to get into serious acting, but with only two or three productions a year, competition was fierce. All would-be participants had to audition before the drama committee and it was not easy to get a part. I wanted to move away from my comedy routines and it was ironic that the first thing I was asked to do at the club was my Figaro mime at one of the Tuesday evening functions. It was very well received and I got asked to do it on numerous occasions. I didn't mind and never refused as it got my face known amongst the club members. Eventually this paid off and I was offered a small part in one of the plays they were putting on.

As time went by, I became more and more integrated with the group, first by hosting a very successful Tuesday evening and eventually being elected to the Arts Club committee. I found myself devoting more and more time to its activities. One Summer, I organised an Arts Club fete which made more money for the club than any of the plays. Then when winter came, I volunteered to organise a fancy dress ball, which was held in the dance hall over Wright Brother's store in Richmond. This not only made money, but was so popular it became an annual event in Richmond.

Having enriched the club in this way, I was unhappy to see the money being spread thinly between all the activities. I wanted to see it used to build a bigger and better theatre group, but it was pointed out that both the fete and the ball had not been confined to any one discipline, although it was mainly theatre group members who had helped me with the organising and running of these events. The view was taken that if the theatre group wanted to expand, it would have to find its own funding.

I found this all rather frustrating as the drama committee tended to be rather conservative and unadventurous in their outlook. I knew that if they carried on as they had done in the past, they would be lucky to break even on their productions, let alone build up surplus funds. I tried to get the other committee members to think big.

"The tenth anniversary of the club is coming up," I told them, "Let's put on a big production that will attract big audiences paying good prices for tickets. Let's try and make some real money." But when they realised the club would have to speculate to accumulate, they once again got cold feet.

I tried to make them see sense in the economics of it but to no avail. In sheer desperation I ended up offering to underwrite the next production. This put the smiles back on their faces and they readily agreed. What had I done? Iris would kill me. I needed some insurance.

"I'll do it on one condition," I announced. "I'll cover the costs of production providing I can choose what we do, I direct it and I cast it." They thought this over for a while, but with nothing to lose they had no real objections. The challenge was on. It was a case of 'Put your money where your mouth is, Buster'.

First I had to decide what the production was to be. I had set my sights on being an actor of substance, so it would have to be a play, and there would have to be a role in it for me. But it was no use choosing something like Shakespeare; it had to be something that would appeal to a large part of the population; something popular. I had to think big.

At that time, Ronald Shiner was appearing in the West End in *Worm's Eye View* and I had read in the newspaper that the run was shortly coming to an end. That's it, I thought, no reason why we shouldn't put that on in the suburbs; the first amateur production of *Worm's Eye View*. Excitedly, I wrote to the publishers for permission. I can only suppose they were impressed by my audacity as within the week I had a positive reply.

I worked night and day to ensure success. I auditioned the players, rehearsed them, helped build the set and designed the costumes. I even went round all the local shops selling advertising space for the programme. For previous productions the audience had been given a free folded sheet as they came in, but I had in mind something much thicker with a glossy cover. I ended up making £50 profit, just on the programmes! I also went from door to door selling tickets, personally disposing of over 200. I contacted the local council and got permission to erect a large hoarding outside Richmond Town Hall advertising the show. I wrote copy for each of the local papers to ensure widespread publicity making it clear we were trying to raise funds for a new theatre and invited people to give donations in return for the best seats in the house. One or two responded very generously. I also sent free tickets to the mayor and council. This was going to be the event of the year in Twickenham or my name wasn't Buster Merryfield.

I am pleased to tell you it was a resounding success both at the box office and on stage. At the next committee meeting it was very difficult for me not to say 'I told you so', but it didn't have to be said. They all appreciated what I had done. They realised it was a landmark in the club's history and we had made a substantial sum of money towards the new theatre club. In recognition, at the next round of committee elections I was appointed Drama Director.

Needless to say, I did not rest on my laurels. There was work to be done on two fronts. Firstly we needed better premises to operate in. I approached the Oddfellows to see if we could have exclusive use of their hall and turn it into a Little Theatre. There was a lot of teeth-sucking before they agreed to let us refurbish the hall, but drew the line at giving it to us exclusively. It would still have to be made available to other organisations who relied on it, like the Spiritualists who met there every Thursday and the Saturday-morning dancing school. I assured them that we could only make the place better, which would be appreciated by all who used it. And so shortly after, with a gang of fellow enthusiasts, I set forth with hammer and chisel to rejuvenate the Oddfellows Hall. Within a few weeks we had completely redecorated it and added a substantial stage at one end.

The other thing I had to turn my attention to was the drama itself. My first action was to enter plays in the annual Thames Valley Theatre Guild Festival for one-act plays which was due to be staged in less than three months time. So when I was not hammering or sawing or painting, I was rehearsing one of the plays or learning my lines. The festival lasted for over a week, with four plays being staged each night, the best four being repeated on the final Saturday night.

I chose two plays. One was called *Festival* and would compete for the Redon Cup. This was presented for the best play put on by beginners. I invited Joan Groves from the Hampton Liberty Players to come over and produce it. The other play was called *The Man of Joy* and would compete for the Guild Cup, awarded by the Guild adjudicator for the best play. There was also a President's Cup for the most entertaining play in the festival. This was judged by a local lay panel. I also made several personal entries with other club members, in the concurrent dialogue competition.

I had first seen the play *The Man of Joy* on children's television and was taken by the deep emotions it evoked. It had been written by Rhoda Power and was based on a twelfth century French poem by Jean de Coucy. It must sound a most unlikely entry for a drama festival, but I knew that if we were to have any chance of success, we would have to put on something challenging and different to catch the adjudicator's eye. It was in four scenes, set in a French village, the monastery, the cloisters and the crypt. It told the story of an itinerant jester who makes his living going from village to village entertaining the public with tumbling and tricks. But alas, he is getting old and he can no longer perform properly or amuse the crowd. He seeks refuge in the monastery where he hopes to be of service to the monks. Once again everything goes wrong for him and in a poignant final scene he performs his tricks in front of the statue of the Virgin Mary before dying.

Having died the death many times with my cabaret act, I knew exactly the way this humble entertainer was supposed to feel and felt well able to play his part with true feelings. I wrote to the BBC seeking permission to use the play and they passed my letter on to Rhoda Power who happened to be in Canada at the time. She wrote back to say she was flattered that I wanted to do the play but it had been written for television and would be impossible to turn into a stage production. There were too many rapid transformations from one scene to another and the lighting effects would be very difficult to achieve.

But, as you should know by now, I do not take no for an answer. The more impossible the circumstances, the more I strive for my goal, and with persistence Rhoda eventually agreed that I could stage it, providing I made no changes whatsoever to the dialogue. It had to be delivered just as she wrote it. There was the challenge.

Needless to say, it was a resounding success, winning the Guild Cup. I felt I had reached the pinnacle of success in amateur dramatics in just a few short years. It is very difficult for me to describe the acclamation I received for my performance as *The Man of Joy* without appearing boastful, so I will let others speak for me. This is a sample of the press reviews that followed our success.

"RARE MOMENT AT DRAMA FESTIVAL - PLAY GRIPS AUDIENCE. Very occasionally in the professional theatre, there is a moment during the performance when a bond is created between stage and audience which is so perceptible as to be almost visible. Even more occasionally, this glorious theatrical experience can be felt at an amateur production, but almost never is it found at an amateur drama festival. Yet sometimes it is, as those who attended the first night of the Thames Valley Theatre Guild Festival at St Mary's Hall, Twickenham on Thursday will know. The last of the evening's plays was *The Man of Joy*, a strange mixture of mime and miracle by Rhoda Power based on a twelfth century medieval poem by Jean de Coucy presented by the Richmond and Twickenham Arts Club. The curtain did not go up on this production until nearly ten-thirty pm. The audience had already seen three plays and were wriggling in their seats, but *The Man of Joy* gripped all attention immediately, an attention which became more and more intense as the play progressed to the climax, a moment which brought sweat prickling to the forehead."

I still regard that night as one of my proudest moments in the theatre, and treasure that newspaper cutting to this day. Having won the Thames Valley festival, the play went on to reach the final of the All-England drama festival, which was staged at the Scala Theatre in London's West End. Unfortunately, rehearsals in the theatre were not allowed and we were only given a very short time to explain the stage directions to the Scala's backstage crew. Rhoda was right. It was difficult to stage and required very precise changes of light and sound, changes which were too complicated for the crew to follow with such inadequate instructions. However, we did not complain. I knew the rules of the competition before we entered and should have learnt the lesson of KISS - Keep It Sweet and Simple - but I didn't.

I had been doing a bit of theatrical freelance work at the

Richmond Theatre with the professionals. When I staged *Worm's Eye View* at St Mary's, I sent a ticket to Alan Miles, who was then Manager of Richmond Theatre. He was a very nice man and I got to know him socially through various theatrical events.

Equity rules are quite strict but did allow him to return the favour and include me as the 'occasional amateur' in his productions when suitable professionals were not available. I found myself playing with Leslie Crowther in *Arsenic and Old Lace* and then in *The Same Sky* written by Yvonne Mitchell. Leslie and I hit it off well and he actually came and did a cabaret turn for me in one of my shows. I was also lucky enough to get a part at the Richmond Theatre in *Storm in Port* which starred Jack Howarth, who played Albert Tatlock of *Coronation Street* but is alas now dead.

Despite the fulfilment I got through my success as a serious actor, the comedian in me still refused to lie down. I was regularly asked to fill in at Arts Club Tuesday evenings either as a stand-up comic or doing my Figaro mime. On one occasion the evening's organiser approached me and asked if she could join in the mime act. How could I refuse? She was a charming twenty-year-old called Patricia May, generally shortened to Ricia. Her father was one of the club's stalwarts. He was a very talented pianist who accompanied all the Tuesday night acts, playing anything from honky-tonk to the classics as required.

Ricia wanted to mime a duet with me based on Fred Astaire and Ginger Rogers' version of, *We're a Couple of Swells*. We rehearsed this and on the night it went down very well. True to the original, we dressed up as tramps and incorporated dance routines in with the miming. Following this success, we developed other similar routines. One I particularly remember was *Lovely Maid in the Moonlight* from the opera, La Bohème, which we eventually performed for the local operatic society.

Another was *Go to Sleep* which Bob Hope originally sang in a film with Doris Day, or somebody like her. For this we occupied twin beds, each popping up when it was their turn to sing. It would have had better visual impact if we could have been in the same bed fighting over the bed clothes and sticking feet out, but in those days the Lord Chancellor's Office laid down a very strict code of conduct forbidding male and female appearing on stage in the same bed together. Which brings me to the point of this story.

For a long time I had nursed a secret ambition to audition as a comedian for the Windmill Theatre in the West End. For the few of you who might not have heard of it, the Windmill was a small theatre which specialised in saucy, risqué acts. Its shows were made up of comic sketches featuring scantily-clad girls and tableaus in which the girls posed nude, but to comply with the Lord Chancellor's censorship the nudes were not allowed to move. In between the sketches and tableaus, comedians tried to entertain the nearly all-male audience whilst the stage sets were being changed. It was a tough school as most of the audience was not there to hear jokes and gave the comics a hard time. Many a promising career was cut short on that stage but a few became big names in the comedy world. Jimmy Edwards and Michael Bentine were just two of those who made good and I wanted to try my hand.

You may remember that on my way back from India on the hospital ship, I had made friends with Major Angel who had connections with the Windmill through his wife's family. Taking advantage of this tenuous link, I wrote to Vivian Van Damm asking for an audition and mentioning my previous connection with Major Angel. Once again my audacity paid off and I got a reply saying they were holding an audition session for comedians the next month and I would be welcome to come along.

My main objective was to show them my solo comedy routine, but to hedge my bets I decided to take Ricia May with me and offer our double miming act as an alternative. I considered our 'in bed' act would be the most appropriate and so I borrowed two collapsible camp beds to take with us. On arrival we were shown where to get changed. A narrow, metal, circular staircase descended from the side of the stage to a large area underneath. It was here that Ricia and I had to change into our costumes, together with all the other hopefuls.

It was quite an education to see the attire of the opposition. Most had realised that it was not enough to stand on stage and crack jokes, their act also had to be visual. There were one or two in full evening dress, but mostly, like me, they were in loud check suits or dressed as tramps. One character had really gone over the top. We watched in amazement as he shed all his clothes until he was stood in just a small loincloth. He then covered his entire body with dark brown make-up, getting a cooperative rival to blacken the parts he couldn't reach. When he was satisfied, he donned large black boots, a white silk scarf and a top hat. We were in stitches just watching him get ready and he certainly helped to break the dressing-room tension.

On arrival we had all given our names to a continuity girl who eventually came to the top of the stairs and called down for the first act. I had made her aware of the double act and it was agreed that Ricia should standby in case they agreed to see both acts, but it couldn't be guaranteed. There were a dozen or more acts all together and I think I was about number seven. I anticipated it would be some time before I was called.

Much to our surprise, the first contestant was back down the stairs within seconds and the two acts which followed lasted very little longer. They told us that there were only three people out front, Vivian Van Dam, his sister and the stage manager. The unfortunate comedians had not been allowed to complete more than one joke apiece before the continuity girl had dismissed them with a curt "Thank you" following a nod from Vivian Van Damm. Their news did little to boost morale below stairs.

Eventually it was the turn of the character in the loincloth and scarf, who was on immediately before me. I followed him up the staircase intending to watch his act. At the same time I hoped to acclimatise a little so that I would not come up blinking in the light like a Christian martyr meeting the lions. It was just as well I was prepared. The call of "Thank you" came before Loincloth had time to reach centre-stage. He was so stunned he didn't know what to do and just stood there with his mouth opening and closing, searching for a suitable response. Before he had time to gather his thoughts, there was another, louder, "Thank you. Thank you for coming."

Disconsolately, he trudged past me with his head down as he disappeared down the iron staircase. I was on.

In the Army we had been taught that surprise is one of the key elements in battle, so without waiting to be called, I breezed out from the wings and went straight into my patter.

"I saw a pal of mine in the pub the other day. 'You don't look well' I said. 'No, I've just been to the doctor's. He says I've got yaws.' 'Yaws? What's yaws?' 'That's very kind of you, I'll have a pint.'" I paused in anticipation of the dreaded "Thank you", but much to my surprise it didn't come. I pressed on with my next throw-away gag and was allowed to continue in this vein for nearly a minute, establishing the survival record so far for that audition session.

When they did eventually call a halt, I was asked about my other act. Excitedly I explained the gist of it and was allowed to bring Ricia and the beds on to the stage. I had already passed the gramophone record to the sound engineer and after a quick signal the music started. Like all the other acts, we were cut short well before the finish, but after a quick consultation between the big three, the continuity girl asked us to report to the office when we had got changed.

You can imagine how excited I felt as we went off stage. None of the other acts had been singled out in this way and I got changed out of my costume in record time. It was all a bit silly really as I knew that whatever they were about to offer I was not in a position to accept, having faithfully promised Iris I would stick with the security of the bank. But even so, it would satisfy the ego and be the ultimate in one-upmanship to be able to say in the future, "Yes, I had an offer from the Windmill, but I turned it down." The reality didn't quite live up to the dream. Yes, they liked both acts but I hadn't done anything that couldn't be done equally well by somebody who was already a member of the cast. Thank you very much for coming, Mr Merryfield.

Chapter 21

The Characters

The Arts Club theatre group went from success to success and two or three years after *The Man of Joy*, we scooped both the Guild and President's Cups at the Thames Valley Festival with *The Bespoke Overcoat*, a one-act play. I was producer and also played one of the lead characters. Unfortunately, the group's success was also the start of its downfall. We began to attract leading players from neighbouring drama groups who were anxious to join a successful enterprise. The trickle became a flood and within a few years the group doubled in size. This was not a problem, but the actors were soon followed by the organisers and producers from the other clubs and before long we had too many people wanting to run the club and direct its policy.

In fairness to the long-serving members, I proposed that nobody should serve on the committee until he or she had been a member of the club for at least two years. Unfortunately, there was already a sizable presence of new people on the committee and my proposal was defeated. Worse was to come. At the next committee elections, most of the old faithfuls were voted out of office. As a gesture of loyalty to them, I felt obliged to step down as Drama Director and I resigned not only from the committee, but also from the club itself.

I suppose at the time I was a bit put out because I saw the new people as usurpers. Over the years I had gradually increased my influence until unwittingly I had become the kingpin of the drama group and it hurt to see my loyal supporters dismissed from office. Having built the club up, I had come to regard it as mine rather than the democratic organisation it actually was. On reflection, there were probably others there who felt just the same way when I displaced them following my success with *Worm's Eye View*. Such is the way of politics and amateur dramatics. I think everybody realised how I felt and there was no ill feeling. On my retirement the new committee voted me life-membership which I was happy to accept.

Although I had resigned from the club, I had no intention of giving up drama. I had some posters made and stuck them up all over Richmond and Twickenham advertising a new drama group called 'The Characters'. I made it quite clear that I only wanted dedicated people who were prepared to work hard to make the new group a success. I had a considerable number of responses, but before I would accept anybody, I interviewed them to ensure they were the kind of people I wanted. In the main I was looking for behind-the-scenes workers. Generally I have found there are plenty of people seeking glory on the stage, but very few who are prepared to make their effort out of the limelight. In all, I selected about twenty, including many of the old stalwarts from the Richmond and Twickenham Arts Club I had just left.

Having set up the group, my first responsibility was to enter three plays in the next Thames Valley Drama Festival which was only six weeks away. The main play was to be *Happiness my Goal* which was entered for the Guild Cup. In the section for new plays, we entered *The White Dove*, written by one of the club members, Cecil Gillard. Cecil later turned professional under the stage name Paul Gillard. Our third entry was *Dark Brown* in the section for beginners.

We had no permanent premises where we could meet as a club but Mrs Vee Sanders, the club secretary, let us use her house for planning meetings. We needed a bit more space for rehearsals and hired a room at the Bricklayers Arms in Richmond. All went well and at the festival, all three of our plays made it to the final night, a feat never before achieved. We came away with the Guild Cup as well as the Redon Cup for beginners and the award for the best new play. As the headlines in the local papers proclaimed next day, "New company triumphs at play festival" and "New group wins three trophies at Guild festival."

Flushed with success on the stage, we now had to turn our thoughts to commercial survival. We needed money to finance future productions, to pay for sets and costumes, to hire regular premises and even to build our own theatre. I had still not dismissed my dream of building a Little Theatre. I charged each member a three guinea joining fee as a mark of their sincerity and dedication, which in 1960 was a lot of money. But with only twenty or so members that wouldn't go far and I didn't think I could call on them for any more. What was needed was one big profitable venture to put us on our feet.

I spent many sleepless nights thinking over how I should go about it. At the old Arts Club I had made money with a West End production, *Worm's Eye View*. Now I needed something similar, only different. I prayed for inspiration and called on my inner strength - through Christ - I can. Eventually my prayers were answered and shortly after, the local paper carried the headline, "Characters will attempt musical *Expresso Bongo*." This would be an extremely ambitious production needing over seventy people to put it on counting cast, orchestra and production crew. We were a company of just twenty.

I managed to contact some of those who had initially been unsuccessful with their application for membership of the Characters, and managed eventually to get a full cast and crew. For music, I went to St Mary's College at Strawberry Hill where they had a thriving amateur orchestra who were only too pleased to help out. I knew there would be a lot of public interest and that with the right publicity we should be able to pull in large audiences if the venue could hold them. I managed to book York House, which was Twickenham Town Hall, and we played to a very full house night after night.

Once again the local papers went to town with, "Buster's Bongo" and "Buster works a miracle." They were right of course. After only seven months, the future of 'The Characters' was assured. We made enough profit to rent a studio where we could store the sets and the other stage equipment we had accumulated. We also banked enough money to cover the expenses of our next production. But what should it be? Having had such a resounding success with *Expresso Bongo* my thoughts naturally turned to other West End musicals and I contacted the agent of the International Copyright Bureau, Doctor Czech, seeking permission to stage *The Threepenny Opera*. Unfortunately this was not granted as it was considered we were too near to the West End theatre where it was still running.

In talking to Doctor Czech, I explained we were looking for something challenging and unusual. She came back to me a few days later claiming to have the very thing. It was a new play, written for the Edinburgh Festival where it had its one and only showing. It was called *The World - My Canvas* and told the life story of the artist, Vincent Van Gogh, in forty-four scenes. She told me it was considered an extremely difficult play to stage. At one time, Rod Steiger, the American actor had considered putting it on in London but had rejected it as too difficult, although much later a film based on Vincent's life was made, called *Lust for Life* and starring Kirk Douglas. Once again the challenge was on. I would play Vincent.

I got very excited waiting for the script of the play to arrive. In the meantime I went to the local library and got out a book called *Portrait of Vincent*. This gave me lots of background information and enabled me to start getting the feel of the character. When the script came and I had time to read it through, I was more than ever convinced that this was the play I wanted to put on. There was a note with the script stating I needed the express permission of the author, Ruth Dixon, before it could be staged. Permission would only be granted if she considered the production could do the play full justice.

There was a London address to write to, but I considered I would stand more chance of acceptance if I could meet Ruth Dixon face to face. I looked her up in the telephone directory and confirmed that the address given was her home. That evening I made my way to her house in Acton through wind and rain and boldly rang her door bell. My ring was answered by a tall, distinguished man who regarded me rather frostily, but when I explained my mission I was invited into the lounge to meet Ruth.

I expected to find a young woman, full of the same vitality that burst from her script and was somewhat surprised to see a small, rather frail, grey-haired lady. She welcomed me in and was quite pleased to think that somebody wanted to stage her play. I gathered she had been somewhat disappointed in that after the initial acclaim, it had been put on one side as all very nice but impossible to perform. In addition to the difficulty of staging forty-four scenes with numerous set changes, there was also the question of endurance of the cast and audience as the full play would take over four hours to perform - plus time for very necessary intervals.

She asked if I had read Vincent's letters to his brother, Theo. I had to confess my ignorance and she proceeded to enlighten me. The two brothers were very close and kept up a lifelong correspondence. Ruth had been taken with the sheer eloquence of Vincent's letters and had written the play around them. She considered him 'an artist in words as well as paint' and most of the play consisted of Vincent reciting the contents of the letters. She had written additional linking material.

As the evening wore on she became increasingly enthusiastic and her enthusiasm rubbed off on me. It was gone eleven o'clock before I left, and as I walked home I felt as if I had been in close communion with the artist himself, such was the depth of her emotion and feeling towards his genius. I longed to be like him, to have that same intensity of purpose that tolerated physical deprivation for the sake of his art.

By the time I arrived home I was so fired with his spirit I had to experience his lifestyle. Iris was already in bed. I knew if I joined her it would break the spell I was under. Without ado, I picked up a blanket and made my way to the garden shed. Clearing a space on the floor, I wrapped the blanket around me and settled down for the night in my imaginary French garret.

Unfortunately, the weather in Hounslow that night was rather more inclement than in Arles and to add to my misery the shed roof was not entirely waterproof. The constant dripping of cold rainwater on to one's back rapidly saps one's resolution and at three in the morning I had to admit defeat and retreat indoors. However, I did not acquiesce completely and spent the rest of the night on the lounge floor, which was where Iris found me the next morning.

I was determined that I would get as close to Vincent's character as possible and realised I would have to learn to paint in his style. I should add that although I had been good at drawing at Sinjuns, I had no idea how to paint in any style. I began to wish I had followed up the offer from William Russell-Flint. At least I would have known what the inside of an artist's studio looked like. I talked of my dilemma to my colleagues at the bank and one of them commented that he often came in on the train with a professional artist and promised to have a word with him to see if he would help.

He was as good as his word and I was invited to visit this artist for basic lessons. In the time available, he could do no more than teach me the rudiments of mixing paints and how to hold a brush in a convincing manner. I quickly mastered this and at least I had had a good look around his studio. I realised that to make the set look convincing, I would need lots of half-finished and completed paintings filling the stage. I bought myself a palette, brushes and tubes of paint and started to copy one of Vincent's pictures. It was his famous portrait of Doctor Gachet which Ruth Dixon had lent me as her contribution to the set. I was of course copying a copy, not the original.

To my surprise I found I was quite good at painting and became totally absorbed in my task. It further helped me to get into the character of Vincent and I felt that his spirit guided me as I wielded the brushes over the canvas. There was just one problem. At the rate I was going, it would take at least a month to complete each picture. I gave this dilemma some thought and then paid a visit to the local technical college. I explained my predicament to the Art Master and he was more than willing for his pupils to mass produce the paintings I needed. Close to, their results were rather crude but from the distance they would be viewed in the play, they looked like the real thing.

This also gave me a good idea for further publicity for the play. I wrote to all the schools in the area advising them that we were putting a play on telling the story of the life of Vincent Van Gogh and inviting them to enter their pupils in a free painting competition. The idea was that all the paintings would be exhibited in York House during the period the play was on and I hoped that proud parents would buy tickets for the play so that they could come and see the paintings. The idea worked well and I even managed to get Tony Hart from the children's television programme *Vision On* to come and award the prizes on the final night.

The difficulty of staging such an elaborate play as *The World - My Canvas* became apparent when we came to final rehearsals. We were only given limited access to York House in which to test out sets and lighting and the dress rehearsal on the eve of production became a marathon affair. It was a succession of stops and starts to accommodate unforeseen difficulties, resulting in cast and crew working on into the early hours. I was almost asleep as I walked back home, London Transport having long since shut for the night.

Next day, after only a few hours sleep, I was back at York House seeing to the final preparations. As well as ensuring the stage crew had everything in hand, there were front-of-house matters to be arranged; usheréttes, programme sellers, box office staff and refreshment organisers. On top of all that, the painting exhibition had to be set up in an adjoining room. I was kept extremely busy all day.

Like many of the others, I had taken the day off work. Those that were unable to do the same, agreed to arrive as soon as they could, after a swift trip home to get changed and grab a quick bite. Fortunately, the Stage Manager was able to be there all day, but about a quarter-to-six he came to me saying he was rather worried, as our sound engineer had not yet arrived. He estimated it would take well over an hour to get everything set up, tested and sound levels checked, which was cutting things fine for a performance at seven-thirty.

As we became increasingly concerned, we telephoned his house. At first we could get no reply but eventually spoke to his wife who assured us he had left at five-thirty, albeit in rather a hurry. Like us, she hoped he had not met with an accident. He only lived two miles away and therefore should have arrived long ago. Our next move was to call the police but they had no news of any accidents in the area. By six-thirty we had members of the stage crew cruising the streets looking for him, but to no avail. By seven o'clock we were alternating between panic and despair. There was no way we could stage the production without him. He was the only one who knew the intricate sound requirements and furthermore, he had all the sound equipment with him in the back of his car. By now the first of the audience were arriving, which would make sound level testing extremely difficult, even if he turned up now.

By seven-fifteen it was apparent that the play would not start on time. Like the rest of the cast, I was in full costume and make-up, but I had to come out and make an announcement explaining our difficulties. I invited people to tour the painting exhibition and hurriedly opened the buffet so that they could while away a little time supping tea. I knew that the start could not be delayed for very long as it was a very lengthy play.

At seven-thirty I was forced to abandon the performance. Although it was not my fault, I found this extremely embarrassing as the audience included many of my friends and relatives as well as the author Ruth Dixon, the mayor and other local dignitaries. Everybody was given the option of free tickets for another night or their money back. Much to their credit, only five people elected for a refund and then only because they couldn't make it on another night.

Soon after, we got a phone call from one of the patrolling stage crew telling us that the sound engineer had been found. Apparently, whilst driving to the theatre, he thought that his delicate sound equipment was sliding about in the boot and had stopped to reposition it. Having opened the boot, it was not clear if he collapsed and hit his head on the way down, or whether the boot lid fell on to his head and caused him to collapse. Whichever way it happened, he had been found by a passer-by unconscious in the gutter beside his car. Help had been summoned and he had been taken into a nearby house and a doctor called. On regaining consciousness, he had forgotten completely where he was going. Naturally the press had a field day, with the headline, "Real Life Drama Stops Play". Fortunately, he made a rapid recovery and we were able to continue with the production for the rest of the week.

The ultimate success of the play depends on one's viewpoint. It was strong meat, not intended for the general play-going public. Some of the reviews in the popular press criticised it for 'being too long and having too many words in it'. Had they but known, I had shortened Ruth's original script by at least an hour. Personally, I was extremely satisfied with my performance. There were some very long soliloquies I had to learn and I was on stage for most of the three hours. I also considered my innovations in the production had worked well. As with *The Man of Joy*, I had to convey a lot of atmosphere with the sets, lighting and sound. I hung a huge gauze net right across the front of the stage which gave everything behind it a soft focus. The climax came in the final scene, set in Theo's flat, when Theo hears that Vincent has committed suicide. It started with low lights and music that gradually faded away into sounds of birdsong and a tinkling stream as the light slowly strengthened to full power as if heralding dawn. This, coupled with the effect of the gauze, gave a magical effect that even the severest critics acknowledged.

I was not put off by the criticism, confident that it was a good play, well-produced and well-acted. Such was my confidence that a year or so later I entered it for an open competition for full-length plays which was held at the Ashcroft Theatre in Croydon. At the same time, I put it forward for consideration for the Greater London Festival of Drama. This festival was not a competition as such. Plays that were entered were visited by one or more members of a panel who then selected six of the plays to be put on as representing the best in London amateur theatre. Competition was keen and it was a great honour to be selected. Imagine my delight when we won first prize at the Ashcroft and were also chosen as one of the six out of forty-two entries for the Greater London Festival of Drama.

Ruth Dixon was there and was enthralled with the production. She came to see me backstage after the performance, threw out her arms and said, "Buster, the play is yours. I give it to you." I don't know if she was serious, but I suspect that I have in my cupboard the only copies of the script still in existence. If anybody out there wants the challenge of re-staging it, I would be willing to give them all the help and advice I could. They would need it.

If further proof were needed of the play's success, I later entered one act in the 1968 Woking Drama Festival and won first prize and best-actor award. My convictions and belief in its merit had been fully justified and I hadn't even had to chop an ear off in the process.

Chapter 22

Margaret

In between the serious drama and the musicals, I was still doing my cabaret act, sometimes at evening functions but mostly for charity. I teamed up with one or two other performers to form a small concert party, so that if any of us were called upon for a function, we could recommend the others to make up the rest of the evening's entertainment. On one occasion I had a telephone call from the governor of Feltham Institution for Young Offenders asking if I could bring some entertainers for a Christmas party. He explained that within the institution he had created the Compass Club, with membership being earned by good behaviour. In return, members gained certain privileges, including attendance at the Christmas party.

I contacted my fellow artistes and managed to put together a programme that would include a male and a female singer, an accordionist, a ventriloquist and myself as compere and comedian. The governor also asked if I would bring my family to the party as he wanted the boys to mix socially with everyday people as part of their rehabilitation process. I put it to Iris and she agreed that she and Karen, who was now a young teenager, would come along.

When we arrived we were shown into the main hall where there was a row of trestle tables set out down the middle of the room, ready for the Christmas tea. The food was fairly frugal consisting mainly of piles of sandwiches and jugs of orange squash, but I think the sense of occasion and the privilege of being there meant more to the boys than the actual food itself. Those not in the club were allowed to attend, but only to wait at table. I supposed that was so that they would see what they were missing and would behave themselves in the future.

At one end of the room there was a small stage and to the side of it, a grand piano. On it, I was surprised to see a large framed photograph of Margaret Rutherford. I asked the Governor why it was there.

"Oh," he explained, "Margaret is our benefactor and Honorary President of the Compass Club. She's coming to the party this afternoon. She should be here any minute." He went on to explain that all the paintings which hung around the walls of the clubroom had been given by Margaret, one every Christmas. No doubt she would be bringing another one with her today.

Whilst we were still admiring the paintings, Margaret made her entrance. There is no other way to describe her arrival, such was her presence. To my surprise, she was not alone. With her were her husband, Stringer Davis, an actor in his own right, who always played a cameo part in her films, Odette Churchill of French resistance fame and Group Captain Peter Townsend, the man who didn't marry Princess Margaret. I felt really honoured to think I would be providing the entertainment for such distinguished guests.

After the meal Margaret stood up and addressed the boys, impressing on them the chance they were being given to start a new and useful life, free of crime. She was a very Christian lady and ended up reciting a religious poem which I found very moving. After that she announced she was not providing the usual painting this year. Instead, she was giving them a souvenir of her recent trip to America. With that she produced signed photographs of Commander Glenn and Neil Armstrong, the American astronauts.

Once the formalities were over, the tables were quickly sided and the chairs arranged in rows ready for the entertainment. I opened proceedings with a comedy patter and after all the acts had done their turn, finished the show with my 'Figaro' mime. It was all very well received and after the show, the governor gave a formal vote of thanks before we retired to our changing room.

But the surprises were not yet over. A few minutes later, there was a knock on the door and in came Margaret and her party. Her thanks were so profuse it was embarrassing and she even went so far as to say she had enjoyed it so much she would like to see it all again. I didn't know if she was being serious or just polite. However, she insisted that I 'gave her my card' as she put it, and after a lot of rummaging in the pockets of my stage suit, I found an old card I had had printed back in the early days at Braunton. It was very dog-eared and I had to cross out 'Lieutenant' and add my telephone number, but she seemed happy enough with it.

I thought no more of it until I returned home from work a few days later to be told by Iris that Margaret had phoned and would be ringing back that evening. I was getting quite excited by the time she rang and it was as much as I could do to concentrate on what she was saying. She wondered if I would be, 'prepared to do it again for her'. She was currently starring in *School for Scandal* at the Haymarket Theatre and wanted to throw a party to mark the one hundredth performance. Could I be at the stage door at half-past-ten next Saturday night?

I assured her it would be no bother at all. Yes, I knew where it was. Yes, I would be there. It wasn't until I had put the phone down that I realised I wasn't quite sure what it was she wanted - just me, or the whole concert party? I hadn't got a phone number to ring back on and in any case I didn't want to appear a Charlie by admitting I hadn't properly listened to her message. In the end I decided to play safe and take Fred, the accordionist, with me. He was a semi-professional and I had to do some fast talking to persuade him to come, as the other thing I hadn't sorted out with Margaret was whether or not we were getting paid. I suspected she might expect the performance for free. However, I explained to Fred that it would be jolly good publicity as he could truthfully add, 'As performed in the West End', to his handbills and visiting cards.

So, at half-past-ten the following Saturday we entered the stage door of the Haymarket. We could hear Margaret's sonorous voice resounding from the stage where the play was still going on. The stage-door keeper was expecting me but wasn't sure why Fred was there. It seemed Margaret had meant just me. After a bit of explaining and persuasion the doorman agreed to look after Fred and directed me to Margaret's dressing room where I was met by her dresser. Within minutes the curtain came down to tumultuous applause and Margaret swept into the dressing room which was positioned immediately off the side of the stage.

She greeted me as though we had been lifelong friends. I was a little overawed but she was completely relaxed and treated me as an equal, one performer to another. Her husband, Stringer, who never strayed far from her side, joined us and shortly after took me out on to the stage. The audience had all departed and the main curtain had been raised again. The house lights were all on and stage hands were busy clearing the stage ready for the party.

"I don't know what you want for your act, Buster," he said, "but if there is anything we can do to help, just say." I looked round at the set which was being dismantled and taken away.

"If you could leave me that central staircase it would help," I replied, "and have you any bunting anywhere?" Bunting was duly found and I had it wound all round the staircase. I also arranged to have several coloured spots trained on it. I envisaged making a big entrance from the top of those stairs. After that there wasn't much else I could do until the party started. The stage hands positioned one of the armchairs in the wings for me and I relaxed in it, watching them at work. Once they had cleared the stage, they put out occasional tables and chairs and set a couple of beer barrels up at the back.

I was still sat there when the first of the actors came on stage and made his way down to the footlights, where canapes and vol-au-vents had been arranged on a series of trolleys. After a quick look round, he helped himself to a handful of bits and pieces before turning and spotting me sat in the shadows. He gave a start.

"I do hope I'm not jumping the gun," he said guiltily, "Are you in charge?" I explained I was Buster Merryfield and that I was there to provide the entertainment.

"How rude of me," he continued, "Let me introduce myself. I'm Ralph Richardson." He was just the first of a multitude of stars I was to meet that night. Not only was the cast of *School for Scandal* there, but also some of the cast of *My Fair Lady* which was playing at the theatre opposite.

The stage gradually filled up with a Who's Who of show business. Finally, Margaret made her entrance dressed in a long clinging chocolate-brown silk dress. The crowd parted in reverence as the star and host made her way slowly across. As she came she looked about her. Finally she exclaimed, "Ah, Buster, there you are," and with that made a bee-line straight towards me and sat beside me holding my hand. I felt honoured and proud to be fussed over by her but at the same time uncomfortable to be singled out in this way. I could see people looking at each other with enquiring glances as if to ask who on earth I was. As each came across to congratulate her on her performance she insisted on introducing me to them.

"This is Buster Merryfield who is going to entertain us," she said to Sir John Gielgud, "He's a very fine actor you know." One after the other they came, Anna Massey and her brother Daniel, Laurence Naismith and Binky Beaumont, the impresario. I was overwhelmed by the wealth of acting talent present. At the same time I was getting a little worried and didn't fully share Margaret's confidence in my ability to entertain such distinguished stage performers.

When she introduced me to the Stage Director I was amazed to find I already knew him. He was Tony Chardet who used to be my boxing second when I was at Sinjuns. I found this quite reassuring. If he could be on familiar terms with the stars then there was no reason why I couldn't do the same. The evening continued in this vein for an hour or so, during which time I was asked if I would like to go with the company to the United States where they would shortly be touring with *School for Scandal*. I don't know if the offer was made seriously or not but I had to turn it down anyway, being fully committed to the bank at that time. Who knows what might have been if I had had the courage to accept?

It was going up towards midnight before I was asked to start my act. Nervously I made my way in the half-light behind the backdrop and up to the top of the staircase. With a flourish from Fred's accordion to announce my presence, the spots were lit and I was on.

"Good evening ladies and gentlemen. I am very pleased to see you all here tonight." (Pause) " I hate being here by myself." (Pause for laughter) And laugh they did. I have never played to such an appreciative and helpful audience. Maybe it was because as show business people they knew how difficult being on stage can be, but I could feel them willing me to do well and with each laugh or cheer my confidence grew. I am completely tee-total, but at the end of that performance I was drunk with euphoria.

I was heartily congratulated as I descended back to stage-level leaving the staircase to Fred and his accordion. He played a selection of popular tunes and before long everybody was dancing on the stage. I was dancing with Anna Massey when Fred broke into the Twist. As you are aware, I do have a slight tendency to show off at times and this was one of those times. Following my successful performance I was high on adrenalin and really went to town. I think Margaret looked on me as her's for the evening as before long she came over and excused Anna and took her place. In no time, the rest of the dancers gave way, forming a clapping circle around us as we writhed backwards and forwards. Although she must have been well over sixty years old, she was extremely fit and matched me twist for twist.

The evening celebrations went on until the early hours with me acting as MC for the proceedings. When it was all over Margaret insisted I stayed with her and Stringer whilst she said goodbye to all her guests. When we were finally alone, she turned and thanked me for the evening and I could see that she had genuinely enjoyed it.

"I'm pleased we danced the Twist like that Buster," she said, "I haven't felt so young in years. Probably regret it in the morning. Tell me, how much do we owe you?" I protested that money didn't enter into it where friends were concerned and that I had enjoyed the evening as much as she had. If the truth were told, I had probably got more out of it than she had and would gladly have paid to do it all again. She continued to insist and I could see that she would feel better if I accepted something. I finally agreed that Fred should be paid five pounds for his efforts, whereupon she insisted that Stringer write him a cheque for twice the amount.

I was well satisfied with our night's work and delighted when Margaret rang up the following day to thank me all over again. She said she was feeling most unhappy because I had refused any payment for myself and would I make her feel better by bringing Iris and Karen up to the Haymarket to meet her? I agreed that we would go the following Saturday afternoon. We arrived soon after lunch as arranged and were shown to the dressing room where Margaret was busy preparing for the matinee performance. She chatted with us for a while before handing us tickets for the best seats in the house.

"Right," she said, "off you go and see the play and when it's over I want you to come back here for tea." We sat enthralled by her performance and as instructed returned to the dressing room for tea between the shows. She had been most thoughtful and invited other guests to keep us company. Whilst I chatted to Margaret about the theatre, Iris conversed with a very nice lady friend of Margaret who was a governess, while Karen was entertained by her ward, a swarthy youth who introduced himself as Prince Manouk of Egypt.

I don't know why Margaret and I hit it off the way we did, but we did. After this third meeting we used to write to each other regularly and we occasionally met in Chalfont St Giles where she lived. I was deeply saddened when she was taken ill and had to go into hospital. Knowing how much she liked poetry, I sat and wrote her a poem and included it with my next letter. It was Stringer who replied, stating that Margaret was too weak for letter writing, but she did insist on adding a PS to say how much she enjoyed the poem. She died a few days later and Stringer joined her soon after. I had lost two very dear friends.

Chapter 23

Byfleet

Most people found the sixties an enjoyable era. In 1963, as I approached my forty-third birthday, I could not have been happier. I had a lovely wife and a beautiful daughter coming up to her sixteenth birthday. With my assistance the health of the Twickenham branch of the bank, where I was Branch Accountant, had been restored. I was fully on top of my job and able to devote much of my free time to 'The Characters' who were going from strength to strength. It was at this stage that I got itchy feet and wanted to move to the country. I had nothing against Hounslow, which in social status was very up-market compared with dear old Battersea where I had been brought up, but I felt a need to get out of the bustle of the city and live where the pace of life was a little slower. Perhaps it was the onset of middle age although I wouldn't have acknowledged it at the time.

At weekends, I would drive Iris and Karen out into the Surrey commuter villages looking for our ideal home. One Sunday we spotted a delightful bungalow in Byfleet with a 'For Sale' sign out front. I made enquiries at the estate agents and was delighted to find it was within our price range. I had very little trouble selling our Hounslow house as it was in a popular area, being handy for Heathrow, yet not so close as to be threatened by aircraft noise. It was also very commutable for those working in the city. And so just before Christmas we moved to 'Two Oaks' at Byfleet.

As with any house-move, it took us a little time to settle in, but by the summer of 1964 I had sorted out the garden and once more had time on my hands. At Hounslow, I had led a very full life and I was now missing my theatre connections. It was time for me to become active again. There was already a small local amateur company called 'The Byfleet Players'. I established who their chief motivator was and one summer's evening I paid him a visit.

"Good evening. I'm Buster Merryfield," I said, as he greeted me at the door, "I've come to talk to you about amateur dramatics in Byfleet."

"Come on in," he replied with a smile, "I'm sure the Players will be delighted to welcome you as a member." It took some little time for me to explain that I had not come round to become a member of the Byfleet Players, quite the opposite.

"I've come because I thought it only courteous to let you know I intend setting up an alternative theatre group in the village." He was quite stunned to hear this but I explained to him that I felt it would be impossible for me to effectively start again at the bottom of amateur dramatics as a new boy in his company when I had been used to having my own company to run.

Having listened patiently to my reasoning, he fully understood my feelings and to some extent agreed with them. We exchanged pleasantries and idle chat about the theatre for an hour or so and parted on the best of terms. However, he warned that he doubted whether there were enough people in the village interested in drama to form two companies and he didn't think I would be able to raise enough support for a new company. What he didn't know was that many of 'The Players' from Twickenham and Richmond were missing their theatre as much as I was and had expressed a willingness to travel out to Byfleet in order to keep the company going.

For our first production I chose *The Miracle Worker* which tells the heart-rending tale of Helen Keller, who was born deaf and blind. I was determined to get the right personality for the part of the girl, Helen. I didn't want a child from drama school who might have preconceived ideas, or even worse, an ambitious mother. I searched for someone outside theatre who looked right that I could train into the part. Eventually I was told of an eleven-year-old girl in the village called Alexia Worley. I went round one evening and explained the purpose of my visit to her mother. She was thrilled. As we were talking, Alexia came to the top of the stairs dressed in a full-length white nightgown, her long dark hair cascading around her shoulders. I knew then that she was what I was looking for.

Alexia not only agreed to play the part, but also adopted Iris and I as aunt and uncle. She would come to the house for drama instruction and stay for meals, helping Iris with the washing up afterwards. She learned her part well, hanging on to my every word. It was a difficult role, as being deaf and dumb, there were no words to learn. It was all done by movement and expression. Three weeks before the production was due to go on, she was taken into hospital with appendicitis, but like a seasoned trouper, she recovered in time for the opening night and was a resounding success as Helen.

However, the warning I had been given about lack of support for theatre in the Byfleet area was correct. On our first night, only

50 of the 200 seats were filled. But those that did come were overawed. To quote the local press, "Those 50 were shattered by the performance. Byfleet residents had never known such polished drama."

As the curtain came down on the final scene, I went forward and thanked the valiant few for their support but told them in no uncertain terms that they had to go out the next day and badger their friends to come and see the play as the company couldn't exist on such small audiences. The next night we had 120 and on the third and final night there was a full house. Every one of the 200 seats were filled. Even so, I had lost all the money I had personally put up to finance the play, and with a new mortgage it was money I couldn't afford to lose. On the final night I had no option but to go out front again and tell the audience that with regret, they had just seen the first and last production by 'The Characters' in Byfleet.

I returned to the dressing room a saddened man and removed my make-up as quickly as I could. I did not intend hanging around to conduct a post-mortem. However, before I had time to leave, the front-of-house manager came through carrying a trilby hat upside-down in front of him. Without a word he tipped the hat over on to the table in front of me, showering down a tinkling pile of copper and silver. The audience had been so moved by the play and the worthiness of what we were trying to do as a theatre group, that they had held a collection on the way out. There was over ten pounds there but that still left me forty pounds out-of-pocket. Later in the week, this unusual gesture was reported in the press and resulted a number of others writing in wishing us future success and demonstrating their support in the form of a cheque. We even got a favourable mention by the local vicar during his service the following Sunday, but he stopped short of sending us the collection.

I now had a difficult decision to make. Having whetted a few appetites, I would have liked to press straight on with another play, but it was the end of the winter season. Plays put on in mid-summer can be quite risky financially. I sent out a letter to all the members of 'The Characters' inviting them to a meeting to discuss the future of the company. I pulled no punches and told them not to forget to bring their cheque books. I wanted to ensure they were as committed as I was. I had a very positive response and the meeting decided we should first devote some time to fund-raising and wait until the autumn before putting on another production.

To raise funds, we put on a night club evening with 'bunny'

waitresses, all-star cabaret, non-stop films and a 'Miss Byfleet' competition. By nine o'clock we had to close the doors of the village hall which was full to bursting point. The event was a resounding success. Throughout the summer, we ran various jumble sales and other small functions to boost finances ready for the forthcoming theatre season. When autumn came, the new season was launched with a swing. Film evenings and outings were held and we laid plans for a dance, annual dinner and pantomime trip.

For our first theatrical production I chose John Osborne's play, *The Entertainer*. Looking back this was a mistake. The play had been made into a film with Sir Lawrence Olivier playing the lead part of Archie Rice. The plot tells the tale of a failing comedian who is forced to play in seedier and seedier venues as his act and his life slowly disintegrate. The trouble was that whilst Archie delivers his patter to an unappreciative night-club audience, the management feel it necessary to have a stripper behind him to provide some interest. Whilst this might have been acceptable to sophisticated West End theatre-goers, it didn't go down too well in Byfleet. One or two people got up and left in the middle of the performance and critical letters were written to the press; one even dubbed it 'profane'.

At the time, I felt a little hard-done-by. The local citizens had entered whole-heartedly into our bunny-club evening and had thoroughly approved of the Miss Byfleet competition, but they drew the line at the first-ever full-frontal nude in amateur dramatics making her debut in their village. In reality, she wore a flesh-coloured body-stocking, but they weren't to know that.

The rest of the company took the setback more stoically than I did and as a gesture of support pooled their money to put on a good family-play which they had been successful with in the past, namely, Wolf Mankowitz's *The Bespoke Overcoat*. For whatever reason, we were not supported by the theatre-going public of Byfleet. The total audience over the three nights the play was performed was just thirty-eight souls. The money put up by 'The Characters' was lost. They were finished as a company. Their resurrection had lasted less than a year.

It was a grim winter and my spirits were further depressed by the death of my father the following February. I have said very little about my father so far but were he here, he would not complain. He was a man who was content to be in the sidelines, an observer of life who got his pleasures through the activities of others such as myself. He had been born into a poor family, one of six brothers. From an early age he had been hindered by poor health and impaired eyesight. As a result his schooling had suffered due to protracted absences, and although he was a very intelligent man, he left school knowing very little. Consequently, the only jobs he could even consider were manual rather than clerical, and his weak heart and chest made even those very difficult for him. Before the war he had been a packer for a high-class catering firm which provided literally everything needed for lunches and banquets in the city. The hours were long and the work arduous, doing further damage to his health. As a boy, I remember him coming home wet and tired to the point of exhaustion.

Nevertheless, he remained cheerful and gained great joy from being a family-man with a loving wife and children. He faithfully handed over his wage packet every Friday, gratefully accepting a few shillings in return so that he could purchase his Woodbines for the week. He was content to take a back seat and let my mother run his life but there were times when he would exert his authority and the rarity of such occasions made them all the more effective.

He took a great interest in sport, something which I inherited from him and when he was able he loved to come and see me perform, particularly when I was having such success with my boxing. Unfortunately, I found it disconcerting to have any close friends or relatives watching, as I would be conscious of their presence and hoping I wouldn't let them down by losing, when I should have been concentrating on the fight. Consequently, I actively discouraged him from attending. Now that he is gone, I realise that this must have been a disappointment to him and he would always be waiting anxiously for me to come home and tell him how I had got on.

On one occasion he couldn't contain himself. I was fighting at the British Oxygen company, Edmonton in a novice competition. I had better explain that boxing competitions are a bit like dog shows in one respect. Just as a dog cannot be entered for Crufts before it has been a winner at lesser shows, which in turn have entry qualifying competitions, so it is in boxing. One first has to enter open novice competitions which are run as knockout contests. One has to win a novice competition to reach Intermediate class and then more competitions at that higher level before one is allowed to enter the open Amateur Boxing Association competitions.

This particular night was my first Novice competition and Dad dearly wanted to be there, but knowing my feelings he reluctantly agreed not to come. There were eight finalists which meant the winner had to box three times during the evening. It was a tough contest but I managed to win and was presented with a quite substantial silver cup which I later sold, but that's another story. I had not been back in the dressing room more than a few minutes when there was a knock at the door. I shouted "Come in" and was amazed when in walked Dad. Unable to resist, he had secretly left home after me and had watched the whole evening from the back of the hall. I sat down and cried out of sheer love for him.

Dad was absolutely devoted to his children and after the death of 'Rene had only me to heap his love on. He had an active interest in all aspects of my sporting career. He took it upon himself to be my unofficial boxing trainer, giving me massages and rub downs after training runs, and once, when I broke my ankle at football, he insisted on carrying me on his shoulders all the way to the hospital.

During the second world-war, he was too old for regular army service but still insisted on making his contribution to the war effort as a full-time civil defence warden. During the blitz he was kept busy night after night helping to rescue the injured from bombed buildings. Again, this took the inevitable toll on his health. When the war was over, the catering firm he had worked for was no longer there and with all the ex-servicemen looking for jobs he had difficulty getting peace-time employment.

Eventually, I was able to use my contacts in the city to get him a job as a messenger for a large insurance company. He was grateful to the company for taking him on and gave them his wholehearted support. In addition to his daytime association, he also joined their sports club and spent many happy Saturdays umpiring cricket matches for them. He was a contented man who asked very little from life. Above all he was a gentleman.

Unfortunately, life is not always fair, and in the mid-nineteen fifties, he had a heart attack. He recovered to an extent but afterwards he was very limited in what he could do. He continued to deteriorate over the next ten years and it was no surprise when I received a phone call to say he had had another serious attack.

I was at work at the time and had to dash across London in my car to get to Battersea to see him. In doing so, I attracted the attention of the police who showed little sympathy as they booked me. I suspect that every other motorist they stopped gave the excuse that they were speeding because they were on their way to visit a dying relative, only in my case it was true. I don't know if it would have made any difference if they hadn't stopped me, but Dad passed away before I arrived. My case eventually came up in court and I wrote a long letter of mitigation to the police inspector in charge, but to no avail. I was fined thirty pounds. Dad was buried amid the flowers and butterflies of Battersea Rise Cemetery, right behind his house in Mallinson Road.

I think that period at the beginning of 1965 was the low point in my life. Ever since leaving school I had known only success, and failure came hard. It was particularly difficult for me to understand as I didn't think it was warranted. I had done nothing wrong. This was still my attitude when I was summoned to the bank's Head Office in Lothbury Street later that year. The bank's affairs were always cloaked in secrecy and one was never given any idea what interviews such as this were about. One lived in hopes that it would be good news, but at the same time worried that it might be the opposite.

In my case it was good news. They were delighted with the way things had gone at Twickenham and were pleased to offer me promotion to Sub-Manager. This was the grade between Branch Accountant and Manager, but existed at two levels. On promotion, Sub-Managers almost invariably worked in a medium or large-sized branch directly under the control of the Branch Manager. More experienced Sub-Managers could be given control of a small branch of their own, with the Manager of a nearby larger branch acting as mentor and visiting periodically. As far as the local customers were concerned, the Sub-Manager had all the status of a Manager and he was referred to as such by his staff. I was amazed when my interviewer informed me I would be going straight to my own branch at Shepperton. I would have a staff of six and answer to the nearby Manager at Walton-on-Thames.

My spirits were considerably raised by this news and received a further boost when some of 'The Characters' approached me and asked if I would have one last try at making a success of the company in Byfleet. After much persuasion, I eventually agreed, but on the understanding that productions would have to be self-financing and therefore less ambitious, at least until we became fully established in the community.

There had also been some confusion between us and 'The Byfleet

Players' with the press calling us 'The Byfleet Characters'. To avoid further misunderstandings, it was mutually agreed that we should change our name to 'The Merryfield Characters'. I booked time at the local village hall having first ensured we would not clash with anything 'The Byfleet Players' were doing.

I chose *The Girl Who Couldn't Quite* ... as the play to carry our fortunes and I am happy to say we got the support of the village, who attended in sufficient numbers to keep us viable. The lead was played by Penny Spencer who at the time was a fashion model anxious to get into RADA. She had been recommended to come to me for drama coaching and this would be her first stage part. In the end she wasn't accepted by RADA but she did go on to success in television, playing the part of Sharon in *Please Sir* with John Alderton. She also appeared in several films including *Grand Prix* with Yves Montand.

'The Byfleet Players' had a production planned for the spring, so rather than overload the local fixture list, we entered one act of *The Miracle Worker* for the Woking Drama Festival and were thrilled when Alexia, still only twelve years old, won the 'Best Actress' award. We continued to concentrate on festival work and the following year entered one act of *The Entertainer* in the same festival. Not only did this win the supreme award, but I also received the 'Best Actor' award for my portrayal of Archie Rice.

In 1968, we switched to the Walton and Weybridge Festival with *The Crucible* and again won the supreme award. Running in parallel, the play had also been entered in the British Drama League Festival and you can imagine our delight when we won the Divisional Finals at The Ashcroft Theatre, Croydon. This seemed to be a successful formula for 'The Merryfield Characters' and in the same year we also won the Supreme Award and Best-Actor Award at the Woking Drama Festival with an act from *The World My Canvas*.

Our involvement with the Woking Festival led to me taking part in a production with the Woking Drama Group. Their director, Arthur Horwood wanted to put on Dylan Thomas' *Under Milk Wood* but didn't have anybody in his company sufficiently experienced to play the part of The Narrator. It required the actor to be on stage throughout the play and to learn an awful lot of words. I was pleased to accept the part and unlike many who have done so, I was able to deliver all the lines from memory without resorting to hidden scripts.

Back in Byfleet, we continued trying to present plays of outstanding merit rather than the run-of-the-mill productions favoured by most amateur companies. I produced one of the first public performances in this country of Tennesee Williams' play, *Cat on a Hot Tin Roof* and followed that with Arthur Miller's *View from the Bridge*. In this, I played the part of Eddie Carboni who meets a violent death following a fight in which he falls from the bridge. We constructed a magnificent set which enabled me to fall seventeen feet from the bridge into the river below. My fall was broken by mattresses and foam rubber skilfully hidden behind a barge moored on the waterfront. Even so, it was an impressive stunt that had the audience gasping.

I was also invited to take part in performances put on by the National Westminster Bank. They first asked me to play the part of Bill Snibson in the musical, *Me and My Girl*, which was put on at the Golden Lane Theatre in the Barbican. In contrast, I played an Ugly Sister in their Christmas pantomime, *Cinderella*. However, in 1971 I gave up my involvement with theatre when I was promoted to Bank Manager and put in charge of the Thames Ditton branch. I decided that I must take the job seriously and devote myself to it full-time without distractions.

I considered myself fortunate to have got this appointment as it was a very nicely-situated branch beside the village green in a picturesque country setting and not too far from home. It was quite a small branch as independent branches go, having been built mainly to cater for the custom of The Milk Marketing Board who had their headquarters nearby. I was there five years in all and during that time built up considerable business with local residents and businessmen.

It was about the time I was promoted to Bank Manager that my daughter Karen met her future husband, Rodney. He came from Hersham where he worked with his father in the family building business. They met at the Hurley School of Dancing in Weybridge. Eventually she brought him home to meet us and we found him a decent, likable lad. It came as no surprise when he came to our house one day dressed in his best suit and formally asked me for Karen's hand in marriage. The wedding took place in St Peter's Church, Hersham, after which the fifty or so guests came back to 'Two Oaks' for a reception in the garden. After a honeymoon in Spain they settled down in a maisonnette in Addleston and have since given me two wonderful grandsons, Stuart and Jonathan.

That summer, Iris and I took a short break in Saltdean, near Brighton. Driving along the coast one day, we passed through Hove. It struck me as being familiar, as though it had some significance for me, but I couldn't think what. I mentioned it to Iris but she couldn't make any connection either. Later, back at the hotel, I realised what it was. It was where Phyllis' brother had told me she had moved to when I had tried to find her in Wales many years before. I told Iris I had solved the mystery and that it would be interesting to try and find her.

"Well if you want to go, you go," she said, "but don't expect me to come with you on another fruitless chase." And so it was that I set off alone the next day to meet the girl I had seen but once, forty years before.

I had remembered the name of the shop that her brother had given me thirty years since and anxiously looked up the address in the telephone directory. I found it straight away. Rather than phone, I decided to go and look through the window, thinking I might see her in the shop. But when I arrived there was a man serving behind the counter. After a few minutes hesitation I went in and enquired if Phyllis was still there.

"Oh yes," he said. "Phyllis, there's somebody here to see you," he shouted over his shoulder. And then to me, "Go on through."

I went round the end of the counter, through a curtain and into the room behind. I was confronted by an elegant, good looking lady in a smart two-piece and blouse. She gave me an enquiring look.

"Hello, how can I help you?"

"I'm Buster," was all I could think of to say.

"Buster," she cried, "You've found me then, at last."

It was clear that her brother had told her of my earlier search. And with that she got a chair for me while she made tea, and we sat down to exchange forty years of news.

"I heard you on the radio," she said surprisingly, alluding to a brief appearance I had made asking a question on 'Does the Team think?', a popular programme of the time. We exchanged a few more pleasantries before her husband, who had not the faintest inkling who I was, came through to check all was well. When Phyllis explained, he too expressed his pleasure at seeing me and tried to join in our reminiscences but the magic of the moment had gone and I left soon after with many things I had been wanting to know still unanswered.

I described the unsatisfactory nature of the meeting to Iris and she suggested I should meet her again, perhaps when Phyllis was not working at the shop. I therefore rang up a few days later and suggested that if she came up to Waterloo, I would treat her to lunch. I was acting out the best of motives but I must admit it reminded me a bit of Trevor Howard and Celia Johnson in Brief Encounter.

Phyllis agreed that we should meet the following Saturday and I was quite looking forward to it. However, on the Saturday morning she rang to say she had changed her mind and perhaps it would be better if I did not try to contact her again. History had repeated itself. I suppose it was asking rather a lot of her husband to let her go on a date with a man from her past, however innocent our relationship had been.

Chapter 24

Holidays Abroad

I don't know if it's because of my personality and approach to life or whether similar things happen to others when they are on holiday abroad, but I always seem to have little adventures wherever I go, and I thought it worthwhile putting a few of them together. I explained earlier that money was tight when we were first married and apart from my trip to France with Tommy, foreign holidays were out of the question.

However, when Iris saw our friends going off, she put pressure on me for us to go. I would have liked nothing better, but where was the money to come from? It was possible for me to work occasional overtime at the bank but it would take many hours work to raise enough to even get to Clacton let alone the Mediterranean and the holiday season was upon us. Eventually I came to the conclusion that I would have to sell something, but what?

The only things I had that were of any value were my boxing trophies. Some of the cups I had won were solid silver and when I became schoolboy-champion of Great Britain, the borough presented me with a gold medal. Much as I treasured them, they would have to go. Without telling Iris, I loaded them all into a cardboard box and took them to a dealer who specialised in coins, medals and trophies.

I think he realised that I was inexperienced in this sort of dealing and looking back he took me to the cleaners. He argued that the value of my cups and medals had been seriously eroded in that they had all been engraved with my name. How could he sell them on to sporting clubs who might want to use them for their competitions? He sounded very convincing and I felt myself lucky to get anything at all from him. It was only a fraction of their true worth, but it was enough to take Iris and me to Cattolica on the Italian Riviera, just outside Rimini.

Being our first time abroad together as well as our first time in an aeroplane, we found the whole holiday an exciting adventure. It was a real eye-opener to find ourselves mixing with the travelling classes of Europe on those exotic beaches and gave us a taste for more. As soon as we returned home, we adjusted our budget so that we could save up for another trip the next year.

Our second trip was to Ibiza. We stayed in a pleasant but cheap hotel just outside San Antonio on the western coast. Iris and I were on our own and in the evenings we had to share a table with another couple for dinner. They were a very pleasant pair. The man was in his mid-forties but the woman, who was his second wife, was much younger.

Having read this far into my book, you will have gathered that I enjoy telling stories and in between courses I kept them entertained with brief tales from my past. As we got to know each other better they asked what I did for a living, but rather than tell them, I invited them to guess. They had several guesses but all were wide of the mark and this developed into a game. Each night when we met they would offer a few more alternatives. One night they came down convinced they had cracked it. "We know what you do," they cried, "you're a writer." They had made the deduction from my story-telling and were most disappointed when I eventually told them I worked in a bank.

After that, they were most insistent that I was in the wrong profession and that I should take up writing, if only as a sideline to start with. Their advice stayed with me over the years and that holiday has been partly responsible for me writing this autobiography.

San Antonio was a charming little town set in a small basin made seemingly smaller by the surrounding hills, which instilled an intimacy and warmth. It was centred around a large square which at the height of summer abounded with tourists of all nationalities. The white stone buildings sported colourful striped awnings which matched the umbrellas spread above the plastic tables set outside the numerous cafés which skirted the square. In between were equally colourful stalls selling fruit and sandals and T-shirts, while holiday makers drifted slowly from one souvenir shop to the next, idly weighing up what small gift they should take home for Aunty Gladys.

Iris and I found it most relaxing to wander the mile or so down the hill from the hotel each morning to sit and enjoy a coffee in the square under the shade of the tamarisk trees. As we turned the corner at the bottom of the steep narrow street we would be greeted by the smell of coffee and the sound of flamenco music drifting out of the open doors as waiters bustled in and out with their trays of refreshments. It was a scene we never tired of.

One morning, the weather was not so good, being rather overcast and stormy-looking, and we did not sit long over our coffee. Instead we wandered up one of the steep, narrow side streets looking at the local leather-work and ceramics laid out to tempt the unwary tourists. As we got to the top of the hill, a hundred yards or so from the square, it started to rain and we had to shelter in the doorway of one of the shops, waiting for the clouds to blow over. We had a long wait.

The rain increased in intensity until the sound of it became a deafening roar. The sky darkened making the lights in the shops stand out as though it were evening. Thunder rolled around the hills. As the rain poured off the surrounding slopes, the street in front of us became first a stream and then a river, with water several inches deep cascading down it. We realised then why all the shop entrances were one step up, even though they were up the hill on relatively high ground.

We had to wait quite some time before the rain abated enough for us to leave cover. It was nearing lunch-time and we were due back at the hotel. To get there we had to descend into the square again in order to make our way up the hill on the opposite side. Braving the elements, we paddled our way down the hill and were met with an astonishing sight when we re-entered the square.

In front of us was a hugh lake about a hundred yards in diameter. The water came halfway up the legs of the cafe tables, every one of which had three or four people stood on top with their heads tucked under the umbrellas out of the rain. The waiters had their trousers rolled up and were desperately trying to retrieve chairs and other items of furniture which were floating away. Two council officials were wading about trying to raise drain-covers to disperse the flood.

Iris and I started to work our way around the edges of the square. This wasn't easy as apart from those stranded on the tables, the tourists had all crowded to the fronts of the buildings to seek cover under the awnings. I was pushing my way through them when I suddenly realised Iris was not behind me where she should have been. I looked around and found her by following the gaze of the crowd. She had got fed up with fighting her way through people and decided to take a short cut. She had tucked her dress up and was wading knee-deep across the lake.

I watched in two minds, wondering whether I should follow or just let her get on with it. Before I could make up my mind there was a loud murmur from the crowd as Iris suddenly descended into one of the drain holes that had been opened up by the workmen. She was chest-deep in the water but fortunately the drain levelled out about eighteen inches below ground. She was not injured, but her dignity was somewhat bruised as she was unceremoniously pulled out by the workmen. As they carried her ashore, I had the job of rescuing her sandals which were floating gently across the square.

We seemed to like the Mediterranean islands and invariably chose one of them for our summer holiday each year. One time we went to Sardinia and stayed in a small hotel near Alghero. One evening after dinner, we were sat drinking our coffee when I was approached by a fellow guest. He explained that he was an amateur film-maker and was looking for people to act out various parts for a story he had in mind. He knew nothing of my acting background and I found it incredible when he told me he had picked me out because I "looked the part".

His name was Leslie Paine, and he and his wife Milred struck up an immediate friendship with Iris and me. Although he was quite skilful with the camera, he was pleased to discover I had stage directing experience. We became a joint production team, writing scripts together and recruiting others to take part in the film. He already had the idea of doing a comedy James Bond take-off and amazingly we hit on the name Basildon Bond long before Russ Abbott thought of it and made it famous.

We wanted to involve the local Sardinians in the film but knew that it would be difficult to explain to them what we were trying to do and they would probably be very camera conscious. To get round this, I would go up to them in the street and start gesticulating and speaking incomprehensible Italian. Using a long-range lens, Leslie would film the puzzled expressions on their faces, getting just the reaction he was looking for.

The storyline involved bandits who were in pursuit of Basildon Bond. We were told that Sardinia was home to bandits who supposedly roamed the central mountains, so one day we took the camera up into the hills in search of them. We didn't find any genuine bandits but did come across a farmer who had been out shooting game. With shotgun in hand, and crossed bandoliers holding his cartridges, he looked every inch a bandit, and through mime and gestures we persuaded him to pose for us and even fire off a couple of shots.

Another scene involved Basildon Bond, who looked remarkably like Buster Merryfield, being chased by the local police. We thought it highly unlikely that we would get the same co-operation from them as we had done with the farmer.

"Never mind," I said to Leslie, "set your camera up opposite the police station and leave it to me." Once he was ready I told him to start filming and boldly entered the station. Inside, the two uniformed policemen behind the desk looked up as I entered. I immediately broke into my pseudo-Italian, making angry gestures. They looked at each other bewildered, wondering how they were going to handle this mad Englishman who had wandered in. When I started shaking my fist at them, they got rather irate and came round the counter towards me. This was exactly what I wanted, and as they closed in, I turned and fled from the police station with them in close pursuit. Once outside, they very soon gave up the chase and shrugging their shoulders, disappeared back inside. Meanwhile Leslie had got his footage.

After the holiday, we kept in contact with Leslie and Mildred, who lived not far away at Woolwich. He invited me over to a meeting of his film club to view the finished film. This was long before I got into television and Leslie often jokes that it was he who was the first to discover my acting talents. He also made a film of my Figaro act for me which I still have, although it has since been transferred on to video tape.

In our travels around the Mediterranean islands, Iris and I became more and more taken with the Greeks. We found them a friendly, hospitable people who genuinely welcomed English tourists. They seem to lack the cynical, mercenary outlook of some other nationalities. I am keen on photography and like to wander into the countryside taking pictures of the Greek way of life. One day I came across a Greek widow, dressed in traditional black costume, who was gathering olives from her trees. Having given a tree a good shaking with a long pole, she picked up the olives from the ground and loaded them into panniers on the back of her donkey. I took a series of photographs but she refused any payment for her troubles, even though the money I offered her was more than she would get for the olives.

On another holiday, in Rhodes, Iris and I decided to go into Rhodes Town on the bus. We had no idea what time the bus went and just made our way to the bus stop when we were ready. When we got to the stop, there was a small aluminium bench to sit on, only it was burning hot in the fierce morning sun. Not knowing how long we would have to wait, I took my shirt off and laid it along the bench so that we could sit down without burning our bare legs. It wasn't until we were on the bus that I realised I had left the shirt behind. It was quite a good one and I was sorry to lose it. Once in town I bought a new shirt and carried on with our day out. It was evening time before we returned, this time by taxi. Imagine my surprise as we drove past the bus stop to see my shirt still lying on the bench where I had left it. What's more, the taxi driver insisted on walking back the hundred yards or so to retrieve it for me, rather than let me fetch it. That is typical of the pleasure the Greek people get out of doing things for others.

Our favourite Greek island is Crete and we have now been there nine times on holiday. Over the last few years we have stayed at the Astir Palace Hotel which lies between Aghios Nicholaos and Elounda at the eastern end of the island. We love going for walks in the unspoilt surrounding countryside or else splashing about in the shallow lagoons and rocky shelves that lie off the coast. There are a whole series of small islands, some of which are inhabited and have small cafés where one can dine by moonlight. On one such island there are three deserted Greek windmills which feature on the cover of many a holiday brochure.

We were surprised one year to find that one of them had been renovated and turned into a holiday cottage, although it must hold the record as the smallest holiday home ever. We got chatting to the young English couple who were renting it and they invited us in to look round. The ground floor was about eight foot in diameter and completely taken up by the kitchen. From there, a ladder led up to a small lounge holding nothing more than a settee and an occasional table. Above this was the bedroom. The walls of the mill sloped inwards, so that at bedroom level the room was no more than six foot across and was completely filled by the bed. The entire place was very small and cramped, but what an idyllic place for a holiday, completely surrounded by water on an island of one's own.

In front of the Astir Palace Hotel was a small private beach at the back of a narrow inlet, set between steep rocky cliffs. One year we went there with our friends Basil and Muriel. Both Basil and I are fairly strong swimmers and we used to leave the two ladies on the beach while we swam out of the inlet to the open sea. One morning, we had gone out as usual and were making our way back along the coast towards the mouth of the inlet when we noticed sinister figures perched on the headlands either side. There were three on either flank, all wearing dark double-breasted suits and trilby hats. We were a little alarmed to see they all sported sub-machine guns.

Whilst we were still trying to sort this out, we were suddenly surrounded by six frogmen who made gestures indicating that we were to stay close to the rocks and turn immediately down the side of the inlet. Who were we to argue? We did as we were told and as we rounded the corner saw that the centre of the inlet was occupied by a bald-headed man surrounded by a further six frogmen. Apart from them, the bay was empty. The original six frogmen escorted Basil and me all the way to the beach.

Once ashore, Iris and Muriel told us that the gunmen had come on to the beach half an hour or so ago and ordered everybody out of the water prior to the bald-headed man and his escorts arriving for their swim. When we got back to the hotel, we found equally strict security measures in place. It appeared that the hotel had been chosen for a meeting of European Finance Ministers. The man in the water was Andreas Papandreou, the Greek Prime Minister.

For the rest of the day the officials and the normal guests were kept in separate parts of the hotel. We had our dinner and then went through to the ballroom where we enjoyed a few hours dancing. Around midnight, we found we were the last ones there and were on the point of leaving when in came the Ministers and their wives. Among them were Nigel Lawson and his wife. We enjoyed a brief moment of glory amongst such illustrious company but it soon became obvious that we were not welcome and we left. It was a little unnerving making our way to our bedrooms past armed guards on every corner and we were relieved the next morning when they all departed as suddenly as they had arrived.

One year we decided to have a change and go to Yugoslavia. To be accurate, it was advertised as a two-centre holiday, with the first week spent at Plat, near Dubrovnik, and then a cruise down the Adriatic Sea to Corfu for the second week. The plane we flew out on had three seats either side of the aisle and I found myself separated from Iris and sitting next to an American called Bob. Although he was in civilian clothes, when we got chatting I discovered he was an officer in the U.S. Navy on his way to join his ship at Dubrovnik. We got on well together during the flight and surprisingly, when we got to Plat we found they were staying at the same hotel as us while he awaited the arrival of his ship.

It was a very large hotel and once we left the reception area we didn't expect to see them again. The next morning when we awoke, there was a large grey warship anchored in the bay. By coincidence, we saw Bob at breakfast and he confirmed that it was his ship and he would be reporting to it that morning. He had official transport coming to pick him up and he asked if we would like a lift with him into Dubrovnik, to go sight-seeing or whatever. It had been our intention to go there anyway and we gratefully accepted his offer. We found the town very beautiful and a refreshing change from the Greek culture. After a very pleasant relaxing day we made our way back to the hotel by taxi.

The next day, Bob sought us out at breakfast-time to tell us that his ship would be coming into harbour that afternoon and there was to be a grand welcoming parade. If we were interested in seeing it, he would once more take us into town in his official transport which would be arriving shortly. So for the second day we joined him for the ride into Dubrovnik. He boarded a small launch which took him out into the bay to where the ship was anchored. Iris and I did some more sight-seeing, including watching the preparations on the quayside for the afternoon ceremony.

At two o'clock we returned to the quay to find that quite a large crowd had gathered. There was a Yugoslav Guard of Honour lined up and a military band in attendance. We found ourselves a viewpoint behind the ropes with the rest of the spectators and waited for the ship to enter port. It didn't come right up to the quay, I presume the water wouldn't have been deep enough, but anchored about a hundred yards off-shore. Three small boats were launched from it and the ship's officers, all in their best uniforms, descended the companionway into them, led by The Admiral of the Fleet. The ship was the U.S. Arkansas which was the flagship of the U.S. Mediterranean Fleet and hence it carried the Admiral. As the launches cut their way across the harbour, a smartly dressed marine stood on each prow like a figure-head, ready to jump ashore and secure the boats as soon as they reached the shore.

The band played 'The Star Spangled Banner', the Guard of Honour came to attention and the Head of the welcoming party saluted as the Admiral stepped ashore. It was all very impressive and once the initial formalities were completed, wave after wave of American sailors came ashore to join in a march-past with the Yugoslavs. We stood and cheered with the rest of the crowd as they all paraded past the podium, particularly when we saw Bob go by, resplendent in his uniform.

After the parade, the crowd slowly drifted away and the Americans and Yugoslavs stood around socialising in small groups. Spotting Iris and I, Bob came across and invited us over the dividing rope to meet some of his fellow-officers. We felt quite honoured to be among such distinguished company.

That evening, Bob returned to the hotel and we thanked him most profusely for his kindness during the afternoon. He could see that we had been impressed and invited us to come with his wife the following day on a tour of the ship. We were delighted to accept and for the third time made the journey into Dubrovnik in official U.S. Navy transport. Once there, we were joined by a dozen or so other guests and taken out to the ship by launch. On board, it was all very formal and efficient but at the same time very welcoming. Having been formally greeted, we were invited to sign the official visitors book before we were handed over to our guide for the tour. It was a very memorable occasion that got the holiday off to a splendid start. If this was Yugoslavia, give us more. But we spoke a little too soon.

During the first week we saw very little of our holiday courier, but didn't really need her except to get the details for the cruise that was to follow. The day before we were due to leave she put up a notice to say she would meet us all in the lounge after dinner. When Iris and I arrived at the meeting we couldn't understand why we were handed a voucher for ten pounds. "It's your refund," she said. "Refund? Refund for what?" we asked some of the others, who had got there before us.

"Oh, haven't you heard, the cruise has been cancelled. We're flying straight to Corfu tomorrow. You've got to be ready for the airport coach at 5 a.m."

I was absolutely furious as the cruise was one of the main reasons we had booked that particular holiday, but my remonstrations were greeted with shrugged shoulders. Next morning found us stood outside the hotel in the dark with about twenty others. It was far too early for breakfast but we had managed to make a quick cup of tea before leaving our room. We expected to get food at the airport, even if we had to buy it, but apart from one check-in desk, the passenger reception-area was firmly closed. Breakfast would have to wait until the other end.

By the time we had boarded and taken off, the sun was up and it was magical to fly along the Dalmatian coast looking down on islands that glistened like jewels set in the clear turquoise sea. Our spirits began to rise. Perhaps it wasn't going to be too bad after all. Landing at the airport in Corfu, we were immediately hustled into a small bus which was waiting outside and within minutes were trundling down the road. I lay back and closed my eyes, thinking of the beautiful hotel at Sidari, with swimming pool and sea views, where we would be sitting down to a four-star breakfast in just one hour's time.

Five minutes later, the coach stopped outside a small hotel and the driver went round to the luggage bay at the back. We naturally thought that this must be the destination of some of our fellow-travellers, but nobody moved. The driver busied himself behind the coach for some time before coming back in.

"Hokay," he announced, "Your 'otel. Everybody get off." We looked at each other, puzzled. Was this a breakfast stop? It certainly wasn't Sidari and it certainly wasn't a four-star hotel. There was no courier on the bus and the driver spoke little English. We had no option but to get off and find out what was going on. When we dismounted we were disturbed to find all the luggage lined up on the pavement. Hotel porters were summoned and immediately started carrying the luggage inside. I stopped one of them to find out what was going on.

"This your 'otel. You stay here," was all I could get out of him. Alarm bells began to ring in my head.

"Iris, sit on top of our luggage and don't let anybody move it," I commanded and with that stormed up the path and into the hotel.

"This is not the hotel I booked," I hissed at the receptionist, "What is going on?"

"Other 'otel is full, Sir. You stay here. Very nice."

"Where is the manager?" I demanded.

"He no here. He come later," was the only reply I could get.

"Is this a four-star hotel?"

"No sir, we 'ave only two star, but very good."

"Do you have a swimming pool?"

"No problem sir, we very near sea. You like swim?"

I had heard enough. "I am not stopping at your hotel. Get the travel courier here. I want to speak to him."

"Courier in Corfu Town, Sir. I telephone him." With that I stormed back down the path to Iris where I explained to the others what I had discovered. I was adamant that I was not going to be fobbed off with anything less than I had paid for and I knew my argument would be stronger if we stayed outside with our luggage. I managed to convince six other people of the wisdom of this and they too sat on their luggage and refused to move. Meanwhile the other twelve or so disappeared inside, resigned to their fate.

At half past nine the manager came out, all smiles, and invited us in for breakfast, but we stood firm. There was a small refreshment kiosk nearby and we managed to get some tins of cola and packets of biscuits when it opened. The manager assured us he was doing everything possible to contact the courier, but he was out at the moment at another hotel. As the sun rose in the sky we began to feel hot and uncomfortable in our travelling clothes. We felt even worse when those who had acquiesced came out in their shorts and sandals en-route to the beach, but were reassured and even more determined when they told us how dilapidated the hotel was. No locks on toilet doors, lights not working and broken windows. Smugly we sat it out.

Around midday, the courier arrived. There was much shoulder shrugging and hand wringing as he explained that every hotel on the island was full and we would have to stay here. By mutual agreement I had become spokesman for the group.

"Either find us a decent hotel similar to the one we have paid for, or fly us back to Dubrovnik," I told him. After more impassioned pleading with us he eventually agreed to speak with his boss in Corfu Town and sped off in his car leaving us still sat on the pavement. I discovered that one of our party worked for a company which had considerable influence in the travel industry back in London. I got him to telephone his boss to see if some pressure could be put on the travel company from that end.

At three o'clock, the courier returned. There was nothing he could do he announced. We would definitely have to stay here. I told him of our contacts in London and for good measure told him we were about to look up the telephone number of the British Embassy and would also be contacting the press. He began to get the picture and once more sped off in his car to see what could be arranged.

At five o'clock, the manager came sidling down the path. "Ah, Mr Merryfield, I have the courier on the telephone for you. He has found you some accommodation." Elatedly I accompanied him back into the hotel. I picked up the telephone but within a few seconds I was back outside again. The courier was prepared to move Iris and me but had nothing to offer the others. I think he hoped that without their leader, the rest would cave in.

There was no further contact during the evening and we began to suspect we might be sleeping the night on the pavement. We managed to find a taverna nearby and dined in relays while the rest watched over the luggage. Then at ten o'clock there was another phone call.

"Mr Merryfield, I have got accommodation for you, for all of you."

"Is it four-star?"

"No, it is only three-star, but it is much better."

"Does it have a swimming pool?"

"No, no swimming pool but it is right next to the beach and the rooms all have balconies overlooking the sea. It is very nice. You will like it." I told him to hold on while I went out to consult with the rest of the party. They were pretty fed up by now and considered we had won at least a moral victory. We agreed that it was worth going and taking a look. "OK," he said with relief, "I will send transport."

Around midnight, a small minibus arrived. The driver unceremoniously piled us and our luggage inside and we set off along the coastal road in the moonlight. It was quite eerie looking out across the glittering waters at the black silhouette of Albania a mile or so away. After twenty minutes or so, we pulled up in the dark at the front of a small hotel that was literally cut into the rocky cliffs.

Wearily we descended and went inside. The reception area

looked clean and inviting but I wanted to see the bedrooms before committing us to staying. I instructed the manager, who spoke good English, to ensure that the minibus remained until we had looked round. This he did and led us upstairs. There were four bedrooms either side of the central corridor and three of those on the seaward side were vacant. They looked clean and decent and I offered them to my companions. Iris and I would have to forego the sea view.

Opening one of the other rooms, we were overpowered by the mustiness of stale air. It was obvious the room had not been used for some time. Going back downstairs, I announced that Iris and I would not be stopping, but much to my dismay, I discovered that the minibus driver had ignored his instructions and was winging his way back to his bed. I had to accept defeat.

Next morning when I awoke, the room was still in darkness, the window being heavily shuttered. Anxious to see where we had finished up, I got out of bed and threw back the shutters. It was like stepping into 'The Sound of Music'. In front of me were Alpine-like meadows soaring skywards through myriads of multi-coloured wild flowers. The sky was blue and the air so fresh you could cut it with a knife. Ponies grazed in the field below. The rooms at the front of the hotel had equally stunning views and we had a superb sandy beach for our exclusive use. It turned out to be one of the most relaxing holidays we ever had and to put the icing on the cake, we all received handsome compensation when we returned to England after the holiday.

Chapter 25

Equity

Although I had made a resolution when I became Branch Manager at the bank not to let the theatre interfere too much in my life, it was not long before I began to miss the tension and challenge it presented, but even I realised that I could no longer give up the time needed for successful direction and acting. Then the solution came to me. I would use the vast experience I had accumulated over the past twenty years by becoming an adjudicator. I applied to The Guild of Drama Adjudicators and was invited on to a weekend course which was a combination of training and assessment.

All day Saturday we were given classroom instruction and then in the evening were taken to a live theatre performance. The next morning we had to give critical appraisals of what we had seen. I found it a very fulfilling weekend and in my inevitable way entered into it whole-heartedly. Rather than just read my appraisal I dramatised the points I wished to make by acting them as I had perceived them and then showing how I thought they could have been improved on. This was appreciated by our assessors and the other aspiring adjudicators.

I was duly given licence to practice and subsequently attended many amateur performances as the adjudicator. It was pleasant and I enjoyed doing it, but I still longed to be on stage with the actors. It was no real substitute for acting, but the only way I could find the time to do that would be to give up my job at the bank and that would be a silly thing to do, wouldn't it? Or would it?

Although I had returned to the bank after the war, it was more out of necessity than choice. At the time I had a wife to support, making a steady income essential. With nearly a million ex-servicemen on the market, I was glad to have any job waiting for me, but working for a bank was particularly advantageous as staff were entitled to reduced rate mortgages. I did the job conscientiously and, as you have seen, with some success, being promoted first to Branch Accountant then Sub-Manager and finally becoming Manager at Thames Ditton.

At all three branches, the bank had customers connected with the theatre and show business. Despite the affluent image they tried to present to the public, I was well aware from their bank accounts, that their's was not the most reliable of professions as far as income was concerned. When I became Manager, I had the unfortunate task of refusing loans to several aspiring thespians who were considered poor repayment risks. Nevertheless, I longed to be one of them.

Each year, as a Branch Manager, I had to complete a report form. The last section was headed 'Additional Comments' and from about 1974 onwards I started using this to ask Head Office what the chances were of getting early retirement. With Karen now married and off my hands, I thought that with a pension from the bank, I might just about survive as a professional repertory actor. Each year I got the same negative reply - that is, until 1978.

Shortly after I had completed that year's report, John Carlisle, my Area Manager, called on his routine monthly visit, and during discussion of the report, I was bemoaning the fact that I expected the usual refusal of my early retirement request. He surprised me by replying, "Well no actually; I think this year might be different."

I was aware that the bank was cutting back on staff at that time with routine work being transferred to computer systems. But each branch still needed a manager, so I didn't think this would have had a bearing on my request.

He went on to explain. "You joined the bank as a lad of 17 in July 1938, and although you are still only 57, three years short of the official retiring age, by this July you will have completed 40 years service, which is enough to earn a full pension. They might just let you go."

He was fully aware of my theatre interests, knowing I had been heavily involved in a successful musical, *Me and My Girl* and the pantomime, *Cinderella*, both of which had been sponsored by the bank. He agreed to sound out the feelings of Head Office for me. A few weeks later, I had to attend a banking conference at Epsom. John Carlisle was there and during the afternoon break for refreshments, he singled me out for conversation. After some introductory pleasantries, he looked me straight in the eye and said, " Are you still keen to leave us to take up acting full time?"

He listened patiently while I again undertook the difficult task of putting my case to him but at the same time trying hard not appear dissatisfied with my lot at the bank. The last thing I wanted was to get on the wrong side of my Area Manager as I fully expected my request to be turned down yet again.

He smiled. "It's OK Buster. I've already discussed it with Head Office. They have agreed to let you go. You will get a phone call shortly inviting you for an interview to discuss the details."

His words made me numb. I didn't know how to feel. After years of carrying the dream, the opportunity was suddenly there. But at the same time there was that excited fear at the pit of my stomach. To talk about being a professional actor was one thing - to do it quite another.

I couldn't wait to get home and discuss it with Iris. After we had talked it through, I went into our hallway and lay down on the cold tile floor, gazing up at the ceiling. What had I done? I had given up a highly respectable job with a good regular income; for what? How did one become a professional actor? What was the procedure? Would I be accepted? Would I be a success?

All this and a thousand other doubts poured through my mind as I lay on the floor. I knew it would be difficult. I had no pretensions whatsoever of being a celebrity or film-star. I just wanted to be a good repertory actor. But at the same time I was not prepared to spend months on tour with a company which would entail me being away from Iris. The one thing I was certain of was that come hell or high water, I was going to do it. I went for my interview the following Thursday and it was agreed that I should leave on the eleventh of July, my fortieth anniversary with the bank.

Meanwhile, I sat down and composed letters to the Artistic Directors of the Redgrave Theatre, Farnham and the Connaught Theatre, Worthing, both places being within reasonable commuting distance of my home at Byfleet. I explained my banking background and my extensive involvement in all aspects of amateur dramatics and asked if they could help by giving me that vital first professional engagement that would enable me to apply for membership of Equity.

The reply I received from Nicolas Young at Worthing was polite, short and not very encouraging, but it did offer a glimmer of hope. It read as follows.

Dear Mr Merryfield,

Thank you very much for your comprehensive letter and photographs.

It is obviously difficult for someone in your position to find a way into theatre, especially as the awarding of Equity cards is as selective as the sword in the stone i.e. we only have one, or possibly two, a year to give.

Theatres like ours are much in need of "weighty" actors who will add texture to the smooth face of youth.

There is the added problem of someone going from a very influential position in business to starting at the bottom in theatre. I don't want to be totally negative and suggest that if you could come down and see a show during the Summer, let me know when you are coming and I will try and meet you before or after the performance. If you ring one morning between half past nine and ten you can check with me and my secretary that I am not going to be in Outer Mongolia.

Yours sincerely,
Nicolas Young

Needless to say, I took him up on his offer and within the week I was driving down to Worthing to see him, having first ascertained that he was not in Outer Mongolia. He gave me a very good hearing, but reiterated all the difficulties I would face compared with young actors coming out of drama school. He explained that newcomers were generally taken on as Assistant Stage Managers and were expected to do all the menial and mundane tasks such as sweeping the stage, making the tea and working long hours for very little pay. Stage appearances would be rare occasions, and then only as stand-ins. He did not see an ex-Bank Manager taking kindly to this.

I listened patiently to all he had to say and pointed out that having been in amateur dramatics for thirty-odd years, formed my own company and run it for the last seven years, I had of necessity done every job from call-boy to Director and was not afraid of work at any level. As for the money, it wasn't that important as I would be getting my pension from the bank. I told him that come what may I would make it, with or without his help. And then, rather cheekily, I added that at least he should give me an audition. "You never know, you could be turning down a new Olivier!"

He found that quite amusing, but it was the catalyst I had been looking for and it evoked a positive reaction from him.

"OK," he said, smiling. And looking at his diary added, "Can you come next Thursday and we'll see what you can do. Can you sing?"

"No."

"Can you dance?"

"No."

"How about Shakespeare, ever done any?"

"A little."

"Hmmm," he replied somewhat more soberly, "you'll need to do some Shakespeare, and a bit of straight drama. What you chose is up to you." When pressed for ideas on the Shakespeare, he suggested I might look at Egeus in *Midsummer Night's Dream*.

I drove home elated at having achieved my objective of getting an audition, and hoping I could live up to my boasts. The problem remained of what cameos to give him at the audition. I recalled a very powerful speech that I had given previously when playing the lead in *The Entertainer*. That should give me plenty of scope. There was also one part in the play in which Archie Rice does his stage act, which involves singing, with one-line jokes interspersed. If singing was mentioned again at the audition, I was sure I could come up with something and hoped that my experience as Archie might see me through.

I went out and bought the sheet music, rehearsed the musical routine and the dramatic speech, and even found the passage in *A Midsummer Night's Dream* that Nicolas had referred to. Setting off for Worthing again a week or so later I was confident that I could do myself justice.

Entering the theatre at the appointed time, I was a little concerned to see a rehearsal in full flow on the stage and even more concerned when in response to my enquiry for Nicolas Young, a young fresh-faced youth in his early twenties came out.

"I'm terribly sorry, but Mr Young isn't available at the moment. He's asked me to listen to you."

My heart sank. I could hear the rehearsal continuing in the background. I had visions of having to do my performance there and then in the foyer. "It's all right," he continued seeing my dismay, "there's a room upstairs we can use."

He was a pleasant young man and took me up to a small rehearsal room at the side of the theatre. I saw at a glance that there was no piano and having spent a lot of time practising the song routine I didn't quite know how to feel about its absence. We decided to start with the Shakespeare and he sat dispassionately at one end of the room as I tried to get into the spirit of Egeus at the other end. I thought I did surprisingly well considering the circumstances, but nothing showed on his face. I tried to break the formality by asking if he was familiar with 'The Entertainer'. He wasn't. I explained the scene I was about to do, of the broken actor trying to justify himself to his daughter whilst full of self-pity and remorse. I was beginning to see a parallel in my own present situation.

However, undaunted, and determined to see it through, I launched into the part. After a few lines I glanced up to judge his reaction, but he was sat with his head in his hands; asleep for all I knew. I had warned him not to interrupt once I reached the emotional climax where the character breaks down completely, and he allowed me to continue. Reaching the end, I approached him in embarrassed silence as I wiped the tears from my eyes. He seemed awkward as though he didn't know what to say.

"It's like this," he said eventually, " We get a regular stream of people through here that think they can walk in off the street and act. It's part of my job to let them down gently before showing them the door. They are usually much younger than you. I think it might be better if Mr Young talked to you."

And with that he took me downstairs again and into the auditorium where the rehearsal was still in progress. He walked over to the stalls where Nicolas Young sat and conversed in a low voice, with frequent glances in my direction. After two or three minutes, Nicolas beckoned me across to him and at the same time shouted towards the stage. "OK, clear the stage everybody. Thank you. I've got an audition."

"Now then Buster," he said, "I want you to get up there and give me the Shakespeare."

Bewildered, but considerably heartened I climbed on to the stage and gave it all. When I had finished, he asked me to do it again but this time as an old man with the shakes. This I duly did, whereupon he got up from his seat and came over to the footlights.

"I'm told you brought some music with you," and taking it from me, sat down at the piano in the orchestra pit and rolled off the introduction. He looked up at me teasingly.

"Ready?" he called. And with that I launched into *The Entertainer*'s stage routine. Nicolas obviously knew it well and paused at the appropriate places for the jokes.

"Don't clap too loud, this is a very old building," I quipped before launching into the final verse. I followed this with the big dramatic scene, but after a few lines he stopped me.

"If I could offer a few words of advice Buster," he said, "When somebody asks you if you can sing, you don't say no. Likewise, when somebody asks you if you can dance, you don't say no. You let them find out for themselves." He paused, and then added, "...that you can't." And with that, he called for the Stage Manager, whom I discovered had been hovering just out of sight in the wings with most of the cast.

"John, meet Buster Merryfield," he said, "Buster's joining the company." Then turning to me he announced, "Here's the deal. I'll give you a contract for 10 weeks' work. Three productions in all, each on for three weeks. First you will play the parts of Egeus and Philostrate in *A Midsummer Night's Dream*. Then you will be both Jacob and Potiphar in *Joseph and His Amazing Technicoloured Dreamcoat* and finally, the stable owner in *Equus*. Is that all right?"

Was that all right? I didn't know whether to laugh or cry I was so happy. Seeing my beaming face and nod of approval, he continued.

"If you write off to Equity applying for membership, I'll send them a copy of the contract and they will issue a provisional card". I knew that to get full membership required 40 weeks of work, which most newcomers took several years to obtain. This was that all-important start, and thanks mainly to further work from Nicolas and the positive response to my letter to the Redgrave Theatre, I became a full Equity member just 18 months later.

And so I started at the Connaught Theatre as Assistant Stage Manager. Sweeping up, emptying ashtrays, making the tea and being the oldest 'boy' in the business. But I was perfectly happy just to be there with the stars, rehearsing for my first performance. Bernard Bresslaw had been engaged to play Bottom and Shirley Stelfox, Hippolyta. The whole cast was extremely kind and helpful to the new recruit and I learnt a lot just from being with them.

When first night came, I found myself in the wings calmly watching the king and queen on stage whilst waiting to make my entrance. As Shirley came off stage, she threw her arms round me, whispering "Break a leg Buster," and plonked a big wet kiss squarely on my mouth.

Before I could blink she was gone and I was on stage and into my opening lines. All I could think of was the lingering tingle from those soft wet lips.

"Full of vexation came I," I proclaimed. What came next? My mind had gone blank. I stumbled on, improvising the words of the Bard. "... stand forth ... standing ... my gracious duke ..."

Fortunately I don't think many in the audience were familiar enough with the words to realise I was ad-libbing and after a few more lines it all clicked back in to place. On I went, gaining in confidence, and finally rounding off with, "Or to her death according to our law, immediately provided in that case."

As I finished I could hear as though from a long way off, the spontaneous applause of the audience. I had survived the opening speech of my professional stage debut.

The second production at the Connaught Theatre was *Joseph and His Amazing Technicolour Dreamcoat*. As well as acting and my comedy routines, I now fancied myself as a bit of a song-and-dance man and was delighted that Nicholas Young had offered me the part of Jacob. My big scene came just before the interval and climaxed when I stepped momentarily off-stage right, only to reappear a couple of seconds later with topper and cane, followed by the twelve Sons of Israel similarly equipped. We then did a dance routine Frankie Vaughan would have been proud of as we gyrated slowly across the stage. When we were fully strung out from wing to wing, our piece-de-resistance was to roll the toppers down the back of our fore-arms and catch them again with the same hand before they hit the floor.

When I first saw this trick demonstrated in rehearsals, I had grave misgivings over my ability to do it, and spent every spare moment practising. Not only in the theatre, but at home before going to bed and again for an hour every morning before breakfast. In the end I could do it with my eyes shut. I reckon if need be I could have done it standing on one leg whilst wearing a snorkel and flippers. My twelve sons were equally diligent in their practising and during a very successful run of over thirty performances, not one topper was ever dropped.

The show was so successful that the company was asked to do a couple of weeks at the Churchill Theatre, Bromley. "This is it," I thought. "The big time. Fame and fortune at last."

But, as they say in the movies, don't count your chickens until Christmas is over. First night at Bromley - Dah de dah, de dah dah dah - across the stage we went. Toppers off, roll and a flip, and horror of horrors I had to pick mine up off the floor. Worst of all was the gasp of sympathy from the audience.

As we trooped off for the interval, there were commiserations all round. "Bad luck, Buster. Could have happened to any of us." Nevertheless, I was mortified. I just couldn't understand how it could happen. We never looked down to catch the toppers. Always head up, smiling out towards the back of the audience. Grab and it was there.

The next night I was determined things should go well, particularly as the Artistic Director was out front gauging how the show was going down with the Bromley audience. I spent the last ten minutes before going on stage practising the topper routine - perfect every time. Came the big moment ... flip, smile, grab. And once again the ends of my fingers hit the brim and down it went.

This time the condolences didn't sound quite so sincere and the Director's congratulations after the show were a bit strained when he got round to me. I lay awake all night trying to fathom out why I could do it a hundred times off stage but not on the night. I saw an ignominious end to my short stage career looming in front of me.

Then all of a sudden I knew the answer and woke Iris up shouting, "I've got it."

"Got what?" she mumbled. "Go back to sleep you silly old fool."

"No, you don't understand. Bromley has got a gallery." But by that time she had turned over and was clearly more interested in sleep than my ravings.

It was so obvious. We had been directed to look out and smile at the furthermost customers during our dance routines, which at Worthing would be at the back of the circle. At Bromley, there was a gallery, which meant we were looking up that much higher and therefore stood up a little straighter. I just wasn't grabbing low enough for the topper. But why weren't the others affected? This puzzled me for a bit, and I could only conclude that, being the leading dancer for the routine, the spotlight followed me across stage, dazzling me into the bargain.

The next night I was still apprehensive but sure I had solved the problem. By now word of my misfortunes had spread and a hush fell over the audience as we approached the point were I collected my topper and cane. Back we came across the stage - one, two, three, shuffle - one, two, three, bounce the cane, - one, two, three, shuffle - one, two, three, topper off, roll it, grab - and it was there! I had done it.

There was a roar from the audience as I proudly replaced the topper at a jaunty angle and with a defiant gesture tossed my head back as I turned to leave the stage. But pride goes before a fall - and the fall was the topper, sliding off, down the back of my neck and on to the floor.

Ever since then I've wanted to return to the Churchill Theatre to lay the ghost of that night, but so far I haven't been invited - I've no idea why.

Chapter 26

Look Mum, I'm on the Telly

When I originally wrote to the Connaught at Worthing for work, I also wrote to the Redgrave Theatre, Farnham. This paid similar dividends. Towards the end of my run at Bromley I received a letter inviting me for an interview. I had an advantage compared with my previous interview with Nicolas Young at Worthing in that I could now boast that I had done some professional work and had an Equity card, albeit a temporary one. Once again the interview was successful and I was given parts in *Mary Rose*, *Murder on the Nile* and the farce *See How They Run*. Once again the money was peanuts, but that didn't matter. It was all good professional experience and contributed towards that magical total that would get me my permanent Equity card.

At that time I did not have an agent and didn't consider myself a big enough actor to warrant one. Therefore any further work would have to come through my own enterprises. I was aware of the notices in *The Stage* newspaper inviting available actors to apply for parts in forth-coming stage productions. I wrote off for anything I considered myself remotely suitable for and did get a few parts. Although I had played a wide range of roles as an amateur, once they read in my CV that I was an ex-bank manager, directors tended to cast me in that kind of role. I was given parts as an industrialist, a solicitor and a vicar. After only a few months as a professional, I was in danger of being typecast.

Whilst I was working at the Connaught and Redgrave theatres I talked with the seasoned professionals about how they went about getting work. They told me of the 'Professional Casting Report' which advertised roles in forth-coming films and television productions. I also found out there were agencies which specialised in casting for advertisements, both still photographs for magazines and hoardings, and films for cinema and television. Once again I got my pen out and wrote to them all. I think I was spending more on stamps than I was earning.

I got a few offers to make commercials, some of which involved travelling abroad. I appeared on hoardings all over Denmark advertising washing powder, and on Dutch television as a Catholic priest on a bicycle advertising soup. I could now promote myself as an international artist!

I continued to seek stage-work in the London area and did a couple of plays at the Theatre Royal, Windsor. The first was *Murder at the Vicarage* and the second, *84 Charing Cross Road*, which tells the story of a trans-Atlantic liaison between a London book-seller and his American client. I also got more work at the Connaught Theatre, Worthing in their Christmas productions, first as one of the Three Kings in *Rock Nativity* and then as the Wizard in *The Wizard of Oz*. I found pantomime an enjoyable break from serious acting and appeared in pantos several years running. It was for the part of Baron Hardup in Cinderella at Windsor that I first grew my bushy beard.

This new image made me popular as a Father Christmas both for charity work and for commercials. The biggest of these was for the chain store C&A. It was quite unnerving to go into one of their stores and see myself beaming down from my sleigh above every aisle and gangway. After that, people in the street used to give me looks as if they knew me but couldn't quite place the face.

Whilst I was still at Worthing in *Equus* we had a small celebratory party for Jan Harvey who was one of the cast. She had just received news that she had been given a part in a major new BBC television production. In talking to her, I made a careful note of the name of the Casting Director and added him to my list of people to write to. I got a reply from him inviting me for an interview with a producer. Surprisingly, he said he already knew of my work in the theatre as he had seen me in *Equus* at Worthing when he had been there watching Jan Harvey. Unfortunately, I did not fit the image the producer had in mind.

On one occasion I dropped in to see a young actress who had played in two of my amateur productions, *The Crucible* and *Expresso Bongo*. She had since married and introduced me to her husband, Peter Jefferies, who was a freelance producer.

Not long after, I received a call from Peter's office asking me to audition for a role in a four-part 'Love Story' production for BBC Television. The play was called *Hannah* and starred Helen Ryan and Tim Piggot-Smith. It told the story of a house-keeper, Hannah, who looks after the vicar's three children and falls in love with a bank clerk, Mr Blenkinsop, played by Tim Piggot-Smith. I was given the part of the children's Uncle Jim, a naval Captain home from the sea. Out of interest, the youngest child was beautifully portrayed by a young teenager called Patsy Kensit, who later took part in several feature films.

By now I was beginning to be known in the profession and was very soon cast in another BBC production. This was A. J. Cronin's *The Citadel*, starring Clair Higgins and Ben Cross, who later played in the award-winning film, *Chariots of Fire*. My next television part came soon after. Anglia Television did a serialisation of P. D. James detective novels, starring Roy Marsden as Inspector Dalgliesh. I played the part of a pathologist in a couple of episodes of one story called *A Shroud for a Nightingale*.

It took me four years to establish myself as a professional actor, but by 1982 work was coming in steadily and I was fulfilling my dream. My happiness was obvious to my friends and family and one day my mother remarked on it when we were out in the garden.

"Buster," she said, "I'm pleased that at long last you are doing what you want to do. You heeded my advice all those years ago and stuck with your steady job at the bank and I am proud of you for that. But it's nice to see you happy making a success of the theatre. I've seen you on television. You're good, Son." Those few words from her meant more to me than all the press reviews as until then she had never approved of me "messing about on the stage" as she put it.

I haven't said much about my Mum since the time when I returned from the war and set up house with Iris, but I wouldn't want you to think I neglected her; far from it. Every Saturday morning I used to make my way over from Hounslow to see her and Dad in Mallinson Road and attend to any little jobs that needed doing. She looked forward to my visits but she was not lonely, having my Dad for company and also her sister Daisy and husband Arthur who moved into the next street after their children had married and left home.

When Iris and I moved to Byfleet it became more difficult for me to visit quite as often as before and I was glad when Daisy persuaded Mum and Dad to sell their house in Mallinson Road and move into the vacant upstairs flat above her and Arthur. This was a fine arrangement for a while but it wasn't long after, that Daisy and Arthur decided to move to St Albans to be near their daughter, also called Daisy. Unfortunately, the woman who bought the house from them was not very sociable and after Dad died in 1965, Mum began to get depressed living on her own. There was no actual harassment, but the owner made it clear that she would like to get Mum out and move her own relatives in.

Mum became increasingly reliant on my visits and would do all she could to ensure I didn't miss. Although I was doing very well in the bank by then, she insisted on pressing a ten-shilling note into my hand as I left each week, " to cover the petrol" as she put it. She stuck it out on her own for a few years but one day she turned up at the bank at Shepperton and demanded to see the manager, me. She had come to the decision that she wanted to get out and she expected me to do something about it.

Now I loved my Mum very much and would willingly have had her come to live with us at Byfleet, but she was a very forceful person and I knew she would not accept this. I therefore wrote to the local council seeking sheltered-accommodation for her. After all, she was nearly seventy-seven years old and had lived in the borough all her life. The council were very helpful and a few weeks later she moved into a self-contained flat in Roehampton. It was nicely-situated on the second floor of a block built around three sides of a grassed area. There was a resident warden and Social Service helpers called regularly to sort out any personal problems.

Mum was very happy there and enjoyed the friendly company of those around her, who came from similar backgrounds. There was quite a bit of excitement one week when the visiting social worker informed them all that important visitors from Russia were coming to look round. The flats were relatively new and were being held up as an example of how the Labour Government looked after the populace. On the day, the balconies were lined with the residents, anxious to get a good view of the proceedings below. At the appointed time, a fleet of black limousines swept round the corner and pulled up in front of the main entrance. Bodyguards leapt out and chauffeurs scurried round to open their doors and usher the black-suited visitors out.

Mum was well-positioned to witness the spectacle and couldn't believe her eyes. As quickly as she could, she made her way down the communal staircase into the vestibule below. As she closed in on the visiting party, an official tried to bar her way and the bodyguard's instinctively reached inside their jackets.

"Hey, Charlie," she called out, "Don't say you don't recognise me. Lily Merryfield, only I was Lily Stone when we went to school together." One of the Labour councillors escorting the party blushed embarrassingly and hurried across, apologising for the outburst. The visiting Russians looked puzzled and Mum's words had to be rapidly translated. Once they appreciated the situation, smiles broke out and they all insisted on coming over to shake my mother's hand. They considered it a wonderful example of socialism-in-action that the councillor had risen from humble beginnings to high office and yet still retained contact with his roots. The incident added to the success of the visit and they all insisted on shaking Mum's hand again as they left.

Mum was always a busy person and could never sit and do nothing. Her main hobby was knitting. She was never without a pair of needles tucked under her arms and would knit anything for anybody. When she was not busy with cardigans and baby-clothes for friends and relatives, she resorted to a staple diet of knitting squares for blankets. A charity organisation would call round regularly to deliver wool and take away completed squares which were then sewn together into blankets and shipped out to the needy in Africa.

During one of my regular Saturday morning visits, she casually mentioned she had to go into town the following week and when I pressed her she mumbled something about it being connected with the squares she knitted. She wasn't clear about the detail and wasn't too keen about going. I promised to look into it for her and rang the charity worker concerned. I was flabbergasted when she told me that because of Mum's prodigious output of squares, she had been selected as one of six people to meet Princess Anne at The Royal Festival Hall.

As far as I can remember, it was to be at a charity concert given by Yehudi Menuhin in aid of the 'Save the Children Fund', of which Princess Anne was President. I dashed straight back to Mum and said to her, "Didn't you realise Princess Anne was going to be there?"

"Oh yes," she replied, "but what a lot of fuss. I'd rather not go." Try as I might, it was very difficult to get through to her the honour that she was being paid. Eventually, I managed to convince her, or so I thought, and took her out to buy a new coat, hat and gloves for the occasion. On the day, I was at work in the bank at Thames Ditton, but nevertheless took the afternoon off so that I could go along. There was only the one ticket, for Mum, but the concert was open to the public. I had to queue outside the Festival Hall but eventually got a ticket for a seat in the gallery. I thought Mum would probably be sat somewhere downstairs near the front if she was going to be presented. I anxiously scanned the heads below looking for her distinctive new green hat, but without success. After all my efforts and persuasion, it looked as though Mum hadn't come after all.

I sat through the concert, enjoying the wonderful skills of Yehudi on the violin, and listening to Princess Anne praising the charity workers and appealing to the audience to give generously in their support. There was no mention of the blanket-knitters and nobody was presented to Anne. Disappointed, I made my way to where refreshments were laid on as part of the inclusive cost of the ticket. The VIPs took their tea in a roped-off area and at last I saw Mum. She was herded forward by a charity official and shook hands with Anne. No wonder I hadn't been able to spot her in the concert hall, she had on the coat and hat that she used every day for shopping.

That evening I went round to see Mum and remonstrated with her for not dressing up. "Why didn't you put on the new clothes I bought you?"

"Well son," she said, "I know they cost you a lot of money and I didn't want to get them messed up." How can you win against such logic? I questioned her about what Princess Anne had said to her.

"She asked me if I had enjoyed the concert and her speech." she replied.

"Well?" I asked, "What did you tell her?"

"I told her I couldn't hear it properly as I'm getting old and deaf." Exasperated I pressed on.

"What did she say to that then?"

"Oh, she offered to send me a tape recording of the whole afternoon, but I told her not to bother." That was typical of my mother. An Evening News photographer took a photograph of Mum shaking hands with Anne and I wrote to him and got a blown-up copy. I then sent it to Buckingham Palace asking if Princess Anne would be good enough to sign it. I got a very nice letter back from her Lady-in-Waiting stating that it was policy to sign only officially-taken photographs, but she conveyed Princess Anne's good wishes to my mother. I suppose if they made a habit of agreeing to such requests for autographs, The Royal Family would be inundated.

Iris and I always invited Mum to come and spend Christmas with us and 1982 was no exception. She had been a little unwell during the week but insisted she still wanted to come. On Christmas Eve morning I was all set to go and collect her in the car when we had a phone call from one of the neighbours. Mum had got worse in the night and they had contacted the doctor. As a precaution, he had called an ambulance and she was now in St John's hospital.

I immediately jumped in the car and drove over to see her. I eventually found her at one end of the ward. She looked extremely frail sat up in bed with her thin nightgown hanging off one shoulder. There was a constant draught as visitors and staff went through the nearby door but although she was practically bare, her body didn't respond to the cold. She just gazed into space and hardly knew me. I remonstrated with the staff and a nurse found a bed-jacket to wrap around her shoulders, and as soon as another bed became free they moved her to a more comfortable part of the ward.

I sat by her bedside all through the Christmas break and visited her every evening thereafter. Although she was frail and found it difficult to talk, she wanted to go over old times with me. All the times we had spent together at Musjid Road and Mallinson Road. I was particularly moved when she pulled me close and whispered, "You were right, Son, Iris was the one for you." It had taken her forty years to forgive me for not inviting her to the wedding. She died on the nineteenth of January, 1983, aged ninety-three. She didn't die of anything except old age. The photograph of her and Princess Anne has pride of place in my lounge but I remember her best as she was when I was a boy, dancing round the kitchen to the sound of the radio, twirling her skirts in the air. I owed everything to that grand lady and I missed her. I still do.

Meanwhile, life had to go on. Iris and I had a comfortable living with my bank pension supplemented by additional income from theatre appearances and the occasional commercial. The latter were harder to come by but paid well considering the relatively small amount of work involved. I did one for a television Father Christmas commercial, for which I was well paid. Then a couple of days later I was called back to the studio as they wanted some additional close-up shots of my hands tying up a parcel. Much to my surprise, I received an additional fee for this. They could easily have used any pair of hands that were handy and saved themselves money, but who was I to complain.

In 1985, I signed up for panto as usual, this time at Windsor, unaware of the drama that was about to unfold. The season was in full swing and it was quite tiring doing two shows a day. By the time I removed my make-up and drove home to Byfleet, I was more than ready for bed. One night as I climbed in, Iris awoke and told me I had received a telephone call from some producer at the BBC who wanted me to ring him back in the morning. This was gratifying but nothing sensational as I had written to lots of television directors asking for work.

However, I was not one to miss an opportunity and I duly made the return call next morning as requested. I was put through to the *Only Fools and Horses* office and eventually the Producer, Ray Butt came on the line. He asked if I could come round that morning to see him. I explained to him that I was extremely busy at the moment doing two shows a day which made it difficult for me to spare the time. I half expected him to apologise for troubling me and to ring off, but he was quite insistent and said he would send a BBC car round to pick me up and then deliver me back at Windsor in good time for the matinee.

I had no option but to agree, and besides, the thought of crossing London in a chauffeur-driven car appealed to me. Being an active person, I had little time for watching television, particularly when my evenings were fully taken up with the pantomime. Consequently, I had never seen *Only Fools and Horses* but I did have a vague idea that it was a comedy series. I anticipated that Ray had some small part in it for me.

When I arrived at Television Centre and announced myself to the receptionist, I was surprised when Ray himself came down in the lift to greet me. He took me up to the office of the Head of Light Entertainment and between them they explained the situation. They told me of the sudden death of Lennard Pearce, who played the part in the series of Del and Rodney's grandfather, and I offered my condolences. But, I became rather despondent. I did not fancy taking over a character that had already been played by somebody else. I wanted to put my personal stamp on any part I played. The fact that the previous player was dead made it even worse.

I think they read my mood as they reassured me that they did not want me to step into dead man's shoes. The author, John Sullivan, had created an entirely new character. All they wanted to ascertain was that I was available and that I could put on a Cockney accent. All they had heard was my everyday bank manager's voice and the similar accent I had used in my previous television roles. I found it quite a laugh and explained that being born in Battersea, a Cockney accent would be no problem. They got me to read a few lines from an old script and with that the interview was over. They thanked me for coming and promised to be in touch just as soon as possible.

Their response came sooner than I had anticipated, right in the middle of Act Two of the matinee performance. As soon as I had a break, I rang back and was answered by a secretary. Could I please come back to the Shepherd's Bush the next morning? Once more they would send a car for me. This time, I was taken along to one of the hospitality rooms where I was introduced to John Sullivan and the main characters from the cast. Over cups of coffee I was quizzed about my background. John Sullivan had in mind a part for me as Granddad's brother who would come to his funeral. I had no idea how big the part would be and whether it would last for more than one episode, and at that time I don't think he did either. It was all very pleasant and once more I was asked to read from an old script, this time with David Jason and Nicholas Lyndhurst joining in.

Eventually it was time for me to leave to get back to Windsor. Ray Butt walked with me to the car.

"You know, Buster," he said earnestly, "If you do get this part you must talk it over with your wife before you accept. If you become a familiar face you will both have to put up with the attentions of the press and the public." I thought he must be crazy but at the same time I found it exciting. I knew I would have no difficulty dealing with publicity but I assured him I would do as he advised.

The cast and production team obviously discussed my acceptability immediately after I left, as that afternoon I got a phone call offering me the part of Uncle Albert. I had had time to discuss the morning interview with Iris during the lunch hour and was able to give my immediate acceptance.

"Good," came the reply, "We want you on the set for filming at seven-thirty tomorrow morning. We will send a car for you. Will six a.m. be all right?" I explained that the pantomime still had two weeks to run. They assured me that they would finish in good time each day to get me back to the theatre and they did. Every day for the next fortnight I was working from six in the morning until gone ten at night.

That first winter's morning I had no idea where I was going, but fortunately the driver did. He took me to the outskirts of London where the cast and crew stood around in the dark drinking steaming mugs of tea, their breath rising in icy clouds. After I was welcomed by everybody, I was handed a single sheet of paper with about six lines of dialogue on it. I had no idea of the plot or how the sequence we were about to film would fit into the story. I was told to learn the lines, but first I had to go into a caravan that was being used as the wardrobe department to select my costume. It was left to me to choose what to wear as long as I looked like a sea-farer.

It took me no more that ten minutes to pick out the duffel-coat, cap and scarf that have since become my trade mark. I put them on and went outside for approval. Everybody seemed satisfied and after a couple of walks through, we were ready to film just as soon as the light was good enough. As I stood waiting to make my *Only Fools and Horses* debut, I reflected on the coincidence that I should be cast as an uncle coming home from sea, just as I had been in *Hannah*. I also thought of the encouraging words of my mother after she had seen me on television in that part. If only she could see me now.

Chapter 27

In the Public Eye

The scene we were filming that morning was for an episode called 'Hole in One' in which Uncle Albert tries to help Del out of his financial difficulties by claiming compensation-money after falling down the open cellar at the Nag's Head. The scenes set in the pub interior were all filmed on a permanent set at the BBC Television Centre, but that morning we were filming an exterior sequence showing our arrival at the pub when Albert first gets the idea. In it, the Trotter's three-wheeler van is seen pulling up outside the pub. Del then releases me from the back and we walk with Rodney past the open cellar-access-hatch in the pavement, exchanging a few words on the way with Mike, the barman, who is down below. In the show, it formed only a thirty-second sequence but it took most of the morning to film it to the director's satisfaction.

It turned out to be part of the second episode in which I appeared. We pressed on filming that while changes were being made to the script of the half-completed episode featuring Lennard Pearce. John Sullivan rewrote it so that the character Granddad also died suddenly and later in the week we went back to that first episode and filmed the funeral at a nearby cemetery on a bitterly cold morning. It was given the title, 'Strained Relations' referring I suppose to Uncle Albert.

Having been in a few television productions previously, I was used to the slow pace of filming, but what I wasn't ready for was the live recording in front of a studio audience. At the TV Centre there were permanent sets of the Trotter's flat and of the Nag's Head interior. All those scenes were performed live in front of a studio audience, with the external footage being shown on large television monitors at the appropriate points in the story. In this way, as the recording went on, the spontaneous laughter of the audience appeared on the sound track.

I managed to get tickets for Iris, Karen and Rodney to come to my first recording session. Naturally, it was a very big event for me and I made the fatal mistake of letting my mind wander to the importance of the occasion rather than concentrating on the character I was playing. Although I had relatively few words to learn compared with some of my marathon parts from amateur days, I suddenly couldn't remember what came next. I made what in my eyes was the unforgivable sin. I dried.

The scene had to be stopped and we broke for a couple of minutes while the cameras were repositioned and the lead-in film was wound back. During that time I truly wished the ground would open up and swallow me. I was convinced I was making my first and last appearance in *Only Fools and Horses*. When we went back on set I was even more nervous than before. I concentrated hard on the job before me, determined there would be no further mistakes. It came as a real shock a few moments later when David Jason got his words in a twist, much to the amusement of the audience. Being the seasoned performer he is, he immediately made capital from his mistake by chiding the audience.

"What are you lot laughin' at then?" he quipped. "You got in for nuffink dint ya?" He knew how to play an audience and they cheered and whistled. I felt relief that even the greatest of them could fluff his lines and maybe it wasn't such a sin after all. We got back into the scene and everything ran smoothly from then on. It wasn't until well after the show that I realised David had seen how tense I was and had deliberately messed things up to put me at ease. He was that kind of chap.

My sudden co-option into the show attracted interest from the press and I gave several interviews to different papers and magazines. It was a strange sensation to see oneself staring out of the centre pages of 'The Daily Star' and it was interesting to see how they manipulated the very mundane statements that I made to them into something news-worthy.

The morning after 'Strained Relations' was broadcast I couldn't wait to get down to the newsagent's to see what they thought of my performance. I walked down with my friend, Basil, who was recovering from a broken ankle and moving far too slowly for my liking as he hobbled along with his walking stick. We made quite a contrasting pair that morning, he tall, shaven and distinguished-looking in his gaberdine jacket and cap, and me short, be-whiskered and scruffy.

As we neared the newsagent's shop I noticed a good-looking young lady coming towards us. As our eyes met she coyly looked away only to jerk her head back again, the light of recognition spreading across her face. So this is what Ray Butt had meant about public recognition, and very nice it was too. Smiling, she headed straight towards us and looking up said, "Excuse me, are you by any chance Brian Wilde off 'Last of the Summer Wine?" She was gazing straight into Basil's eyes and ignored me completely. My time had not yet come, but my pride was saved by the favourable reviews in the papers and I did not begrudge Basil his moment of false glory.

After those first two episodes, I was given no indication of being wanted for more and it was some time before I received a phone call asking me if I was free for another episode. I was never told that I was a permanent member of the cast but as time went by I started to get bigger and better parts. John Sullivan is an excellent writer who has the knack of getting to know the personality of the actor as well as the character he has created and writes exactly the right thing for each person. His lines come naturally and are very easy to interpret.

He took a great interest in the show and appeared at most of the rehearsals, picking up vibes and characterisations all the time. I remember once arriving at the rehearsal-room before anybody else and amusing myself on the piano while I was waiting. I still can't read a note of music but my early efforts on Mum's harmonium back at Musjid Road enabled me to pick out a tune and I had often stood in as impromptu pianist for Army concerts. I was still tinkering away when David Jason walked in.

"I didn't know you were a pianist," he remarked.

"I'm not," I replied, "I'm just killing time."

"Sounds like you're killing the tune at the same time," he joked. I thought no more of it, but he must have mentioned it to John Sullivan who later asked me to play something for him. I gave him a rendering of *My Blue Heaven* to which he just grunted. However, when I received the script for the next episode, it opened with Albert sat at the piano in the Nag's Head. During rehearsals I was flattered when the director told me I was playing too well. I needed to make more mistakes to be in character with Uncle Albert. After that my piano-playing became a joke on the set. Whenever it was mentioned, somebody would put on a pained expression and plead, "You're not going to let him play again are you?", but from time to time they did.

Towards the end of the year I found myself in the first of nine Christmas specials, 'To Hull and Back'. This was my first full-length production, the normal weekly episodes being only thirty minutes long. The story involved us sailing a small fishing boat across the North Sea from Hull to Amsterdam to collect some illicit diamonds. We did location work in both ports but most of the filming was done on the boat.

Each day we sailed from Hull out of sight of land and despite being seasick I thoroughly enjoyed it, as Albert was the one who had to steer the boat. However, the real skipper was always there, just out of camera shot in case I did anything stupid. For one sequence we had to hail an oil rig to ask the way. In reality it was a British Gas platform. The engineers on it found our filming an interesting diversion and invited us back to the rig after we had completed filming. They sent a helicopter for us and we had a mutually enjoyable day as their guests.

The following year, 1986, the Christmas special was 'Royal Flush' which was filmed in Salisbury. It was while this was being made that we heard we had been chosen for that year's Royal Variety Performance. David, Nicholas and I were to perform a sketch in front of The Queen Mother and The Duchess of York at the Theatre Royal, Drury Lane. We were a late inclusion and were not given much time for rehearsals. John Sullivan wrote us a script, which we rehearsed in one of the hotel bedrooms in Salisbury after the day's shooting.

Our inclusion had not been announced to the press and the secret was kept right up until our appearance on stage. On the day before the performance, we were smuggled up to London and secreted in a dressing room at a theatre opposite the Theatre Royal while the dress rehearsal was in progress. At midnight, after everybody had left, we were taken across to the Theatre Royal for a quick run through and sound level tests.

On the night, we received a tumultuous welcome and stole the show with John's brilliant sketch in which we had supposedly lost our way and stumbled into the theatre by accident. Pretending to be dazzled by the lights, we took some time to spot the occupants of the Royal Box, after which there was much nudging and forelock tugging before we left the stage.

At the final curtain call I found myself stood next to the famous violinist Stefan Grapelli. Glancing along the row I could see Dame Vera Lynn, Cyd Charisse, Petula Clark, Max Bygraves, Paul Daniels and countless others. My one regret was that my mother had not lived to see my proudest moment on stage. If only she could have been there, my night would have been complete. After the curtain came down, we had to line up once more to be introduced to the royal party. We were thrilled when The Queen Mother stopped and told us how much she and the rest of the Royal Family enjoyed watching *Only Fools and Horses* and turning to me she remarked, "So the beard is real then."

"Yes, Ma'am," was the only reply I could think of.

We got a second hasty call back to London when we were at Ramsgate making another Christmas special, 'The Jolly Boys' Outing'. While we were filming, word came through that we were in the running to receive an award from BBC Television as the most popular show among children. Votes were still coming in, but if we were top, they wanted to film us receiving the award.

We were on a very tight schedule and turned the request down as we could not afford to lose a day's shooting, but as the votes were counted, it became more and more apparent that we were the winners. In the end the BBC hired a helicopter to fly us up to the Television Centre and back. The helicopter touched down in a field just off the end of the promenade and waited for us to finish filming. Naturally, the local holiday-makers were quite curious as to why it was there and by the time we came to leave, we had to push our way through a large crowd of fans. It was a relatively small helicopter, just a bubble of perspex large enough to hold the pilot and the three of us. I had not flown in one this small before and I found the flight along the Thames very exciting.

The highlight of the trip came as we started to descend towards the London Westland Heliport. Those of you familiar with London will realise that this is right next to Battersea where I had spent my childhood. The first prominent landmark I spotted was my old school, Sinjuns, and as I excitedly pointed it out to David and Nicholas, the pilot took us down for a closer view. At one stage I thought he was going to land in the playground and I had visions of getting out and calling in on Jet and his staff, but of course, they had all long since retired. Later in the evening we made the trip back to Ramsgate by moonlight with all the lights below making the countryside look like a scene from a Disney spectacular. The whole round trip made a very lasting impression on me and is now one of my treasured memories.

After I had been in *Only Fools and Horses* for a couple of episodes, Ray Butt took me on one side and hinted strongly that he thought it was time I got myself an agent. When I had been invited to join *Only Fools and Horses* I hadn't bothered too much about fees, in fact I think at the time I would have paid them had they asked. As the show had grown and my popularity had grown with it, he thought an agent might be able to negotiate a better deal for me.

When I first become a professional at the Connaught, I had

seen an advertisement in *The Stage* from a firm of agents who were opening a new office in Richmond. That being my old stamping ground, it seemed like an omen, so I decided to write and ask them to take me on. I got a letter back from one of the partners, Tim Combe, saying they would send somebody along to the theatre in Worthing to discuss it with me. A very pleasant young lady came to see the show and met me for a meal afterwards.

A few days later I received a very nice letter from Tim explaining that they already had a number of people on their books who were straight actors of my age group. As they tried to spread the limited amount of work they received evenly amongst their clients, they didn't think it fair to me or to their other clients to take me on. Therefore, up until the time Ray spoke to me, I continued to be my own agent. However, I now gave Tim a call and he was only too pleased to take me on. He put my career in the safe hands of Sandy Ross-Brown and they have served me well ever since. I found Sandy to be a very good friend as well as an agent and she and her husband have been down to stay with Iris and me, to see me in pantomimes at Bath and Bournemouth.

Although there has not been a series of *Only Fools and Horses* since 1991, and the last Christmas special was in 1993, Sandy has keep me in the public eye and I have made numerous appearances on various chat-shows and game-shows. One of the first of these was on *Robson's People* which is a chat show similar to *Wogan*, but put out locally on Tyne Tees Television. My fellow guests were Eddie the Eagle, the Olympic ski jumper, and Hughie Green who used to present *Opportunity Knocks*.

When I was a Bank Manager at Thames Ditton, I saw a notice in *The Stage* saying that Hughie would shortly be holding auditions for *Opportunity Knocks* at Kneller Hall, Twickenham. As this was virtually next door to where I used to live and within walking distance of the bank, I decided to go and try my luck. I asked my Area Manager for the afternoon off and with his agreement set off to try out a brand-new act I had put together.

In this act, I played the part of an American industrialist who is visiting Britain and has been invited on to a late-night chat-show. I came on stage and sat talking to an imaginary host who was interviewing me. I thought I had written it most skillfully by repeating the hosts questions as part of my replies.

"My views on Mrs Thatcher? Now there's a lady. If only we had somebody like her. Ronald Reagan? Dear old Ronnie. He does try, doesn't he? Well he certainly tries me." I went on with this monologue and gradually got around to talking about an important speech I was to deliver the next day on the future of the world in the nuclear age. I am persuaded by my host to give a preview of the speech, but explain that it so depresses me that I have to take pinches of a special 'happy powder' to keep my spirits up. I give him a sample of the speech, but in doing so overdose on the powder, finishing up in hysterics on the floor.

As I did this act at Kneller Hall, the stage crew and other contestants could not restrain from laughing. I got to my feet and looked down at Hughie and the Producer, sat in the stalls.

"Next Please," was their only response. I was reminded of the Windmill auditions where many had suffered a similar fate.

On *Robson's People*, when I was introduced to Hughie in the hospitality-room before the show, I pretended to be annoyed with him for rejecting me all that time ago. For a while I had him going but eventually I had to own up that I was kidding. When Hughie came out for his interview, he got his own back by pretending he had been insulted by me before the show. He eventually had to admit that he couldn't remember my audition, it being only one of several thousands he had had to sit through during his career. He went on to say he had turned down bigger names than me, having rejected both Alma Cogan and Engelbert Humperdink, the latter no less than three times.

Once one becomes known, there are innumerable spin-off appearances one can make. Since joining *Only Fools and Horses* I have been invited on to no less than seventeen other television shows. Out of interest, I have listed them for you at the end of the book. I have been interviewed for several women's magazines and have had my garden photographed for gardening magazines. I have twice taken part in Jersey's Battle of the Flowers, opened countless fetes, old folk's homes, a garden centre and two chip shops. Is there no end to this man's talents?

I had been warned by Ray of all the attention I would get from the public, but far from being a nuisance, I quite enjoy it. Most weekends I am asked to make at least one appearance for charity and providing I am not working, I never refuse. It gives me a deep satisfaction to be able to do something for the community no matter how small. Most of all I enjoy meeting fans. I always know when somebody in the street has recognised me by the double-take followed by the nudge to their companion. Some just smile and nod as they go past while others ask for autographs. People are quite funny in that way. Over eighty per cent of those who ask, say they want it for somebody else and the higher their social status, the less likely they are to admit it's for them. Rather than just sign, I always ask for a name so that I can personalise the message. That's when a lot of them nonchalantly say, "Oh just put my name down. That will do."

Some of them are quite funny. Some won't believe its me. One chap insisted that if I was who he thought I was, I wouldn't be walking down the street with ordinary people. I think he must have been confusing me with royalty. Sometimes, if they are unsure, I play a little game with them by pretending to be a foreigner who doesn't understand what they are saying, but that rarely works.

Another man I met once at Clapham Junction also had a bad case of mistaken identity. "Del Boy," he shouted, pointing his finger at me.

"No," I explained, "I'm not Del Boy."

"Yes you are," he insisted. "Isn't he Del Boy?" he appealed to a couple of passers-by. By the time he had finished, quite a crowd had gathered, but nothing could convince him that I was other than Del Boy. He ended up asking if he could shake my hand, just in case I was.

Many of those who ask for my autograph don't even have anything for me to write it on. We were in Ramsgate shooting 'The Jolly Boys Outing' as a Christmas special, when a teenaged girl approached me on the promenade. She asked for my autograph but when I got my pen out all she could offer was her arm. When I refused, she lifted her skirt and said, "Well stick it on here then," proffering her thigh. I laughed and looked for the hidden photographer knowing of others who have been caught unawares.

But she was a genuine fan and when I again refused she went to see what she could find. She was back a couple of minutes later with a supermarket check-out receipt that she had picked up in the gutter. It had a large imprint from somebody's trainer on it and once more I told her it was not good enough. By now I was running out of patience and decided to move on. She caught up with me, panting, five minutes later. "Will this do?" she enquired. She had been into one of the shops along the sea front and emerged with a picture postcard and a pen. How could I refuse her?

I think the award for outstanding cheek must go to a youth on Bournemouth beach. I had been asked to take part in a sponsored swim for charity, from one pier to the other. Now if you know

Bournemouth, you will appreciate that is a distance of well over a mile. I've always enjoyed swimming as a way of keeping fit, but being over seventy, I wasn't sure I could make the distance. It isn't just a straight swim as you first have to swim out a hundred yards or so to clear the ends of the groynes and get out of the breakers. Anyway, together with my friend Charlie, I decided to have a dummy run. It was a cold and miserable September day and after half a mile or so we decided to pack it in.

Coming ashore we realised that our towels and clothes were down the other end of the beach and we would have to run back, cold and wet, in nothing more than our bathing trunks. The beach was practically deserted, but about half way along we were joined by a couple of youths asking for my autograph. They were very persistent and eventually I stopped.

"OK," I said, "give us your pen."

"Oh dear," he replied, "I was hoping you might have one!"

I find the most appreciative fans are the old folk. One day I met an old lady, even older than me, as I was coming out of the newsagents. Having confirmed I was who she thought I was, she was keen to engage me in conversation. I was in rather a hurry but I spent as long as I could with her but eventually I had to excuse myself, explaining that I had an appointment to keep.

She thanked me most profusely for talking to her and then added. "Wait till I tell my husband I've been talking to you. He's a real big fan of yours. He never misses a show. Since he lost his legs, he only has the television to occupy him." Later, I regretted I hadn't got her address and visited him, but at the time it just didn't occur to me. Even so, it warmed my heart to know that I could bring such pleasure into people's lives.

A couple of years ago, Iris and I went on a touring holiday around Bavaria. All the other people on the coach were either American or Japanese and I was able to travel in peace, unrecognised. That is until we got to Hitler's Berchtesgaden. As the coach backed into a parking spot in the car park, passengers were alighting from another coach parked next door. The lettering on the side indicated that it came from Belgium.

As the people walked down the side of our coach, one of them looked up and saw me. She gave a yell and banged on the window, shouting something in French or Walloon that I couldn't understand except for the words "Uncle Albert". Immediately the rest of her companions gathered round the window and started chanting, "Uncle Albert, Uncle Albert." Meanwhile the passengers on our coach looked on in amazement, unable to comprehend what was happening.

I got down from the coach and spent the next ten minutes signing autographs and having my photograph taken with my new-found friends. What was most remarkable was that the Belgian driver was a devoted fan of *Only Fools and Horses*. The inside of his coach was equipped with a video player and the passengers had been subjected to a non-stop showing of *Only Fools and Horses* videos all the way to Berchtesgaden. He even had a large sign on the front of his coach saying, 'Oncle Albert' which I presumed was the Belgian spelling. It goes to show what a truly international show *Only Fools and Horses* has become. It is now shown on television in fourteen different countries including Australia, Greece and even, would you believe, Angola. Public acclaim is the price one pays for fame.

Chapter 28

This Is Your Life

I have appeared on several chat-shows where the main features of ones life are covered in five or ten minutes. Similarly, I have been interviewed for articles in magazines which occupy no more than a single page. In both cases, the result has been an over-simplification, often giving the wrong impression.

The favourite point which these interviewers latch on to is that I didn't become a professional actor until after I left the bank at the age of fifty-seven. In order to give more impact to the interview or the resulting article, they foster the impression that I stepped straight from the business world into the theatre and achieved almost instant success with Uncle Albert. Having read your way through my autobiography, you should now be aware that this is not the whole truth. Over thirty years of amateur stage work cannot be ignored.

Although they are not as frequent as they used to be a few years ago, I still receive a steady trickle of letters from fans. They all say how much they enjoy watching *Only Fools and Horses*, praise my performance as Uncle Albert and then ask when we might be doing another series. Whenever possible, I try and write back and my standard answers are "I'm pleased, thank you," and "I don't know". But a considerable proportion of writers add that they too would like to break into show business, as I have done, and please could I tell them how to do it.

Now that is something which cannot be answered in a few lines in a letter and it is partly for them that I have written this book. Here I have not only shown the way I went about it but hopefully I have given an insight into my character and the qualities which I think led to success. The best advice I can give these would-be thespians is to go back and read the book again and look for these characteristics. The answer you seek is there, but in case you find it too obscure I will summarise my philosophy for life and the necessary ingredients for success in these closing paragraphs.

The first thing one needs is luck. There are probably hundreds of actors out there who could make an equally good job of playing the part of Uncle Albert, but they did not have the luck to be chosen. Having said that, luck is concerned only with the things over which one has no control. Many of the things which others attribute to luck are not luck at all. How many of the other would-be Uncle Alberts had their CV and photograph on Ray Butt's desk at the time the opportunity arose? How many of them were Cockneys? How many of them had forty years acting experience? How many of them had my record of acting awards? How many of them had my talent? The only luck connected with my big break was that the opportunity arose, through the untimely death of Lennard Pearce. What most people call my lucky break was mostly of my own making.

To take advantage of luck, or opportunity as I would prefer to call it, one needs talent. It is no good being the right man at the right place at the right time if you are unable to take advantage of the opportunity when it arises. I could well have come in to *Only Fools and Horses* as a minor character for just the one episode. But I like to think I had the talent to take full advantage of the chance I was given. It surprised me how much leeway I was given in the characterisation of Albert, from the choice of his costume to the way he jerks his head as he speaks. I was able to mould him into the believable lovable human character that he became, and more to the point, that the writer and director of the show liked. I would like to think that it was my originality that kept me in the series.

Hand in hand with talent, comes experience. Both are essential for a polished performance. Latent talent must be developed. There is no such thing as an overnight success. Invariably when the press reports the instant success of a new talent that appears in any walk of life, there is in reality a background of extensive hard work and practice. We all make mistakes and it is only through repeated practice and experience that one eliminates them and gradually improves one's performance in whatever chosen field. The higher one rises in any profession; the better the performance expected. Before reaching the dizzy heights, one needs room to experiment and make the mistakes where they don't matter so much. I shall be forever grateful for the Tuesday evenings spent at the Richmond and Twickenham Arts Club where I was able to develop my ability in a forgiving environment.

Of course, one first has to discover in which direction one's talents lie and to do this one must not be afraid to experiment. There are countless fields of human endeavour and one cannot possibly try them all. It is possible that there are undiscovered Grand Masters of chess who have never played the game or potential Olympic marathon champions who have never run further than to catch a bus, but in general we all tend to like doing the things we are good at and the talents needed for these chosen activities becomes apparent at an early stage. I have often wondered about the great acting families such as John Mills and his daughters or the Fox brothers. Is it that they have inherited their talents for acting through the genes of their parents, or is it that being born into theatrical families they have the opportunity to practice acting and gain experience? I suspect it is probably a combination of inherent talent, experience and opportunity that led to their success.

Us lesser mortals must experiment to find our talents and in doing so must be both fearless and thick-skinned. Of course you will die the death, of course you will be booed off stage. This has happened to all the great actors and comedians at some time or other in their careers. If however you continue to get the bird you should realise that the audience knows best and maybe you need to try something else. For years my ambition was to be a great stand-up comic after the style of Max Wall or Jimmy Durante, but I had greater success with acting. It is ironic that my major acting role so far has been in 'Only Fools and Horses', a comedy. I found I needed my full range of stage experience, including my stand-up comic and miming routines, to do justice to the part of Uncle Albert.

It goes without saying that to succeed on the stage one needs ambition. One must continually set targets to strive for. If they prove unattainable then at least you will have tried and you can always change your goals. Even if the target is attained, one must not sit back satisfied, but set new targets to aim at. You might think that at the age of seventy five, I should be content to have got as far as I have, but I am still ambitious.

If any producer is interested, I have ideas for my own television show, but a show with a difference, and I promise not to play the piano.

In experimenting to find one's niche, do not be afraid to be original. Most people who make it to the top in any profession involving public recognition have originality. Who cannot instantly recognise a Gauguin, a Van Gogh or a Constable? Whoever is the first to do something gets the recognition even though those who come after might do it better. Elvis Presley once came third in an Elvis look-alike competition but he was still the greatest. Think of the voices of Bing Crosby, Vera Lynn or Gracie Fields. They are all unique and instantly recognisable. It is this same search for uniqueness that spurs comedians to develop catch phrases. But a word of caution. There is a fine line between uniqueness and gimmickry. All too often nowadays, the latter is used as a substitute for talent.

Once you have decided where your future lies, you must be prepared to work endlessly towards achieving perfection. Do not settle for second best. It is all too easy to accept mediocrity, but only the best is good enough to reach the top. The top performers in all activities make what they do look easy, but their apparent spontaneity or nonchalance is usually the result of hours of practice. There is a lot of truth in the saying 'Practice makes Perfect'.

You must have determination and single-mindedness in pursuing your goal, letting nothing deflect you. This is not easy to do when one has commitments to others. I look back on the time when Karen was a child and know I should have spent more time with her and Iris rather than wrapping myself up in the theatre in the way I did. You may consider this is too great a price to pay for success, that is your prerogative, but without an absolute dedication that puts it above all else, it will be very difficult to attain your ambition. I have talked to many people who have told me they would have liked to have gone into the theatre, adding, "I think I would have been good at it". My response is to ask, "Well why didn't you then?", which usually evokes a shrug of the shoulders and some comment about not wanting to lose the security of their regular income. Absolute commitment is essential. To paraphrase a well-known saying, 'A faint heart never won a part in My Fair Lady'.

Coupled with determination is persistence. Do not take 'No' for an answer. There are many who use rejection as a reason for giving up. I am fortunate in that I inherited both determination and persistence from my mother. In those early days when her life was hard in Musjid Road, she had the determination to strive for something better for her family. Despite having two young children to bring up, she persisted with her evening work as a waitress until she had accumulated enough to move to Mallinson Road. It was her determination that got me to Sinjuns and her persistence and refusal to accept defeat that gave me my second chance after I had failed my exams.

This brings me to my next point, the help of others. I forget who first said, "No Man is an Island", but whoever it was knew a thing or two. It is impossible to achieve success without the help and support of others. Although I have not always given her the attention I should have done, I have throughout my career had the full backing of my wonderful wife, Iris. In our early married life she uncomplainingly put up with a house full of actors night after night, preparing piles of sandwiches and cups of coffee, while they planned and schemed over our next production. At the same time, if you will excuse the mixed metaphor, she has been the wise head that kept my feet on the ground.

I have also had great support from all the actors I have worked with, both amateur and professional, and would not have survived without them. There was a period when I was giving my all to 'The Characters', but getting little support from an unenthusiastic public. At that time I seriously considered abandoning the theatre altogether, but was persuaded to carry on by others who still had faith in what I was doing. I would like to take this opportunity to thank them all.

If you have not been deterred and still wish to pursue a career on the stage, there is one more attribute needed, perhaps more important than all the rest. You must have faith, a belief that what you are doing is right. Very rarely is the road to success a smooth one. There will be setbacks and adversities and it is only belief in ultimate success that will carry you through. One needs a strength to draw on.

In my youth, that strength came through my religious beliefs. I have told you of Leslie Page's drawing of the gnarled hand and my adoption of his text, 'Through Christ - I Can'. Whenever I had doubts or fears I would think of this and it would give me the strength and belief to carry me through, particularly during the war.

As I grew older I began to question the traditional view of Christianity and formed the belief that whatever God was, there was a part of Him or It in me. I saw God as some inner strength I could call on in times of trouble. I didn't have to know what it was or where it came from, as long as I could rely on it being there for me to use.

Now, as I approach the end of my life, my views change yet again. I look back at my God and realise that I created him to meet my needs. I needed something to give me strength and comfort and I created him in that image. Is this what mankind has always done? In the beginning, did Man create God? It seems that all civilisations have a concept of God that satisfies a need of some sort and the poorer their life on Earth, the more fervent their belief in life-after-death or reincarnation.

If that brings comfort to those that believe, then so be it and I am glad for them. For myself, I believe that Heaven is here on Earth. I look at life around me and I marvel at its beauty and its complexity. Whether it is the creation of a superior being or the result of chance and selection is immaterial. It is here and we should be thankful for it and enjoy it for what it is. This quotation from an unknown epitaph sums it up well.

"The universe is unfolding as it should. Therefore be at peace with God, whatever you conceive Him to be, and whatever your labours and aspirations, in the noisy confusion of life keep peace with your soul. With all its sham, drudgery and broken dreams, it is still a beautiful world."

Although I do not believe in Heaven in the accepted sense, I do not fear death. The consciousness that is Buster Merryfield will return to wherever it was before I was conceived in 1920. I have no recollection of that being a fearful place even though it may be black nothingness. As for life here-after, I shall live on through my daughter, my grand-children and the happy memories I have given to others.

I believe there is only one performance on the stage of life. This is not a rehearsal for Heaven. This is your life. I commend you to live it to the full as I have tried to do. I wish you well.

Television Appearances

BBC Television

Love Story, 'Hannah'

The Citadel

Strangers and Brothers

Only Fools and Horses
(4 Series and 9 Christmas specials)

The Royal Variety Performance

The Laughter Show

Points of View

B.A.F.T.A. Awards

Blankety Blank

Wogan

Family Fortunes

Noel's House Party
(2 Appearances)

Third Age

Pebble Mill at One

The World of Paul McKenna

The National Lottery

That's Showbusiness

Big Break

Esther

Anglia TV

Shroud for a Nightingale

The Time, The Place

Paul Daniel's Magic Show

TVS

The Bobby Davro Show

Channel 4

The Third Wave

LWT

Surprise, Surprise

Tyne Tees

Robson's People

Meridian

A Tale of Four Ports